A Journey of Days

of Days

Relearning
Life's Lessons
on the
Camino de Santiago

Guy Thatcher

To Richard Shantz

Guy Thatch 2008

Enjoy your journey

GENERAL STORE PUBLISHING HOUSE
499 O'Brien Road, Box 415
Renfrew, Ontario, Canada K7V 4A6
Telephone (613) 432-7691 or 1-800-465-6072
www.gsph.com

ISBN 978-1-897113-99-8

Cover illustration, design and layout: Magdalene Carson / New Leaf Publication Design
Printed by Custom Printers of Renfrew Ltd., Renfrew, Ontario
Printed and bound in Canada

Library and Archives Canada Cataloguing in Publication

Thatcher, Guy, 1937-
     A journey of days / Guy Thatcher.
ISBN 978-1-897113-99-8
     1. Thatcher, Guy, 1937- --Travel--Spain--Santiago de Compostela.
2. Santiago de Compostela (Spain). 3. Christian pilgrims and pilgrimages--
Spain--Santiago de Compostela. 4. Spain--Description and travel. I. Title.
DP285.T48 2008   263'.0424611   C2008-901807-9

To my wife, Carroll, my life companion,
who is always there for me.

FOREWORD

Dear Reader,

The pilgrimage to Santiago de Compostela in Spain is a trip of almost 800 kilometres. It has been described as a journey, not only to a physical destination, but to the interior of oneself. Every pilgrim undertakes this journey with his own baggage and objectives—sometimes shared, sometimes kept within.

Join in as Guy Thatcher shares some of his reasons and many of his experiences with us.

I hope that you learn something new about Guy and yourself as he takes you on his journey.

Paul O'Hagan

ACKNOWLEDGEMENTS

I want to start by acknowledging two people, Carroll Thatcher, my wife, and Meredith Thatcher, my daughter, whose quiet and insistent persuasion, in spite of my repeated intransigence, convinced me to take with me and keep a journal of the events of my journey, without which there would have been no book, no record at all of the weeks of my adventures in northern Spain. I was strongly — and wrongly — opposed, for a long time, to the very idea of keeping a journal. I thought that it would detract from my experience. I was wrong and I appreciate their persistence in this matter — although I didn't at the time. They also spent many, many hours searching by phone and via the Internet for my lost backpack and forwarding my e-mails to interested friends, and they set up the Weblog from which this book is derived.

Thanks to Ali Black, Marjory Cort, and to Jim and Sandra Gervais, who shared their previous experience, books, and material on the camino. They gave me an abundance of good and useful advice over dinner and good red wine. To Marilyn Carty, who loaned me one of her treasured books about the camino. To the front desk staff at the Hotel Maissonave in Pamplona, Henrik, Ander, Raquel, Pilar, and Aitor, who tried their best to help solve the missing backpack problem and were helpful in finding replacement items in Pamplona. To José Luis Garcia Cuartero in Madrid, who gave up most of a day to help me deal with the lost baggage at the airport, then treated me to lunch at Atocha station while I waited for my evening train back to Pamplona.

To the people I met on the camino, Martin from Constance, Hannelore from Hamburg, Walter and Roswitha from Cologne, Eva and Richard from Augsburg (who gave me his only fleece), Heinz from Munster, Vicente, Miguel and Vicente, the three compadres from Spain, the Aussies from Brisbane who brightened my days near and in Santiago, Sturla Pilskog and Mari Bjørnstad from Oslo, who are preparing a documentary about the camino, and to Adrie from Holland. To the people with whom I walked, Georg from Bremen, Wayne from south of London, Veronica and Julian, the teachers from Normandy, Tina from Germany, Andreas from Germany, Ferran from Barcelona, Eva Papp from Budapest, and especially to three people: Paula from Bremen, Karsten from Berlin, and Marina from Hamburg, with whom I walked for almost three weeks. They gave me a glimpse into another generation and gave me permission to quote their words in this book.

To Kirsti Antila from Finland, who loaned me her cell phone to call Canada on my wedding anniversary, and Suzie from Montreal, who talked with me and brightened my day while I was recuperating from a walking injury and who suggested that I should write a book—this book.

To the *hospitaleras* and *hospitaleros* at all the *albergues* on the camino, many of whom are unpaid volunteers, for their warm welcome, love and care, dry, clean beds, security, food, advice about the camino, and laundry facilities.

To my dear old friend Fern Charbonneau of Quebec City, for his engaging commentary on my blog while I was travelling. To my book club, who asked that they be allowed to use my draft book as one of the books they discuss.

To my family, to my sister-in-law Maryan O'Hagan for her encouragement and unconditional love over the years, to her son and my nephew Paul O'Hagan for his interest and encouragement, to my English cousin Dr. Roger Sage, of Whipsnade, for his medical advice early on—drink a lot more water— and for his offer to come and help when I was briefly laid up, to his wife, Jackie, for her review of an early draft of this book and her excellent advice, to my brother Ance Thatcher of Candia, New Hampshire, for his manuscript review and his comment on scythes, and to Jim Holmes of Ottawa and John McGee of Atlanta for their careful reviews of the draft and their perceptive and helpful criticism.

To my daughter-in-law, TJ Sharp, who produced the wonderful artwork for the cover of this book.

To the Confraternity of Saint James, London, **www.csj.org.uk**, for a wealth of good advice about the camino and for their permission to quote from *The Pilgrim's Guide: A 12th*

Century Guide for the Pilgrim to St. James of Compostella,[1] and to the Canadian Little Company of Pilgrims, **www.santiago.ca**, for more good advice closer to home.

To my publisher, Tim Gordon, for his faith in me; to my editor, Jane Karchmar, for her sensitivity and excellent advice; to Magdalene Carson, who designed my book and its cover, for her beautiful work; and to my publicist, Alison Roesler, for her enthusiasm and good ideas, without all of whom this would still be just a dream.

And thanks above all to my wife, Carroll, for her constant love, quiet encouragement, and practical advice, without whom the journey itself would probably not have happened, and without whose abundant tolerance this book would certainly not have been written.

---

1   Aimery Picaud, *The Pilgrim's Guide: A 12th Century Guide for the Pilgrim to St. James of Compostella*, translated by James Hogarth, originally published ca. 1140 (London: Confraternity of St. James, 1992, 1996).

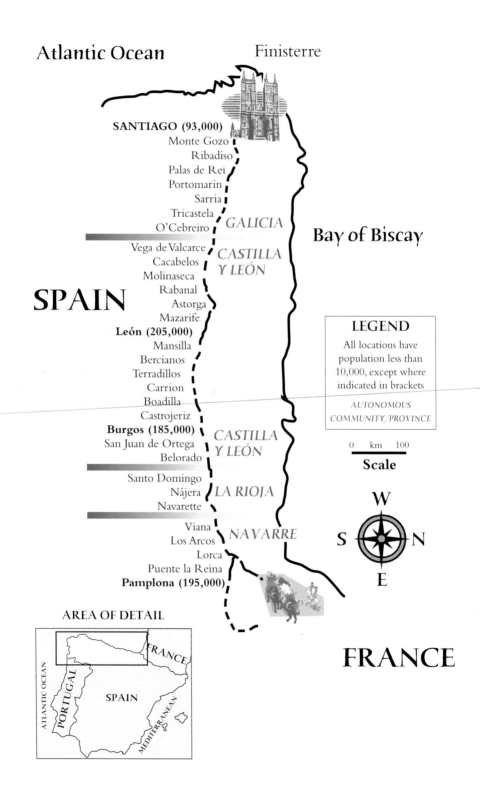

Atlantic Ocean

Finisterre

SANTIAGO (93,000)
Monte Gozo
Ribadiso
Palas de Rei
Portomarin
Sarria
Tricastela
O'Cebreiro

GALICIA

Bay of Biscay

Vega de Valcarce
Cacabelos
Molinaseca
Rabanal
Astorga
Mazarife

*CASTILLA
Y LEÓN*

León (205,000)
Mansilla
Bercianos
Terradillos
Carrion
Boadilla
Castrojeriz

SPAIN

Burgos (185,000)
San Juan de Ortega
Belorado

*CASTILLA
Y LEÓN*

Santo Domingo
Nájera
Navarette

LA RIOJA

Viana
Los Arcos
Lorca
Puente la Reina
Pamplona (195,000)

NAVARRE

LEGEND

All locations have
population less than
10,000, except where
indicated in brackets

*AUTONOMOUS
COMMUNITY/PROVINCE*

0   km   100

Scale

W

S   N

E

FRANCE

AREA OF DETAIL

ATLANTIC OCEAN

PORTUGAL

FRANCE

SPAIN

MEDITERRANEAN

INTRODUCTION

This is not your typical vacation. It starts normally enough; an international flight, a connecting flight, a train to an old European city, a nice hotel, a few days of wandering around the city. Then one April morning I step out of the hotel, turn left, and start walking by myself for hundreds of kilometres across country I have never seen before, using only a rudimentary map from a guidebook. How bizarre is that? But that is exactly how it happened. This is the story of that journey.

This book is organized into six sections: the Prologue describing the preparation for the journey; four sections representing each one of the major political regions that I walked through: Navarre, La Rioja, Castilla y León, and Galicia; and an Epilogue.

PROLOGUE

I am going to Spain to walk 800 kilometres of "el camino de Santiago," or the road to Santiago, also known as the Way of St. James. I have never been to Spain. I plan to start at St. Jean Pied-de-Port, across Spain's northern border with France, just on the northern side of the Pyrenees. The camino is a thousand-year-old pilgrim[2] path that runs across the northern part of Spain from east to west, ending at Santiago de Compostela in the northwest corner of Spain. Santiago is where St. James is reputedly[3] buried, and his tomb and shrine has been a major site for Christians. It is not clear to me why I am doing this, except that I feel a compulsion to make this journey. I do not think that I am religious, so this is not a "pilgrimage" for me, although I hope that the journey will have spiritual overtones. I do not, however, expect that this will be Shirley McLean's camino.

I intended from the start to walk it alone. I would do it either in the spring, mid-April and May, or in the fall, September to mid-October. I figure that I need about five weeks to complete the walk. The choice of dates is based on two major considerations: the weather and the volume of people. For the past thirty-five years, the numbers of people on the camino have been increasing steadily, from a low of six in 1972, to 2,500 in 1986, to 20,000 in 1995, to a high of 100,000

---

2   In early medieval times—this was before Lourdes and Canterbury—the three major Christian pilgrimage destinations were Jerusalem, Rome, and Santiago. A pilgrim who arrived at Jerusalem was known as a *palmero*, a pilgrim who achieved Rome was known as a *Romero*, and a pilgrim who struggled through to Santiago was known as . . . a *peregrino* (a pilgrim).

3   There is no evidence whatsoever that St. James was ever in Spain, either in his lifetime or after his death, but that does not matter, because a lot of people thought that he was buried in Santiago and that gave them courage in the centuries-long fight against the Moors. The fiction likely arose because an eighth-century Spanish monk, St. Beatus, read a document, the *Breviarium Apostolorum*, about where the apostles preached, which had been mis-transcribed. St. James likely preached in Hierosolyman (Jerusalem), which morphed over time into Hispaniam (Spain). Beatus picked up this version and spread the good news.

in 2006. Holy Years[4] in Spain see a significant jump in the numbers of pilgrims. In 2004, the most recent Holy Year, the numbers almost doubled to 180,000. The busiest months are July and August, Spain's typical months for vacation from work or school.

June, July, and August are also the hottest months in northern Spain, so those three months are definitely out. November, December, January, and February are cold, snowy, and unpredictable. That cuts them out of contention. September and October are pleasant months, but I want to visit New Orleans in late October, and I do not want to have to walk the camino to a tight deadline, so that leaves March, April, and May. In March I will be coming back from a couple of months in Arizona, so, by exclusion, I am walking in April and May. Since I have read and been told that the Pyrenees, where I will be starting, will likely be snow-covered and can have blizzards in March and into April, I plan to start by mid-April and finish by the end of May. That ought to give me the best weather and the least volume of people.

The tomb of St. James was "rediscovered" here early in the ninth century (834 AD) and authenticated, if that is the correct term, by Theodomirus, the Bishop of Iria Flavia. This was a stroke of good luck for the local Spanish nobility and clergy, who were having trouble keeping the Moors[5] at bay. The Moors had a magical edge, a piece of the arm of Mohammed, and with it to inspire their troops, won enough of the important battles to discourage the Christian defenders. Once the bones of St. James were discovered, having been lost for eight centuries, the Spanish troops had their own magical relic to inspire them, and the *Reconquista* began. St. James, that mild-mannered apostle, became known as St. James Matamoros, the Moor slayer. He is often portrayed in Spain wearing Conquistador armour, on horseback on churches and cathedrals, wielding a sword with the heads of dead Moors around the horse's feet. In this world lit only by fire, the belief in an all-powerful and often vengeful God was almost universal.

---

4   A Spanish Holy Year of St. James is one in which the Feast of St. James, July 25, falls on a Sunday. The most recent was in 2004 and the next will be in 2010, when you can expect about twice as many pilgrims as in off-years.
5   The term "Moor" is a derogatory early Christian name for Muslim, much as "Eskimo" is a derogatory Cree name for Inuit. Eskimo means "raw meat eater" in Cree.

It turns out that, like so many other Christian rituals and myths, this journey across northern Spain may well have been a pagan pilgrimage thousands of years before the Way of St. James was initiated. The older Celtic pilgrimage is to a point on the coast just west of Santiago, Finisterre (Land's End or the Edge of the World), which was seen as a magical place by Celts, who thought that paradise existed beyond the far horizon where the sun set every night. The scallop, for so long an article of the Christian faithful, resembles the setting sun, and was the focus of pre-Christian Celtic rituals of the area. All of this to say that the pre-Christian origin of the camino de Santiago may have been a Celtic end-of-life journey, always westwards towards the setting sun and terminating at the Edge of the World (Finisterre).

St. Francis of Assisi made this pilgrimage to Santiago in 1213–14, as did Charlemagne,[6] earlier, and Pope John Paul 23rd, more recently, so I am walking in good footsteps.[7] Of course, not only the good guys walk the camino. In former times, all kinds of people could be found on the camino. There were genuine pilgrims, traders, thieves, medical people, criminals who had been sentenced to make the pilgrimage, other people who, for a fee, would walk the camino in place of someone else (often a wealthy criminal). It appears that heretics also used the pilgrimage route to reach the western part of Iberia.[8]

Even fictional heroes like Diego de la Vega, better known as Zorro, walked the camino, during the peninsular wars, disguised as a pilgrim, with two beautiful—of course—young women and their *dueña* (chaperone) as fugitives from the French and their traitorous Spanish allies.

I have moments when I say to myself, "What are you thinking, to commit very publicly to walking 800 kilometres across Spain by yourself?" Carroll reminds me, lovingly, that I am seventy, and young

---

6   Charlemagne must have had the gift of prescience, since, if he walked the camino as a pilgrimage, he did so about fifty years before the bones of St. James were discovered. No wonder he was known as "the Great"!

7   Other famous pilgrims include: King Alfonso II in 813, El Cid in 1064, Louis VII of France in 1154, Hermann Künig, author of a German guide, in 1495, James III of Scotland and England in 1719, Giovanni Roncalli, later Pope John XXIII, in 1957, and, of course, more recently, Shirley MacLaine.

8   "Despite preaching, excommunication, interdict and a crusade, the Albigensian heresy continued to flourish in Languedoc, and the Waldensian movement was by no means dead. The pilgrimage to Compostela apparently served as a route whereby these heresies penetrated into the western part of the peninsula." Joseph F. O'Callaghan, *A History of Medieval Spain* (Ithaca: Cornell University Press, 1975), p. 498.

people will see me as old, even if I don't see myself as old. Other than my failure to reduce my own weight by about twenty pounds—I am just under 190 pounds—I think that I am ready. I have trained hard over the past twenty-four months and have reduced the pack weight as much as possible. It feels very normal and comfortable wearing it. My hiking boots are well worn in.

My preparation included a very careful selection of items to go in the backpack. Weight is a major issue when one has to carry everything one needs. It is normal for people to carry their own gear with them, although one can join a tour group and have one's gear carried from point to point. That makes it, in my view, into something resembling a hike and not something resembling a pilgrimage. But that is my opinion, not a dictum for others.

I have a blue Osprey Aether 70 (for seventy-litre capacity) backpack, which has a separate zippered section at the bottom for my one-pound three-season sleeping bag. In the top flap of the backpack, I have a Camelback collapsible one-litre plastic container, which allows me to drink water any time I want from a plastic tube extending over my shoulder to a mouthpiece in easy reach. My clothes—two complete sets of shirts, pants, underwear, and socks—have all been chosen for easy washing and drying, which means all synthetic. For rain, I have a red Mountain Hard Wear Typhoon rain jacket and pants, breathable, waterproof, and lightweight. For cold, I have a long-sleeved fleece pullover. For sun: sunglasses, sunscreen, and a Tilley hat with my cloth pilgrim scallop shell sewn on it by Carroll. I had her sew this on at the last minute, since I did not want to display the shell while training. I am saving it for the actual camino.

My boots, a critical component, are Lowa light hikers with Birkenstock orthotic insoles. I am on my second pair, since I wore a pair out while training for this walk in the countryside near my home in Kanata and for two months walking the hills in the sere, mountainous country north and east of Mesa, Arizona. I used a pedometer and recorded my step count to encourage myself to walk the distances that I figured would prepare me for the camino, although I never walked more than eighteen kilometres a day in training (a little over three hours), and that seldom. My Leki trekking poles are collapsible, which has two advantages. I can carry them in my baggage and I can change the length depending on whether I am going up (shorter) or down hill (longer). I got most of the gear at either the Mountain Equipment Co-op and the Expedition Shop in Canada or at REI in the United States.

The pack also includes my trusty guidebook, Brierley's *A Pilgrim's Guide to the Camino de Santiago,* complete with maps, a rather complete set of utility items, such as a headlamp, a Swisscard—like a Swiss army knife but in credit card shape and size—, compass, whistle, all the usual hiking stuff, and emergency medical items to combat the most likely problems encountered over a period of weeks in a strange country.

15 April, in Ottawa

It is 1435 hours and I am at the Ottawa airport waiting at departure gate 18 for the Air Canada flight to Toronto at 1600, en route to Madrid via Munich. I checked in and got my boarding pass online. When I arrive at the airport, courtesy of my daughter Meredith, I am able to get my checked baggage—my backpack—packed in plastic and checked through to Madrid. I let go of it very reluctantly, since if it doesn't arrive in Madrid, I will just have to wait for it. I am very ready to go, although I am a little trepidatious about what I have embarked on.

16 April, Ottawa to Madrid

The flight is very pleasant, considering that it is a red-eye. Manage to get my seat changed from row 32 to row 22, but I need not have bothered. We are at the gate at 1000 hours on the dot, and I go through passport control and security and am here in twenty minutes. Didn't have to take my boots off in Ottawa or here, so that is a pleasant change from air travel in the U.S. these days.

Yesterday evening, I reread *The River of Doubt, Theodore Roosevelt's Darkest Journey* (a gift from my sister-in-law Maryan O'Hagan), in which he and a small group of companions, in 1913, went down four hundred miles of a tributary—the "River of Doubt"—of the Amazon that had never been gone down by anyone not an indigenous Amazonian before, and for very good reasons. And even the native Amazonians may not have travelled the entire river. The co-leader of the expedition was an authentic Brazilian hero, Colonel, later Marshal, Cândido Mariano da Silva Rondon, who was most famous for his exploration of Mato Grosso and the Western Amazon Basin and for his lifelong support of

Brazilian native populations (his mother was indigenous). Rondon and Roosevelt's team lost three men (one murdered, one drowned, one, the murderer, left in the jungle), starved (Roosevelt lost twenty-five percent of his body weight), and were threatened by caimans, piranha, catfish capable of swallowing a man, biting insects, malaria, snakes, previously undiscovered—and deadly—Indians, not to mention waterfalls, rapids, and really bad logistics. It all makes my carefully planned trip look like a walk in the park.

I am feeling good, not tired, although I only dozed through the night. The blow-up neck support really makes a difference.

It is 1020 and I am sitting in the Munich departure lounge. I am still concerned about my pack arriving in Madrid when I do, but there is nothing I can do to influence that. Spent some time last night listening to my Spanish lessons. They seem very pertinent all of a sudden. The weather here is gorgeous—clear, warm, sunny. I hope that it is a sample of what's to come. German being spoken all around me—I catch a few words now and again.

Thinking about why I am doing this, I still don't have a definitive answer. Certainly there is the physical challenge—that much is obvious. The psychological challenge is also pretty clear—spending a lot of time over a period of weeks by oneself is likely to bring up interesting stuff. Beyond that, I can't say. Is there a spiritual aspect to my evident need to do this? I don't know, but I expect I'll find out over the course of the next five weeks.

Now 1205—We are supposed to be airborne, but we are sitting on the tarmac in Munich after our Lufthansa aircraft hits a canteen truck with its left wingtip while being pushed back out of the gate. There are three ground crew at the end of the wing now, on a lift, try-

ing to fix what the captain is calling a "scratch" on the winglet, the vertical fin at the end of the wing. Good thing that I have about five hours in Madrid before the train to Pamplona leaves.

Ground crew in Munich repairing the damaged left winglet on my Lufthansa flight to Madrid.

1230—They have removed the left wing winglet and we are going to Madrid without it. The captain, who speaks fluent English, says that it is perfectly safe to fly; it just increases fuel consumption slightly. Since the winglet is only added to reduce drag, that makes perfect sense to me. Of course, I can't help but think about the L1011—or was it a DC–10?—that crashed about twenty years ago near Paris after the ground crew battered a baggage door shut, only to have it open and tear off in flight—although I am not feeling morbid.

1740—I have arrived in Spain and everything has worked flawlessly, except for one thing. My backpack has not arrived and there is no plan B. The Lost Baggage woman at the airport here in Madrid is very helpful and solicitous. She takes down all the details, gives me a case number and phone number and says that she will call my cell phone or the hotel in Pamplona when they know anything. She figures that it will come in on the 2230 flight from Munich tonight. I sure hope so, because I will have to completely re-equip if it is seriously lost. I even left my detailed guidebook for the trip in the backpack, since I am not going anywhere without it.

Now I am in the Atocha train station in Madrid, waiting for the 1930 train to Pamplona. The train station is simply gorgeous. The old, or original part of the station, is a botanical garden inside—tropical trees and shrubs, hundreds of turtles in a pond.

Botanical garden in the Atocha train station in Madrid.

The people here look and dress exactly like they do in North America, but there are three noticeable differences. Very few blacks, very few Asians, and, out of thousands of people, exactly three fat ones. Agribusiness and high-fructose corn syrup have evidently not arrived here yet.

The train leaves at *exactly* 1930. Well, I AM in Europe, where one expects the trains to run on time. It is a fast, very smooth ride. I am travelling in Turista, a nice car, next to the cafeteria car. The trip from Madrid to Pamplona is 3.5 hours, rural all the way. The last sixty minutes seem extremely long in subjective time. I am very tired and it has been dark for a couple of hours.

I arrive in Pamplona at about 2300 and get a cab to the Hotel Maisonnave. It turns out to be located in the heart of the old city and is a three-star, with exceptionally pleasant and helpful front desk staff. They make a photocopy of my lost luggage report and will follow up with the folks in Madrid for me. Only one of three desk staff speaks English, not like the Europe I'm used to. I go to bed, expecting to have my backpack by tomorrow morning.

17 April, in Pamplona

In the morning, still no sign of baggage, I must come up with a plan B. I am reluctant to buy stuff that I either have to carry or throw away when my baggage arrives. You can see that I am still hopeful that it *will* arrive. I am heading off to the Pilgrim office to find out what I can do here to re-equip. What I find is an *albergue* (pronounced al-ber-gay, with the emphasis on the last syllable) — a hostel — closed, of course. It does not open until 1300 hours. I am in the very old part of Pamplona: narrow, winding streets, very medieval in appearance and feel. Of course, this town was established in Roman times.

It feels as if I am suspended in amber. I have to stay available so that my luggage has a place to come to. I am staying here for another night. The hotel has been calling Madrid for me every couple of hours, because they are aware of my problem. I can't start the camino without my pack or some substitute for it. Later today, after 1630 when the stores re-open (*siesta*[9] is alive and well here, just as all my books reported), I am going to find a sports clothing store to see what I can find.

In the afternoon I go for a walk, meet two local men, probably in their fifties or sixties, who think that I am lost. They suggest that I try the local wine, vino de Navarre, *vino del año* (this year's wine). I find a lovely, large square, Plaza del Castillo, with open-air bars around, so I order local wine and it is good. Similar to nouveau Beaujolais. Not much of a surprise, that. I sit and talk to a couple, Elizabeth, English, from Taunton, and Stefan from Germany — married, doing a few days on the camino. He is wearing cords and old boots, one of which is

---

9   *Siesta* is the afternoon nap that is popular and widespread in Spain.

Plaza del Castillo in Pamplona with shaded patios.

failing. They are planning to do twenty-eight kilometres tomorrow as their last day, but they are worried. If the boot fails en route, in the villages, no repair and no bus equals big problem. They came in yesterday from the north, said that they had met at least forty people on the camino and that it was very muddy and that you really need at least one walking pole. There has been a lot of rain, although it is lovely now, warm and sunny. They tell me that the camino is quite busy, which surprises me, this far away from Santiago and this early in the season. So I guess I do have expectations, after all.

An observation: there are almost no cars in the whole area where I am walking in the city. It is delightful, only a few delivery vehicles. It is a good thing, since most of the roads are extremely narrow and winding, with three- to five-storey buildings up tight on both sides. It is the old city, which is a pedestrian-only area, except for deliveries, which are restricted to a few hours every morning, and taxis.

I go to the tourist office and get a map that includes the camino route through Pamplona. This will be handy when I finally get underway. Also visit a department store and pick up polyester underwear and a hat, in case my luggage stays lost. This store also has backpacks and poles, so if worst comes to worst, I can re-equip there.

My Spanish is sufficiently good—or bad—to convince people to try their English, so communication is possible, although there is one lady, a pharmacist of a certain age, who simply speaks Spanish to me and repeats herself when I say, "*no comprendo.*" I am trying to fill a prescription for medication that is in the missing backpack. Other people waiting in line after me are able to tell me what she is saying. So

I manage. Like Scarlett in *Gone with the Wind*, I always rely on the kindness of strangers. Everyone I talk to is exceptionally kind and helpful.

A few notes on pronunciation: V is B, as in *vino blanco*, pronounced "bino blanco." Unlike the rest of the Spanish-speaking world, here in Spain "C" is "th," as in the word for "five," spelled *cinco*, pronounced "thinko." The letter "R" is rolled, even more than in French, when at the beginning of a word or doubled in the body of a word. Using the "C" sound instead of the "th" sound marks one as being from away, although I suspect I will give out more clues than just that one!

At 1900 hours I am back in the square, sitting on a bench and watching the scene unfold before me. This square has shaded arcades around most sides, to help protect against what must be brutal summer sun. They also work pretty well, I discover, for rain. They look just like those surrounding the square in Santa Fe, New Mexico, which of course was built on the Spanish pattern. All the buildings that surround the square are between three and five storeys high, obviously built prior to the invention of elevators. There are lots of people, many small children playing, only a few teens, many smokers, many cell phones, overwhelmingly Caucasian — few African, few Asian, and no fat people at all. There is an occasional police presence, a couple of cops strolling by, but not overt, and the people seem to ignore them, so they are not seen as a threat at all. Some of the stores have security guards, who look much like those at home — police wannabes, except these carry large and conspicuous truncheons on their belts.

At 2000 hours, I decide to eat dinner and go into an elegant restaurant, the Iruña,[10] on one edge of the square. It turns out that Hemingway wrote about this very restaurant in *The Sun Also Rises*, which he wrote here in 1926. I know this because he is quoted on the menu: "*Tomamos café en el Iruña, sentados en comodos sillones, mientras desde la fresca sombre de las arcadas contempabamos la gran plaza.*" "We take coffee in the Iruña, seated in comfortable chairs, while from the dark shade of the arcades, we contemplate the great plaza."

The walls are the same stamped tin as the ceiling tile that we have from the old doomed Daly Building. This place predates the turn of

---

10 Iruña is the Basque name for the city of Pamplona.

the past century, noisy but with great ambience: one huge room, about sixty by forty feet, a twenty-foot ceiling, ornate columns on a twenty by ten grid, large, ornate chandeliers. Where the walls are not stamped tin, they are enormous mirrors, probably six feet wide by twelve feet high. They feel just right in a room this large.

I order the daily special, the "*menu del dia,*" for twelve euros: asparagus appetizer and veal cordon bleu as the main course. It comes with water or wine included, so I, of course, order wine. When it arrives, it is a full 750-ml bottle of local wine, Irache Tinto 2005 — a full bottle of red wine for a single diner. No wonder there are so few cars around! These guys don't fool around when it comes to wine with dinner. If red wine is really good for me, I should be in great shape five weeks from now.

When the asparagus (*asparragus*) arrives, it is five chilled white stalks, attractively presented with sour cream, grated carrots, and corn niblets on the side — delightful. Also a very large crusty roll arrives on the table — no plate or butter, just the roll.

The veal arrives with French fries. It is good, seriously fried, no other vegetables. This is carnivore country. I have read that vegetarians have a difficult time on the camino, and this would seem to reinforce that. I am not one, so it ought not to be a problem for me. Dessert is lemon sorbet — in a tall narrow glass like we use at home for champagne cocktails — and a straw. It's a thick drink here. Very nice.

The restaurant crowd consists of many ladies of the blue-haired set, a few men of the same age with them, a few couples, a long table obviously reserved and set up in advance, and me. It looks like tea time in the Empress Hotel in Victoria. This is apparently the early bird special time in Spain, which confirms what I have read about people here eating *really* late. The restaurant at the hotel where I am staying does not even open until 2030 hours.

Sitting here alone, watching the activity at the tables around me, emphasizes for me the enormous importance of relationships in our species. I have no idea what any of them are talking about, but they are doing a thorough job of it. Eavesdropping is easy, understanding is not. Two couples, one a generation younger than the other, are sitting next to me. The younger couple arrives, two-cheek air kiss — very French. The younger couple are showing digital camera images and an actual photo to the older couple. Parents, aunt and uncle, friends, in-laws? I'll never know.

Pamplona is, of course, the city that Hemingway made famous in *The Sun Also Rises*, because of the bullfights and because of the Running of the Bulls, an annual festival held from 7 to 14 July each year in honour of St. Fermin, the patron saint of Pamplona and Navarre and of bakers, wine, and wineskins. Each morning, six bulls are released into a narrow corridor of streets, where thousands of mostly drunk or drugged young male tourists run frantically in front of them, fulfilling, at least in their own minds, some kind of manhood ritual. In the afternoon, the bulls are released into the bullrings for their ritualized execution. Officially, one is not allowed to run if one is drunk, but that does not seem to be taken seriously or seriously enforced. Personally, I would not get out in front of a half-dozen half-ton desperately frightened and therefore unpredictable bulls *unless* I was drunk. You can probably tell that I am underwhelmed by this activity, although it doesn't matter, because the running of the bulls is going to happen three months from now, and I will be long gone.

18 April, in Pamplona

Carroll has sent me faxes of two prescriptions and I have been able to fill both here in Pamplona, so that concern is eliminated. As of this morning at 1100, there is still no sign of or news about my luggage. The hotel front desk staff continues to be extremely helpful, but to no avail. For some reason, the Lost Luggage people in Madrid had noted that I was staying here until 25 April. I have no idea where they got that from. The hotel guy this morning reminds them that I am leaving for el camino as soon as my backpack arrives, so their date is incorrect.

Of everything that I have planned and packed, I actually have with me only the rain jacket and the boots, along with one set of clothing, which I have on. This is definitely a problem.

19 April, in Pamplona

There is still no sign of my missing backpack after three full days, so I am staying here in Pamplona. I am going to wait one more day, then re-equip, as I need to move on. I find and have put away at a department store here a backpack, sleeping bag, trekking poles, pants, and shirt that I will need to continue my journey. I am still hopeful that the missing backpack will miraculously turn up.

The upside is that I am getting a really good introduction to this part of Spain. As always, I am finding that speaking as much Spanish as I can encourages the person or persons with whom I am speaking to try English, if only to stop my barbarous Spanish.

Yesterday was my jet lag day. I woke up at 1030 and went back to bed at 2000. I did not eat at all because I never got hungry. I spend a restless night but wake up refreshed at 0830. Have breakfast here in the hotel at the restaurant El Txoko, pronounced "Choko." It's Basque for "corner."

The Basque culture is fascinating. It is generally accepted that Basques are a remnant of the Palaeolithic inhabitants of Western Europe, and Basque tribes were mentioned in Roman times by both Strabo and Pliny. It is the only language in Europe that predates the Indo-European invasions. Evidently it is the only culture that the people who are our ancestors (if you are German, English, French, Spanish, etc) were unable to conquer or assimilate, likely because they live in inhospitable country, very hilly and rugged, and, like the Afghan or Kashmiri hill tribes, were just too difficult to conquer.

The Basques are the same folks who wiped out Charlemagne's rearguard at Roncesvalles. *The Song of Roland*, written in the 1100s, memorializes this battle. It turns out to have some basis in fact. In 778, Charlemagne was fighting the Moors in Spain when a disturbance on the Rhine forced him to return home. He retreated through the pass at Roncesvalles, and the rearguard force was destroyed by the fierce and fiercely independent Basques of the region. (They deserved it. His army had pillaged Pamplona, which was a Basque city, and the Basques were, nominally, on the same side as Charlemagne's troops in the war.) Among the slain was Count Hruodland, prefect of the Breton March. Over time, the Frankish name Hruodland became the Roland of the poem.

More recently, there has been another upsurge of Basque nationalism, which includes, unfortunately, murders and kidnappings, performed mostly by the ETA — *Euskadi Ta Askatasuna* or "Basque Homeland and Freedom," a Marxist–Leninist group founded in 1959, considered by itself as a paramilitary Basque nationalist group and defined as a terrorist organization by the European Union, the United States, and the United Nations. The violent nationalism is surprising, given that, after Franco's death and the end of the dictatorship, autonomy was restored for the Basques (as well as for the rest of Spain), and they achieved a level of self-government without precedent in Basque modern history. The Basques manage their own public finances and have their own police force. While I am here, there is a truce, but it is shaky. There are some 500 ETA militants held in prison in Spain and France.

Pamplona is the largest Basque city that I will visit on this journey to Spain. Here in Basque country, the street signs are bilingual (Castilian Spanish and Basque), as are many of the commercial signs on buildings and vehicles. There are sprayed-on slogans on some surfaces, presumably Basque separatist sentiment, but there does not appear to be any sense of danger here. Of course, my radar for that type of situation has never been very good!

Here is a Basque tidbit to mull over: Recent genetic studies have confirmed that about seventy-five percent of the people of the British Isles have bloodlines that can be traced to inhabitants of the Basque areas of Spain and France. So apparently most Britons are actually of Basque descent or are, at the least, related.

Today, I spend from about 0900 until about 1300 trying to get some resolution about the missing baggage. No success. Then I go out, find out where I can get the *credencial* (the official booklet with many spaces for stamps for pilgrims) and go to visit the cathedral. To my surprise, there is an entry fee of about six dollars for the cathedral. That is a first for me, and one that I decline to pay. I take a couple of pictures of the outside, for which there is no charge.

I visit the Plaza del Toros, the bullring, but do not go inside. It's about the same shape and size, with about the same seating capacity, just over 19,000, as the Corel Centre in Kanata. Outside it there is a statue of Hemingway, a life-size bust on top of a plinth. They liked the fact that he publicized Pamplona and the bullfights. There is also a loading dock with a ramp leading down to a high door. It is likely the last thing the bulls see before they get the surprise of their young lives. Evidently, they are never exposed to a man on foot while they are being raised. The budding matadors always train with heifers, not

*Hemingway bust
at Plaza del Toros
in Pamplona.*

bulls. The theory is that if the bulls were accustomed to men on foot, the matadors would not stand a chance. So the men go in fully trained while the bulls go in cold. Seems a little unfair to me, kind of like duck hunting, in which the ducks don't get to carry weapons.

On a happier note, I visit the Parque de la Taconera, just down the road from here. It is an old fortification, and now one of the prettiest parks in Pamplona. The moat is now used for deer—very large ones, little shaggy goats, domestic geese, swans, and peacocks. I watch as a peacock displays all his finery for an apparently indifferent peahen. He is magnificent with his feathers all displayed. In the end, of course, he is just an oversized chicken with a super-sized opinion of himself. He reminds me of an actor who has begun to believe his own press releases. A keeper is feeding them all and he has to keep shooing the goats and deer away so that the geese, including one lame one, can get enough to eat.

Then I go to the Ciudadela (literally The Citadel). It was built between 1571 and 1645, ordered by King Felipe II, to a very sophisticated design, in a pentagon, with five bastions with overlapping fields of fire. It reminds me of Fort Henry at Kingston, Ontario, with some important differences. It is larger and was tested under fire, as Fort Henry never was. It eventually failed the test, since the French took the Ciudadela by force in 1808 (during the Peninsular Wars). I walk around the top of the ramparts, which are all covered with wild grasses and some wild flowers. There is one blood-red poppy standing alone. I think about all the men who fought and died here, both Spanish defenders and French attackers, some instantly, many more in agony and at length, and think about the stupidity and futility of war. It seems that we never learn.

After dozing for a while, seated on a bench in the Ciudadela, I walk back to the Plaza del Castillo (this is turning into a favourite haunt; I can see why Hemingway liked it) and have two very small—cup size—local beers while I sit under an awning and watch the world unfold. There is a small, sturdy, swarthy busker playing an accordion and singing what sounds like songs about tragedy and loss. There is also a little girl, about three or four years old, in a blue dress, walking very slowly along this side of the Plaza, shoulders shaking, face contorted and obviously in distress. I think that her parents are lost and she cannot find them. I want to help, but realize that with almost no Spanish, my actions could be easily misinterpreted and I could find myself in a world of trouble. She eventually passes out of sight.

I notice that there are many fewer people than the night before and I wonder what the difference is—and then I notice that many of them are carrying open umbrellas. It is starting to rain, so I leave the square and go home to bed.

Carroll calls to say that she has had a return call from Stephen in Munich Baggage and he has told her that my pack was on the manifest from Munich to Madrid. She urges me to go to Madrid and insist on a much more thorough effort to find the baggage. I catch the 1900 train from Pamplona to Madrid.

Just south of Pamplona, which was wrapped in darkness when I came up a few days ago, there are hundreds of windmills on every ridge in both directions, along with arrays of solar panels. These Spaniards are serious about alternative energy, as we Canadians, shamefully, are not. NIMBY (Not In My Back Yard) seems to be the rule in Canada. We could be world leaders in alternative energy technology, but we remain hewers of wood and drawers of water. We have for so many generations been a resource-based economy that we, as a country, can't imagine any alternative. We will pay for our complacency and lack of foresight.

At 2230, I arrive at Atocha station in Madrid and find a hotel nearby. Did I mention that they showed an Adam Sandler movie on the train? He isn't any better in Spanish. The hotel has a room available and I take the elevator which ought to be—and often is—in a museum, to the fifth floor. The room is Spartan, small, spotlessly clean, and the right price. I call Carroll and tell her where I am, then I go to sleep.

At midnight, the hotel phone wakes me. It is my daughter Meredith with a message that she is faxing me some contacts in Madrid that she has gotten from a friend, Linda Beverley in Houston. The contacts here all speak English and will likely be happy to help. Thank you both, Linda and Meredith, for caring enough to create this positive feeling.

20 April 2007, Madrid to Pamplona

The fax that Meredith sent me last night is waiting for me at reception in the morning. I call and get the administrative assistant of José Luis Garcia Cuartero. She puts me through to him at home via the switchboard. He is head of EuroFM and the managing partner of Grupo CADAR, which is a facility management (FM) consulting firm like ours, Carroll Thatcher Planning Group, back in Canada, only much bigger, with architects and engineers on board. He offers to help in any way he could and I tell him my plan: Go to the airport, demand to personally see the lost luggage area and determine what is going on. We will meet later in the day if nothing shows up.

I go to Terminal 1, Arrival Lounge 2, and find the lost luggage booth where I first reported the missing baggage four days ago. The man on duty checks my precious baggage ticket, checks the computer file and says there is no new information. I tell him what I have been told. I check his lost luggage room—not there. Back to the Lost and Found.

After I have spent a lot of time going back and forth, José arrives. He goes immediately into action, like the successful, powerful businessman that he is. Eventually, they admit that no one has the slightest idea where my baggage is. At least I am satisfied that the bag is not physically here at the Madrid Airport and now I can move on.

José drives me back to the train station, graciously waits with me while I get a ticket for Pamplona, and we eat lunch together. Since the menu is in Spanish only, he explains what each item is so that I can make an intelligent and informed choice. Anything *"a la Romana"* is breaded and deep-fried. This is good to know. *Tortillas* are potato pancakes here, unlike in North America, where they are made from cornmeal. This is also good to know. I have a small wedge—a *"pincho"*—of a tortilla. It is not great—and José assures me that they will be better in the villages on the camino. I sure hope so.

He spent his last year of high school on an exchange program in the U.S., then another four years at a college in Iowa. His wife is from Idaho, so that is where they and their three children spend their summer vacations. For a Canadian, it seems strange for Spaniards to spend their vacations in Idaho, but family ties trump everything. Even though I still do not have my baggage, José has been an enormous help. I am satisfied that I am not missing any subtlety about the baggage due to my lack of fluent Spanish.

He has arranged that when the bag is found, they will contact his office and he will ensure that it is sent to wherever I want it to go. So now I am again waiting for the 1930 train and I call ahead to make sure that I have a room at the Hotel Maisonnave. They are so good to me; they assure me that my room is secure.

Here in the train station, they have a people mover, a shallow moving platform that moves people up or down two floors on four angled and moving ramps. It reminds me powerfully of the shooting galleries at carnival midways of my youth. Remember the ducks? If you shot down a predetermined number of them, you won a prize of a large and gaudy stuffed animal, which you then promptly gave to whoever was the love of your life at the moment. Anyway, it looks just like that, except the ducks are people.

As I am sitting here in the Atocha station, a couple and an older gentleman sit down near me in the restaurant. The couple is smartly dressed, but the older man, likely in his eighties, is elegant. He is wearing a three-piece velvet suit, either brown or loden green, I can't tell. Striped shirt, smart tie, a wooden cane with a dark red wood handle, a gold band separating it from the dark brown cane itself. Did I mention the brass buttons on his suit? I thought that era had vanished, but it is still alive, though elderly. When they get up to leave, I approach them, excuse myself, *"Disculpe, señor,"* and ask if I might take a photograph of him.

"Of me?" he asks (in Spanish) and I reply *"Yes."*

"Why me?" again he asks, and I reply *"Because you are so elegant."*

He smiles and sits back and allows his photo to be taken. We introduce ourselves: he is Nicolas, and I am Guy from Canada.

"What part?"

"From Ottawa."

"Oh, yes, I have friends in Toronto."

"I was a little boy in Toronto."

That is all, we say goodbye and then they leave, but I have a permanent reminder of what elegance still looks like.

On the way back north on the three-and-a-half-hour train ride to Pamplona, I sit with Guillem Huguet Serra, a twenty-eight-year-old Spaniard with a doctorate in mathematics, specializing in "attitude mechanics." He is leaving next week for Darmstadt in Germany, to join the European Space Agency and work on the problems of unmanned resupply of the International Space Station.

When I ask him, he explains how one determines attitude in space. One needs three coordinates to fix oneself in space. The first coordinate is the sun. The second coordinate is the target, in this case, the space station. The third coordinate uses the first two as the x and y axes and heads off at right angles to both of them to form the z axis. Easy enough in concept, as he explains it to me, but a little more challenging, I would think, in execution.

He is brilliant, personable, handsome, and looks and sounds like he has the right stuff. He grew up in Mallorca, mother tongue is Catalan, speaks English, Spanish (Castilian), French, German (all fluently), a little Arabic, a little Chinese. He wants to be the second Spanish astronaut, and he might just do it. The first one worked for the same company and did much the same job as Guillem does now. I am going to watch for his name in the news in the coming years. I find this chance meeting a little bizarre. I am going off to walk for five weeks and he is working on devices that travel in space at 18,000 miles per hour.

Tomorrow it is time to pick up gear and get moving. The first part of the original planned trip, from St. Jean Pied-de-Port in France, is too late to start now—I don't have enough total days left—so I will start from where I am, which is in Pamplona. I will miss about 100 kilometres, including crossing the French-Spanish border and the high climb and descent over the Pyrenees.

I want to get back on track for what I came here to do—although I have really enjoyed Pamplona. Perhaps I could just stay here for five weeks and send fake messages about the trip. It is tempting.

21 April, in Pamplona

It's 0930, it's sunny, and I am sitting on a concrete bench in the plaza of the Palacio de Congreso y Auditorio de Navarre waiting for El Corte Ingles (a large, multi-storey department store) to open. I have already been to the archbishop's palace to collect my *credencial*, but the palace is closed. No clue as to when it will open. I was told that the Corte Ingles would open at 0900, but evidently not. Since everything is closed tomorrow (Sunday), I have to get what I need today, even if I don't leave today. When I look at my planned schedule, I see that I am fine, even if I leave tomorrow. I think that I will have lots of opportunity to practise patience on the camino, not one of my strong suits—yet. The weather is lovely and I would like to take advantage of it while it lasts.

This morning I pick up replacement gear at El Corte Ingles (it opens at 1000). I am well and pleasantly served by Iñaki, who speaks sufficient English so that, mixed with my rudimentary Spanish, we can communicate successfully about my needs and their stock. He is Basque, hence the name. I pick up my *credencial* at the archbishop's palace, check out of the Hotel Maissonave with my new backpack on, step down onto the narrow street, turn left, and head out. I am on my way by 1230. It's very late in the day to start, but I want to be gone.

What do I have? A new small backpack, new sleeping bag, new collapsible poles, one new complete change of clothing, a new second pair of socks, a new hat for sun, a rain jacket, new water bottle, camera, iPod, cellular phone, new sandals, one pair of reading glasses—don't lose them or break them—and, thanks to good planning and luck, my well worn-in boots. I wore them on the trip because they took up too much space in the backpack and I carried the rain jacket as a utility jacket. I search for but cannot find Footglide, so I have acquired instead a small plastic jar of Vaseline for my feet.

SECTION 1

NAVARRE – PAMPLONA TO VIANA

Navarre is one of Spain's seventeen autonomous communities, based on the constitution of 1978. These communities have wide legislative and executive autonomy, with their own parliaments and regional governments. Unlike Canada, the U.S., or Europe, where provincial or state powers are the same, the distribution of powers is different for every autonomous community. The objective of the 1978 constitution, following Franco's death, was to appease separatist forces and disarm the extreme right, so a highly decentralized state was established. Navarre is one of the two autonomous communities that I will be walking through that consists of exactly one province. The other is La Rioja. It is at the same time one of fifty provinces. Tricky, isn't it?

Navarre is small, at about 10,000 square kilometres compared to Castilla y León, but twice the size of its neighbour, La Rioja. In the northeast of Spain, Navarre is bordered by France to the north, Aragón to the east, La Rioja to the south, and the Basque country to the west. I will be walking southwest until I get into La Rioja. Pamplona is the capital of Navarre, and the greater Pamplona region holds about half of the population of the entire community. There are many Basque in Navarre, especially in the north.

Navarre, in the western Pyrenees, is mountainous and green in the north and has rolling hills with long vistas and valleys in the south. The south is dry and dusty, but I won't be going there. The people in Navarre are very proud of their wine, although it is not as famous as that of La Rioja, south and west of here.

21 April, Pamplona to Puente la Reina

I walk twenty-three kilometres[11] between 1230 and 1900 hours today. First hour, out of Pamplona, past the Ciudadela and the Universite de Navarre and out of urban. The trail is extremely well marked. I take pictures of typical marking, some formal, some just yellow arrows painted on every available surface. A friend told me before I left Canada that I

Typical official signage on the camino.

The yellow arrow—typical and much more common unofficial signage on the camino. Yellow arrows are everywhere.

could walk the camino without a map, and she is probably right. Then I start up the ridge, the Alto de Perdón, south of Pamplona. The word "*Alto*" should have given it away, as should the vertical profile map. This is the toughest climb I've ever done—worse than the Appalachian trail that I was on with TJ and Relma, my very fit daughter-in-law and her equally fit mother. The vistas are breathtaking, but it just goes on and on and up and up. At one point the camino skirts around a section of land, perhaps fifty metres across, that has recently slipped and has left an ugly scar on the landscape. I can see where the old path was in the slipped earth. Hope no one was on it when it slipped. It would have been an interesting experience.

And it is sunny, very hot, no shade, and not a breath of wind. I drink copious amounts of water—there are *fuentes* (fountains) along the way—and I still can't piss a drop. I take baby steps on the way up and have to stop frequently to keep my heart rate from getting too high (more than three beats per second is okay for young guys, but not for me). I pass two Dutch women sitting at rest under a small, lone tree and think that they are going to have trouble getting over the Alto at all today. One has stripped off to her bra to cool down and puts her blouse on hurriedly as I approach.

---

11   A kilometre is about two-thirds of a mile.

They are horrified when I say that I think it is four hours to Puente la Reina (which is exactly what it turns out to be).

As I continue the exhausting climb, I pass a memorial to a Belgian pilgrim, incongruously named Koko, just the one name, who died here in 1996. I think I know why. Finally, I arrive at the summit at 1630 hours, a vertical climb of about 1,000 feet. What a glorious relief! At the summit, there is a larger-than-life-sized 2-D sculpture in metal of a medieval party of pilgrims.[12] Of course, I am also taking pictures of the vistas and of the trail itself. In most places it is wide enough for a wagon or motor vehicle and is used by local farmers. In other places it is one person wide.

A man from Pamplona at the summit tells me it will take an hour to get to today's destination and points to a village in the far distance. He tells me that it is Puente la Reina. It isn't. This experience is one of the few that I have with someone sounding sincere and well-meaning and giving me bad information.

However, this may be a very old, entrenched habit in Navarre. Aimery Picaud travelled the camino sometime before 1140–1150, when he wrote his *Pilgrim's Guide*.[13] He had a lot to say about the Navarrese, none of it good:

> This is a barbarous people, different from all other peoples in customs and in race, malignant, dark in colour, ugly of face, debauched, perverse, faithless, dishonourable, corrupt, lustful, drunken, skilled in all forms of violence, fierce and savage, dishonest and false, impious and coarse, cruel and quarrelsome, incapable of any good impulses, past masters of all vices and iniquities.

---

12 This sculpture was commissioned and placed by Energia Hidroelectrica de Navarra, who also placed the forty giant windmills here in 1994. The windmills generate twenty megawatts of energy each year.

13 From *The Pilgrim's Guide*, written about 1140–1150. The Guide is part of a twelfth-century Latin manuscript known as the *Codex Calixtinus*, attributed to Pope Calixtus (d. 1124). The *Codex* was designed to promote the pilgrimage to Santiago de Compostela. Although the *Guide* has a number of anonymous authors, the work is usually attributed to a French prelate, Aimery Picaud. The tone of the *Guide* and its focus are from a French point of view, as you will see from the scathing comments that the author makes about the local populations as he makes his way to Santiago. The *Guide* includes references to many of the towns that I will walk through. The version from which this quote is taken was published by the Confraternity of St James, London, Great Britain, 1992, reprinted in 1996. The translation from the Latin is by James Hogarth.

This is what he wrote in the *Guide*, which was intended to *encourage* people to make the pilgrimage to Santiago. Imagine what he might have said if he were trying to *discourage* them from going!

The relief at the top is short-lived. The trail down is equally steep or steeper and is down what appears to be a dry stream bed. Round stones of every size. You have to pick your way. It is very rough going. I had not expected this. I am very grateful for my hiking boots and my poles. I keep expecting to arrive in Puente la Reina. When I get to the village that I could see from the summit, the first people I ask tell me it is six kilometres to Puente la Reina. About a kilometre on, there is an *albergue* with a bar, which I gratefully visit for water and a beer. Tap water is *agua del grifo*, and they are very pleased when I want that, not bottled water. I think that when you ask for local water, you are acknowledging that they are First World, not Third World,[14] and they appreciate it. Anyway, they get a chuckle out of my attempts to say *agua del grifo*. The bad news is that they say it is seven kilometres to Puente la Reina. Ever had one of those dreams where something that you are trying to reach recedes forever into the distance? It is like that.

Eventually, at about 1900, I arrive in Puente la Reina and find the Hotel Bidean on Calle Major, 20. Since *calle major* means "main street," I expect a wide thoroughfare. Wrong. This main street was laid out perhaps 800 years ago. It is narrow and quite dark. The hotel building is much newer, only about three centuries old, but renovated in 2000, with a very modern small glass and metal elevator to take me to my third-floor room. Luxury: a hot shower, private toilet (which of course was pointless, since I still can't piss a drop), and a comfortable bed.

The town of Puente la Reina grew up around the Queen's Bridge, built in the early years of the last millennium, around 1185, by King Sancho III, and named for his wife, Doña Mayor; or, perhaps, by his successor, Garcia el de Nájera and named for *his* wife, Doña Estefania. It was built here over the River Agra to assist pilgrims coming from the passes through the Pyrenees at Roncesvalles and Somport. As you will read below, there was a desperate need for a bridge. Before the bridge was built, the pilgrims had to use the services of a ferryman.

---

14   There is a French saying, attributed both to Napoleon and Alexandre Dumas, that "Africa begins at the Pyrenees." It has to do with the 750-year occupation of most of the Iberian Peninsula by the Moors.

Statues of pilgrims at the top of the Alto de Perdón, near Pamplona.

Here is what a pilgrim travelling about the year 1120 has to say about the ferrymen of that time on the camino:

> Although the rivers are quite narrow these men are in the habit of taking a piece of money for each person, rich or poor, whom they ferry across, and for a horse they exact four unworthily and by force. Their boat is small, made from a single tree-trunk, ill suited to carry horses; and so when you get into the boat you must take care not to fall into the water. You will do well to hold on to your horse's bridle and let it swim behind the boat. Nor should you go into a boat that has too many passengers, for if it is overloaded it will at once capsize.
>
> Often, too, having taken their passengers' money, the boatmen take such a number of other pilgrims on board that the boat overturns and the pilgrims are drowned; and then the wicked boatmen are delighted and appropriate the possessions of the dead.[15]

This town, Puente la Reina, is where two of the major camino routes over the Pyrenees from the rest of Europe merge, so the bridge is well sited.

The route that I am on, which passes through France and winds over the pass through the Pyrenees to Roncesvalles, then through Pamplona, is known as the "Camino Frances," or the French camino. The other route goes a little to the east through the Somport Pass.

---

15   Picaud, *The Pilgrim's Guide.*

The bridge for which Puente le Reina is named.

After a shower and lots and lots of *agua del grifo*, I walk down the main street to the bridge for which the town is named and get a couple of arty photographs, then back to the restaurant at the hotel for dinner. I order some *pescado* (fish) for €17, expecting a wonderful dinner. The presentation *is* wonderful, a lovely, tasty, small piece of fish baked in some kind of sauce with a thick red pepper sauce on the side and parsley sprinkled artistically around the border of the oversized plate. That is it. No vegetable, no potato, no wine; I even have to ask for bread. But it is beautifully presented. The good news is that the beer was good and only cost 1.5 euros. It helps that I am not particularly hungry, which surprises me.

My bill for lodging, dinner, and breakfast is €66.60, just a little more than $100. Not part of the plan!

I need my *credencial* stamped. The young woman in the hotel very carefully sets up her stamping machine and presses down firmly, putting the stamp in my book upside down. She is properly horrified and wants to stamp my book again, this time right side up, but I demur. This way I will never forget her . . .

So far, no blinding light from the heavens or psychological insights, just tired legs and feet, but it is early yet. I have lots of thoughts about how the camino is analogous to life, but they will have to wait for later.

What is important is that my legs, joints, and feet are fine. I picked up some funny-shaped Dr. Scholl's gel things for between the toes and, along with Vaseline, they work really well. Bless you, Dr. Scholl, wherever you are!

22 April, Puente la Reina to Lorca

After breakfast in the morning, I set out at 0900 for Estella, another eighteen kilometres along the way. The path runs along the edge of fields of crops and, even now when it is very dry, has muddy sections. It must be truly dreadful when it is raining. To my surprise, I turn a corner and there are the same two Dutch women, sitting again partway up a long hill. They got in very late to Puente la Reina and ended up in a room to themselves at an *albergue*; left again about thirty minutes before me. The path goes over an old Roman bridge—I guess that's redundant, since Roman bridges are always old—as it winds back and forth using tunnels to pass under the highway, the N111 between Puente la Reina and Estella. I walk through one town, Cirauqui,[16] where the *new* church is thirteenth century.

When I get to Lorca,[17] smaller than a whistle stop, I pause for needed water and a beer at a bar/*albergue* and like it so much that I decide to stay here for the night. How different my experience is from the days in 1120, when Picaud's experiences were very difficult.

Leaving Puente la Reina in the morning over the bridge.

At a place called Lorca, to the east, there flows a stream known as the Salt River. Beware of drinking from it or of watering your horse in it, for this river brings death. On its banks, while we were going to St James, we found two Navarrese sitting there sharpening their knives; for they are accustomed to flay pilgrims' horses which die after drinking the water. In answer to our question they lied, saying that the water was good and drinkable. Accordingly we watered

---

16   The town's Basque name means "nest of vipers," likely based on its location on a rocky ledge that might house either vipers or bandits (or both).

17   Lorca's name is from the Arabic *alaurque*, a term for "battle." The particular battle was fought here in 920, when Sancho I of Navarra was beaten by Muhammad Abenlope.

our horses in the river, and at once two of them died and were forthwith skinned by the two men.

I can and do drink water anywhere here without fear of death or disease. The people through whose land we pass have learned that warm and honest hospitality is better business than thievery or deceit. I could wish that this lesson were more widely understood. It would make everyone's life a lot easier and more pleasant.

The overnight charge is seven euros. I am, at the moment, the only occupant in a bright and airy spacious room with two bunks, with pillows! And I have access to a *lavadora* (washing machine) and a *secadora* (dryer). I had no idea that those Spanish lessons at Algonquin College would come in so handy. The people that I pass and meet on the way are very tolerant of my Spanish and are pleased, I think, that I make the effort. So that is where I am at the moment, taking an easy day after only about a dozen kilometres. Tomorrow I will either go to Estella or beyond it.

At 1530, same day, I am sitting at the open front of a little *albergue*, Albergue Ramon, in Lorca. The young fellow here is José-Ramon, son of José Ramon. The sound system is playing Vivaldi's *Four Seasons*. It's sunny and warm, a little breeze. I have a comfortable chair, a table, and a beer to sip on. A wonderful sense of peace—no stress, no pressure. This is a tiny village with two small *albergues*. I am in the smaller one, directly across the street from the larger one. No road names or signs. Not needed. There has been no traffic in three hours. As I note this, two vehicles come slowly by, then no more.

My laundry is drying on a collapsible rack in the street—can't do *that* in Kanata. This is the first time for washing for the Tilley pants and Sportif shirt since leaving Ottawa a week ago. They are holding up well, although I note that people tend to stand off a little. I have managed to wash my underwear every day, because it dries quickly, or at least every other day. Here I asked about a washer and dryer; "*Si, si.*" It turns out the dryer is just the spin cycle of the washer—that's why my stuff is in the street drying in the sun. Good thing it's a sunny day or I would be in trouble. José-Ramon is busy teaching me Spanish. He says that he is not a good teacher, but he is. He has very little English, so we are working together on this. I ask about the difference between *muy* and *mas*. *Mas* is "more," and *muy* is kind of like "very," as in *muy bueno*, very good.

I did not think that I would enjoy keeping a journal, but I do. I am sending it via e-mail to Carroll, whenever I can get access to Internet and my ass isn't dragging, and she sends it on to whoever is interested. I find the technology is almost like magic. When I was serving in the military in Cyprus forty years ago,[18] I could not talk to Carroll or the kids for six months. Now we speak almost daily, especially about my missing baggage, on the cell phone and I set up a Yahoo account so that I can send and receive e-mails without the need to carry a computer. I have to carry whatever I need. So far, it's working well. Internet access is widespread here.

When I travelled here, I kept my camera, cell phone and iPod on me, so I have the technology. I am not using the iPod at the moment (although it was great on the train trips between Madrid and Pamplona). When I have it on, I cannot use my hearing aids, so I lose bird sounds. My senses seem to be accentuated — colours are brighter, sounds are sharper, although my senses of taste and smell aren't any better . . . yet.

I now have two roommates, Carlos, fifty-five, and Juan, thirty-nine, from Valencia. They walked today from Pamplona, about thirty-four kilometres, and will do the same tomorrow. They tell me that it was very hot from Puente la Reina on. I don't doubt it. That distance and the hills would probably have killed me — literally. As I mentioned, I passed yesterday on the way to the summit a memorial to a Belgian who died there as he climbed the Alto. As if I needed a reminder to go slowly. That is one reason why I decided to cut today short.

Thoughts about language: It seems that different parts of the brain are responsible for different levels of competence. When I search for a Spanish word, I get German, but I don't get French. Turns out my French is quite strong and is therefore stored, at least conceptually, in a different part of the brain from the part where less strong or new languages are stored.

A brief cultural note: The massacre of thirty-two people on 16 April 2007 at Virginia Tech was a short-term wonder here. Nothing about it in the news after a couple of days. It appears that Europeans are just not surprised at or fascinated by this kind of horrific violence in America.

---

18   I was the deputy commander of an armoured reconnaissance squadron of 100 men
        for six months in 1968.

I am in Lorca watching, on a TV in the bar of the *albergue* across the road, my first game of Pelota—two players, although I am told that it can be played with teams. It is something like squash, except only one side wall, one front wall, no back wall or right side wall, very high, about as wide as a squash court but three or four times as long, and, most important, they play with their hands—no racquet. Usually this game is played with some kind of racquet, but this particular game is "*main nue,*" or bare hand. It has to be extremely difficult to play. The server plays off the front wall and the return can only be to the front wall. There are several local guys of indeterminate age who are watching the game, and it is from them that I get my information about how Pelota works. The players are Olaizola in blue and Eugi in red. As you can see from the names, this is a Basque game. Long white pants and white shoes seem to be "*de rigueur.*" The game requires enormous physical strength. If these two are typical of young Basque men, no wonder they whipped Charlemagne´s rearguard in 778.

Later in the afternoon, I meet the whole family, José-Ramon, his father, José Ramon, his mother, and his sister. I ask about the possibility of having dinner from the *menu del dia*, a fixed-price menu. José-Ramon looks at his mother, and she says the equivalent of "why not?" So they make a special dinner for two of us.

I eat dinner with Irmtrud from somewhere near Cologne in Germany. We eat an excellent meal, served with the ubiquitous bottle of red wine, which we demolish over a couple of hours. Irmtrud, a mother of two and grandmother of three, is a fiftyish German housewife—or was, until she left her husband after twenty years of bipolar disorder. His, not hers. Now she has another man in her life, but he is a mama's boy. This comes out, all in German, after we had gotten most of the way through the wine. She would just like to meet a *Mann* who is a *Mann*! I have not seen her again, except briefly in

A more difficult section of the camino. There were a few sections like this, but the uneven surface is not typical.

passing on the trail. I think about a dear friend of mine who lost her husband to cancer—I met her through my volunteer work with the Hospice at May Court in Ottawa—then ended up with a mama's boy in her life. After a year or so, she invited him to leave. I think it might be better alone than with someone who is so totally dependent, but I don't know and won't judge.

An Extremely Short History of Spain

Why would this be relevant to what I am writing about and why ought you bother to read about the medieval history of Spain?[19] Well, modern Spain —and modern Spaniards—have been shaped to a remarkable degree by their history. And the camino and its destination, Santiago, have been shaped to a remarkable degree by Spanish history. The peninsula that is now known as Spain and Portugal was populated by Celts migrating from Gaul, who mixed with the indigenous Iberian people, then by the Carthaginians (Cartegena was populated and named by Carthage), by Romans, succeeded by Visigoths, and invaded in 711 by Islamic Moors from Africa and the Middle East across the Straits of Gibraltar. This 7,000-man Berber invasion was intended only as a reconnaissance, but was so successful that the Moors stayed and expanded until they held almost all of Spain by 714. To give some idea of the astonishing impact of this, imagine if the abortive and bloody raid on Dieppe by Canadians in 1942 had, instead, been successful and been followed almost immediately by the complete capitulation of Vichy France.

By 714, the Moors temporarily held León, Astorga, and Pamplona in the far north—these cities are all on the present-day camino—and were raiding north through the pass at Roncesvalles—also on the camino—into Gaul. They were stopped by Charles Martel at Tours in 732 and retreated south across the Pyrenees, never to seriously threaten the rest of Europe again. But they stayed in Spain for over 750 years, until 1492, changing the course of history. Why didn't the Moors complete the conquest of the peninsula? It was probably a question of return on investment. The northern land was mostly mountainous, not worth much as agricultural land, the tribes were very troublesome, and

---

19   Serious historians may object to my very broad brush treatment of Spanish history, but I am just setting up the backdrop against which the current events take place.

it probably did not seem economically worthwhile to winkle out all the tribesmen from their hills and mountains. One early Muslim leader dismissed them, saying; "What are thirty barbarians perched on a rock? They must inevitably die."[20] Big mistake. It took over 700 years, but those thirty barbarians perched on a rock finally drove the Muslims out of the peninsula.

In 997, a raid on Santiago gained the Muslims the bells of the church at Santiago, which were transported back to Cordoba by Christian captives and installed, much to the Christians' distress, in a mosque and used as lights. This act of deliberate religious humiliation acted as a catalyst in the fight against the Muslims.

> The vicious burning of the city, and the carting away of all the church bells back to Cordoba to be used as mosque lamps, helped catapult Santiago from local to near mythological importance in the subsequent century. The city became the very symbol of Christianity on the peninsula and a legendary pilgrimage site of international proportions, both of which remain largely true today. [21]

In 1236, when Cordoba was retaken—remember, we are talking two and a half centuries later—the bells were repatriated to Santiago, carried by unwilling Muslim captives. Nice touch, and long, long memories.

Only a narrow tier of northern Spain was held by the Christian defenders, originally in the kingdom of Asturias. To protect its eastern flank from Moorish assaults—and from anyone else who was a threat—the rulers built many castles in this region, which became known, therefore, as the county of Castilla. Over time, the Castilians became so powerful that they overwhelmed Asturias and the other emerging Christian states of León, Navarre, Aragon, and Catalonia, while at the same time all these states were fighting against the Moors in what became known as the Reconquest, the "*Reconquista.*" It was a great psychological help to the Christian defenders of this northern tier of states to have many, many pilgrims walking from the rest of Europe through the Pyrenees, then west to Santiago every year. The pilgrims

---

20 As reported by Ibn Hayyan, an eleventh-century Muslim historian.
21 Maria Rosa Menocal, *The Ornament of the World* (Boston: Little, Brown, 2002), p. 97.

Map of Spain showing Muslim and Christian areas, around 1000 CE.

also became a signal to the Muslims that they ran the risk of a larger war if they tried too hard to complete the conquest of the peninsula.

The reconquest was, in my view, the single most important factor in the shaping of the Spanish culture of pride and honour, to the point of recklessness. For almost three-quarters of a millennium, the Spaniards in the north fought an intermittent border war with the Moors, creating a frontier mentality that dwarfs, in size and duration, the American frontier culture of the nineteenth century. A person's worth, for generation after generation, was measured in how well he or she could withstand the rigours of war. As the frontier was slowly and inexorably pushed southward, the land newly occupied by the Christian forces needed to be settled, and they were always short of settlers. Unlike the rest of Europe, which suffered from too many people and not enough land, Spain had exactly the opposite problem.

Of course, it was not always war. There were long periods when both sides accommodated each other, intermixed, traded, and even intermarried at the level of the highest rulers. There were also treachery, assassinations, outright betrayals, and as much infighting on both sides as there was fighting the official enemy. There were incidents of horrifying barbarism and cruelty. (For example, one of the official

Christian punishments was decalvation, or scalping by fire. Ouch. It makes a strong argument for very short hair. I am glad that that one isn't on the books anymore.) The internal wars, on both sides, were about succession, tribal differences, and land. El Cid, that great Spanish hero, at one point defended a Muslim city against a Christian besieging force. But he always remained true to his king, even when that king exiled him, probably for becoming too popular with the masses.

The Peninsular War[22] started when France occupied Spain in 1808. The two armies were allied until Napoleon ordered his troops to turn on their Spanish hosts. Pamplona fell early in the war. You will recall the Ciudadela that I visited, where the fortress failed to stand against the French. Another connection is at O'Cebriero—a town I will pass through on the camino—where the British paymasters had to dump wagonloads of gold coin down the mountainside to reduce the impediments to the appalling winter retreat to La Coruña, where the British commander was killed before some 23,000 of his 30,000 troops could get back to their boats.

The twentieth-century Spanish Civil War,[23] like most civil wars, was exceedingly uncivil. The summary execution of wounded, prisoners, and of civilians was widespread. Estimates of 500,000 to one million dead during the war include from 100,000 to 200,000 who were assassinated by both sides, prefiguring the terror tactics of the Nazis and the Russians[24] during World War Two. For many, it stands as a proxy for the wider war that followed almost immediately after. The Republicans under General Franco won, followed by a dictatorship that lasted until Franco's death in 1975. This legacy of repression supported by the military has led to a general distrust of the military in Spain, even today. They keep a very low profile. On a deserted and lonely wooded hill on the camino, I passed a black stone memorial to civil war soldiers executed, not in battle, but afterwards, in 1936, by the opposing forces at that point. There were fresh flowers on it as I passed.

In 1978, after Franco had died peacefully in bed, a constitutional assembly was held that created the current overlay of autonomous communities with remarkable independence of action.

---

22 1808–1814.

23 1936–1939.

24 The Germans provided Stuka dive bombers, as part of the Condor Legion, to the Nationalist side, while Russia provided NKVD (secret police) to the Republican side. The NKVD participated in the executions of Nationalists.

23 April, Lorca to Los Arcos

The next morning, I am up and on the road at 0700, heading for Villamayor de Monjardin,[25] about eighteen kilometres. Just before Estella, I pass a memorial to a Canadian pilgrim, Mary Catherine Kimpton, killed here on 2 June 2002. As I understand it, this sixty-one-year-old woman was struck and killed by a drunk driver while resting with her husband and another pilgrim in a clearing about five metres off a road, near where the camino crosses the road. The driver lost control on the curve, hit the guardrail and veered towards where they were sitting. She was unable to get clear and was killed instantly. The other two were injured. The two occupants of the car walked out of the vehicle unhurt.

Estella is described in Pica-ud's *Pilgrim's Guide* as "fertile in good bread and excellent wine and meat and fish and full of all delights." My experience here tells me that the wine, meat, and fish produced in this part of Spain is still excellent, 850 years later. I cannot speak about "full of all delights," since I did not sample all of them.

I stop at 0900 in Estella for *cafe con leche* and a croissant. That, along with lots and lots of water, is all I eat until evening. It is a hot and sunny day today, with not a lot of protection from the sun.

The famous free wine fountain at the Irache winery.

---

25 One of the many legends that surround Charlemagne is based here. On his way from Puente la Reina (before the bridge was built) to fight the Moorish giant Ferragut, he attacked and defeated the Navarran ruler who held the castle on top of the hill. The night before the battle, Charlemagne prayed to God to show him which of his knights would die the next day. When the soldiers shrugged on their armour in the morning, some of them were marked with a glowing cross upon their backs. Taking this as the sign, Charlemagne left them behind. On his victorious return from battle, he found all of them mysteriously dead in the camp.

After leaving Estella, I go to Irache, which is famous for two things: an enormous ruin of a Benedictine monastery, set up prior to 1000 AD, and, more relevant to me, a *bodega* (winery) that has a wine fountain for pilgrims outside. There are two taps, right for water, left for red wine ... and it is free for the taking. It is, like many things on the camino, run on an honour system. There is no one there checking to see if you take too much or have a second swig of wine. Just a tap that pours good, new, red wine, as much as you want, for as long as you want. I am here alone, so I do not know if anyone abuses this, but I suspect not. I can vouch that it's the real thing, although I don't have much. I don't have strong feeling for a lot of red wine first thing in the morning, but it is welcome. And I love the trust.

Shortly after, I meet Wayne, from just south of London, England. He looks much like Mick Jagger: tall, very lean, enormous mouth, big grin, and an accent that allows me about sixty-percent comprehension. He is forty-one, bald on top, long hair on the sides, and dreadlocks on the back. If I met him on the street, I would likely just hand him my wallet to avoid the inevitable confrontation. But I would be wrong. He is a plumber by trade—a philosopher-plumber. We walk and talk together as we climb through dense woods, following the camino markers. When we come over the top, we can see a town in the distance.

Once in the town, I ask a workman if this is Villamayor, confident that it is. He says, "*No, it's Lorquil.*" We go on, stop at a small restaurant,

The camino running west towards Los Arcos with a vineyard on the left.

and ask again if this is Villamayor. Once again, "*No, it's Lorquil.*" We are about four kilometres south and west of Villamayor. We are beyond our planned destination. How could we have missed it? We followed the yellow arrows and other markers faithfully.

We sit in the restaurant and study our maps, and I relearn an old, old lesson. The map is not the ground. Both Wayne and I have maps that show one camino. It turns out, from our discussion with the woman serving the bar, that there are two camino options here. They diverge just after the monastery and rejoin just before Los Arcos. And the one we are on does not go through Villamayor. This is devastating. I did not want or intend to go to Los Arcos today. It's too far, almost thirty kilometres. But it turns out that from here, the option, based again on advice from our lady on the ground, is to backtrack four kilometres uphill to Villamayor or go on eight kilometres, level or downhill, to Los Arcos. It's no contest. We go on, which Wayne had intended to do anyway.

It is very hot and the sun is beating relentlessly down. There is no wind and little shade. After another hour, we stop for a rest under a small tree. I am going to just take off my boots and lie down, but Wayne blows up his air mattress and gives it to me to lie on. Then he cooks up his lunch, which he offers to share with me. I decline, with thanks, since I am not hungry. After a half hour or so, we go on to Los Arcos. *Los arcos* means "the arches," which may mean the arches of the bridges over the river Odron, which splits the town in two, or it may mean the arches of the large church here; I don't know which.

Wayne stops at a small Austrian-run *albergue*, and I decide to go on and try the municipal one in Los Arcos. It is just across one of several bridges in close proximity, on the west side of the river, much larger than the Austrian one, but I think that I should experience this, at least once. It's only four euros, has a pleasant staff, one of whom speaks English, and the place is large, with many bunks crowded together ("togever," Wayne would say), mattresses covered in plastic (just in case, I guess), two showers, and two toilets, for God knows how many people. I get a bed space, number twenty-two, upper bunk, unpack my stuff, shower, change into dry clothing and sandals. I am going out to find a restaurant or a bar where I can get a large, cold beer. Now I'm hungry.

I speak with Carroll on my trusty cell phone while I am still at the municipal *albergue*, and she tells me that the husband, David, of a very dear friend in Houston, Linda Beverley, has been shot and killed in an act of workplace violence. The killer was a guy whom the husband had warned because he had broken a corporate policy about no weapons in the workplace. The guy went home, simmered to a boil, then came back and killed him. I grieve for him and I grieve especially for her. She is younger than either Carroll or me and they were looking forward to spending their remaining years together. Suddenly all their dreams and plans have vanished in an instant of incomprehensible violence. I will be praying for her and for him, as well as I can, being not religious, as I walk this journey.

I find a little bar off the beaten track (like that touch?). It is the Hotel Bar Ezequiel. I ask the young, pretty, blonde barmaid, Anna, if she *habla Ingles*. She laughs and says yes, but I am not Spanish, I am Polish. We chat and I have a large beer and a large *agua del grifo*—I am learning. After that a fellow patron, in fact the only fellow patron, asks if I have had the local drink. Of course I have not and of course I must. He suggests the *sidra*, made from apples. Yes, you've guessed it: apple cider. Then I try another local drink, the *Pacharon*; it's also local but much stronger and sweeter. It is an after-dinner aperitif made from the berry or fruit of a local shrub. I have no idea which shrub. It turns out to be made from anisette.

It occurs to me that this place might have a room. I ask Anna, and it does. They are twenty-two euros (about thirty-three dollars), and the room is everything the municipal *albergue* is not: private, comfortable, spacious, secure . . . and I don't have to use my sleeping bag, and they have towels! I had thought that I should experience the municipal *albergues* at least once, but when I checked in, I realized that I *had* experienced this before—about fifty years ago in the military, and the military had more space between bunks and way more communal showers, toilets, and washbasins. Altogether I am very glad to be out of that *albergue*. I realize that I don't have to repeat that particular experience at this stage in my life.

Checking my trusty pedometer (42,262 steps), I learn that I have walked farther today, thirty kilometres, than ever before in my life. Thank goodness I had my hiking boots on as I travelled to get here, because this would not have been pleasant in new boots. The only reason I wore them on the flight was because they were too big to fit in my pack. That turns out to have been a stroke of good luck.

24 April, Los Arcos to Viana

It is 24 April 2007, and I am on the road at 0730. It is much better to get in several hours before the sun gets high in the sky. I stop after a couple of hours in Torres del Rio for breakfast — part of a baguette, a banana, and an orange, but there is no *cafe con leche* (strong coffee with hot frothed milk)! There are several people here; a French couple I passed yesterday and a young German, Andreas, whose shin is so badly abraded that he is taking the bus to Logroño.

I hear that there have been at least two deaths this month on the camino. I also hear that this happens every few years with boring regularity. On 5 April, ignoring local advice about conditions high in the pass, an English pilgrim, a wealthy banker of about fifty, started to walk over the high trail from St. Jean Pied-de-Port to Roncesvalles alone. He met with two Italian pilgrims later, but got separated from them in the fog and dark of night and was found the next afternoon lying face down in waist-deep snow, near Ortzanzurieta and less than three kilometres from Roncesvalles. He was alive when found, but died in the hospital in Pamplona. There is also an unconfirmed report of a young male pilgrim of around twenty who has died of exposure this week in the Somport pass. I find out later that in 2002, in January and again in April, two pilgrims died as a result of exposure attempting the same Roncesvalles pass. It makes one pay close attention to the weather . . . and even more to local advice.

Just after I leave Los Arcos, I pass a small, enclosed cemetery with a sobering and thought-provoking text carved in stone over the entrance. It says, in Spanish,

Yo que fui
Lo que tu eres.
Tu seras
Lo que yo soy.

The translation? "*I was what you are. You will be what I am.*" That's food for thought — a kind of memento mori for every day.

The view to the north as I walk between Los Arcos and Viana. The crop is wheat.

In the heyday of the camino, around 1200–1300, when half a million or more pilgrims walked these paths every year, the towns, even the little ones, each had up to a dozen pilgrim hospitals,[26] run by various religious orders, to minister to the sick and dying who were not going to make it to Santiago. Of course, many of them were sick unto death when they started their journey. That is why they were on it, looking for divine intervention.

I walk with the French couple for a while. He is Julian, she is Veronica—*"Beronica, in Spanish,"* she laughs. They are teachers from Normandy. She offers to take a picture of me, so I will have at least one of me on the camino. I am wearing the dorky hat that I acquired in Pamplona. This is the exact hat that I rejected out of hand last year when Carroll spotted it in Florida. It has a big, floppy brim. I said then that it makes me look like a dork. Well, I have it on. It does make me look like a dork, but it works to keep the sun off.

They walk on, and I am alone for a bit. Then I meet Tina from Germany. Her English is pretty good, so we manage between her English and my German. When I tell her my name, she doesn't understand, so I write it in the dust with my pole—GUY. She laughs wildly and says she has only seen it spelled

Me in my dorky hat. It really makes me look dorky, doesn't it?

---

26   The term "hospital" in those times meant all hostels, hotels, hospices, and hospitals as we understand them today.

before with an "a," as in "gay." Then she confides that she is gay, which is not as big a surprise as she thinks. She says she is poor in languages, even though she took eleven years of English in school in East Germany, then lived in what she referred to as a community of Germans, Russians, and Poles. It may have been some kind of refugee camp. The only common language was English, but there were no native speakers, so she is unsure of pronunciation.

We walk together into Viana and stop for water, beer, and bread. Somewhere we have passed the French teachers. They come up, sit for a few minutes with us, then go on. They are doing the camino in stages and will end in a day or so. I am sorry to see them go. I get good vibes from them. I am staying here in Viana, after nineteen kilometres today, so Tina says goodbye and heads off for Logroño.

Viana has an interesting history. It was founded in 1219 as a forti-fied hamlet on the border between Navarre and Castilla. The king at the time depopulated a number of local towns to create Viana, kind of like Joey Smallwood closed down the outports in Newfoundland, although for, I think, different reasons.

Guess whose hometown this is! César Borgia[27] of the infamous family was born here (or perhaps in Rome; I'm not sure) in 1475, was made Bishop of Pamplona at fifteen — yes, you read that right — a car-dinal at eighteen, did his power thing in Rome as general of the papal armies (Daddy was the pope), and had a more-than-close relationship with his beautiful but ruthless sister Lucrezia (when she was annoyed with someone, she didn't pout, she poisoned). He died here in 1507 in his early thirties in a siege during an internal struggle of Navarrese nobility and is buried in the atrium of the church. Big banners cele-brating the 500th anniversary of his death are fluttering around town. I guess if you wait long enough, everyone gets rehabilitated.

Tomorrow, all being well, I will leave the province of Navarre (don't forget to roll those rrr's) and enter Rioja. I have walked about eighty-five kilometres in the past four days. My legs are fine and my feet are holding up. When I arrived here, after my shower I gave myself a little foot massage with Lubriderm — sheer bliss!

---

27   Machiavelli was an admirer of Borgia's and used many of his exploits and tactics as examples in *The Prince*.

The ruins of a monastery in Viana.

After going out, I visit the church here. Like many on this route, it is very large and very ornate. As I enter, I see a woman leaving, wiping her cheeks. When I leave she is nearby and I ask her if she is all right. She says that she is, but she isn't. After a brief discussion I ask her if she would have a beer with me. She says that she will.

Over the beer she tells me a horror story. Her name is Hannelore. She was a palliative care nurse in Hamburg, married, couple of kids. Her husband was murdered by his girlfriend when he tried to break off the relationship. Then she suffered what she refers to as "burnout" and was hospitalized. She could not return to work and fell through the cracks in the welfare system. She lost her house and had to sell her car to buy food. After that, she slowly sold her possessions via eBay to buy food. She is fifty years old, and no one is interested in hiring her because of her history and her age. She gives me the very real impression of being really alone. She stays in the cheapest *albergues* and always declines when people ask her to come out to eat because she can't afford it. I ask her if she would join me for dinner, and, after some hesitation, she agrees. We are eating the standard *menu del dia* and she says that she has not had this much to eat in two weeks. I realize that she is slowly starving on the camino. After dinner I very carefully ask her if I might give her a gift. She looks at me and, again warily, says yes. I then give her some euros, enough to have a decent night's sleep or two and get some decent food. She looks at me and says, and I quote, "You are not normal." She says that I have helped her enjoy the first day in a long time. We hug, say good night, and go our separate ways. I think about her a lot and think how unfair life often is.

SECTION 2

LA RIOJA – VIANA TO SANTO DOMINGO DE LA CALZADA

When one thinks of La Rioja, one probably first thinks of the wine of the same name. La Rioja, a small (5,000 square kilometres, just a little smaller than Prince Edward Island), autonomous community with one province, is one of the most important wine-producing areas of Spain, and the wine is the best-known Spanish wine outside Spain. La Rioja is located west of Navarre and directly south of the Basque country. The country is gently rolling, with a Mediterranean climate perfect for the production of grapes. Half of the population of just over 300,000 lives in Logroño, the capital. The coat of arms of La Rioja bears, in the bottom left quadrant, both the cross of Santiago and the scallop shells that are a mark of the Camino de Santiago.

The scallop shell is worn by pilgrims on the camino as an expression of their faith. Since the twelfth century, almost all images of Santiago or his followers include a scallop shell on hat or tunic. There are conflicting views on the origin of the scallop as a symbol of St. James. One is that a drowning man at Finisterre was saved by St. James and was borne to shore, nearly covered in scallop shells. Another is that the scallop was a symbol of an older Venus fertility cult and was then co-opted by the church as a symbol of spiritual rebirth and resurrection. I had an embroidered scallop shell on my Tilley hat, which never made it to Spain, so in a fit of pique I did not carry one on the journey.

25 April, Viana to Navarrete

Last night I slept soundly from 2200 until 0700, so I get on the road about 0800. I intend to go as far as Logroño, only two or three hours. The country is changing; the vistas are not so grand and sweeping. I meet up with Andreas, the young German with the bad leg. He is walking again, and we walk together for a couple of hours, then he falls behind. Just outside Logroño, I come across a tiny welcoming spot. It is too small to call it a restaurant or bar and it is an unofficial border post to La Rioja. It is run by Maria and her daughter Felisa, where they offer to stamp my *credencial* and offer *cafe con leche*—and YES, toast and marmalade in return for a donation. If you have no money, no donation is expected. I have my picture taken by another pilgrim with the mother and daughter. The person who takes the picture inadvertently positions the horns of a mounted deer head directly on Felica's head in the photo. When she sees the picture on the camera's viewer, she is delighted.

Andreas catches up here, but he is using his stick as a crutch. He is not going to be able to go on. I give him my e-mail address. I walk on into Logroño, the capital of La Rioja, on the River Ebro. As I enter, I cross a bridge over the river. On my left there are several people on the bank fishing. Evidently the fish is edible here now, unlike, according to Picaud, in his time:

> All the rivers between Estella and Logroño have water which brings death to men and beasts who drink it, and the fish in these streams are likewise poisonous.[28]

To be fair, Picaud also identifies the rivers that are "sweet and good for drinking." It makes one think about how we take our good drinking water for granted. In his day, the water was whatever it was and it was clearly a deadly serious consideration for pilgrims at that time. Now, I can ask for *agua del grifo* and never have a second thought about its quality. Of course, there are many places in the world where that does not hold true, such as Waterton, Ontario, or many of our aboriginal reserves in Canada. Now that's a disgrace.

---

28 *The Pilgrim's Guide*, p. 14.

Logroño is a city much the same size as Pamplona, about 145,000 inhabitants and, like Pamplona, a university town. I find it noisy and disturbing after days of relative quiet. I decide to continue to Navarrete. It is much smaller.

As I walk, I have some thoughts about noise. In our genuine desire to allow people as much freedom as possible, we have allowed the freedom to create noise to trump the freedom from noise. We must balance freedoms with responsibilities. I think that noise like this is only a product of the past century, and Messieurs Ford, Mercedes, and Renault and their kind have a lot to answer for. As I walk, the wind is blowing directly into my face and causing my hearing aids, especially the left one, to whistle. I find this annoying and take them out. This cuts the wind noise and the traffic noise . . . but it also means that I cannot hear the birds. On balance, I would rather hear the birds.

A paved section of the camino between Logroño and Navarrete.

Today, most of the path is paved. While it makes navigation and walking easier, it does lose some of the mystique. Wherever I can, I walk on the shoulder of the path. The weather is overcast for the first time since I started. It is comfortable and cool, but feels like rain. I had intended to buy a pair of rain pants if there was a Corte Ingles department store in Logroño. It turns out there wasn't, but the weather has improved, so I don't care. It's kind of like, "I don't need to fix the leaky roof, since it isn't raining."

En route to Navarrete, I walk beside a road separated from the camino by a wire fence in which are woven hundreds of pieces of twigs and branches in the form of crosses. I will see a lot of this in the days ahead. There is a lot of speculation as to why modern pilgrims walk the camino. Much of it is about active tourism, but the evidence of all these crosses, and the many piles of stones elsewhere, indicates that a lot of the people who pass this way still have some form of faith. This is an old and honourable tradition, going back to the earliest days of the camino. Here is Picaud on this subject:

> And so pilgrims are accustomed to kneel here in prayer, looking towards the country of St James, and each then sets up a cross. Sometimes as many as a thousand crosses are to be seen here.[29]

I am in Navarrete. In earlier times, this town was a flash point for the ongoing quarrels over territory between Castilla and Navarre. One difference between Viana and Navarrete is that Viana is built on top of a hill, fully walled and level in the town, whereas in Navarrete, only a few streets are level—most are steeply up or down, depending on where you are. It is 1730 and I am sitting in the plaza with some locals, enjoying a beer. There are no other pilgrims here, as far as I can tell. We are pretty easy to spot. It is overcast and the dark clouds are heading this way. I think we are going to get serious rain and I hope that it is only for this evening or overnight. Did I mention that I don't have rain pants?

Realistically, I know that someday soon I am going to have a rainy day . . . or two or three. My clothing is hanging on an outside line at the *albergue*. I am in a room by myself, with bath and toilet. I need the clothing to dry by tomorrow morning, so if it starts to rain I will have to go and rescue it.

I wander into the church. It is huge and only 100 metres from the plaza. Navarrete is a one-plaza town. The interior of the church is dark, only a tiny bit of light at the altar area, and the few windows are very high up and very small. One can barely see to walk around. There is organ music playing quietly. I sit in a pew and contemplate while I listen to the music. Then after a few moments, the lights go on, and I am presented with a spectacular display of Baroque gold and statues that goes up five

---

29   Ibid., p. 21.

storeys or more in front of me. The correct word for this is awesome — it is a deeply emotional experience, and not religious in the slightest.

As I leave the church, there is a bar offering a *menu del dia* just below it. I go in and there is a middle-aged couple sitting by themselves. They, of course, are fellow pilgrims, from Germany. We talk, and I ask if I might sit down for a few moments. They are gracious people, Hans-Walter and Roswita Burkard. They both speak fluent English, so I am free to try out my German. He was thirty-five years with Ford in Germany, she is a fashion designer; they have been married thirty-six years. We have a most wonderful evening. Two other German women, Erika and Erika (this makes it easier for me), join us for dinner. We discuss everything, including my theory on *now*, which I shall repeat here.

When we look at time, we seem to see a continuum from distant past through now to the future. But it really isn't like that at all. All of us experience an endless series of moments that we call *now*. When Viana was established in 1219, it was now. When César Borgia died in a siege there in 1507, it was now. When each of us was born it was now. As I write this, it is now for me. As you read this, it is now for you. But as Carroll would say, as my favourite and best Devil's Advocate, "So what?" What does this concept of time as an endless series of *nows* have to do with anything? Let me explain.

I often hear people talk about how they were happy at some point in the past, whether it was on a Caribbean vacation, or at the birth of a child or grandchild. But past memories are fickle. They can be and often are distorted over time to give us a rosy view of the past or a sombre one, depending on the event. I also hear people talk excitedly about some plans for the future. But the future is only a set of potential *nows* that may or may not turn out to be real. They might not happen or they might not happen as we expect. The only real now that we have is the one we are experiencing in this moment, and so it becomes important that we are mindful of now and experience the sense of happiness in the only moment that we have — *now*.

I am sitting with Walter and Roswita as we discuss this idea, and it occurs to me that I am the happiest man alive. I am happy now and I am fully aware that I am happy now. As important, I am tranquil and satisfied with what is happening in my life right now.

When we leave the little bar where we had eaten, it is raining lightly but steadily, and I think, a little despondently, about the laundry that I had left outside to dry. Rats! So I am extremely pleased to find when I get back to my room that some anonymous person has moved all my clothes from the exposed line they were on to another drying rack on my balcony, out of the rain. I never do find out who did this, but it was a generous and thoughtful act, in this, my now.

26 April, Navarrete to Nájera

It is 26 April, day twelve. I am up for breakfast at 0730. There is a fellow here from Montreal. He says that the weather forecast is for thunderstorms, but there is no evidence at the moment. It is overcast, so I decide to go as far as Nájera. (Pronunciation note: The accent over the "á", as in Nájera, does not change the sound, but it does indicate where the stress on the word is put, so this is pronounced NA-hay-ra. The default is the second-to-last vowel.) It is only about fourteen kilometres, so it should be an easy walk. I have my rain jacket on and my pack has its rain jacket on. My wallet, passport and *credencial* are wrapped in a plastic bag, from yesterday's strawberries, and my clothing and sleeping bag are also wrapped in plastic bags I kept from Pamplona, so I am not concerned about stuff getting wet.

As I leave town, there is a cemetery on the left with an ornate gate, which turns out to be the transplanted twelfth-century gate from the old pilgrim hospice of San Juan de Acre, the ruins of which I passed as I entered town yesterday. The tombs here are ornate, above ground; it reminds me of cemeteries in New Orleans.

I expect an easy day, but about six kilometres along, there are two options; the first is to walk two sides of a triangle to go via Ventosa to the south. The other option is to walk one side of the triangle — a shortcut — to walk beside a divided highway. I choose the short option, and boy, is it the wrong choice! Less than a kilometre along, the highway is under repair and they are using this section of the camino as a service road for the construction crews. It is about two inches of soft mud, churned up by tracked vehicles into a sea of mud. There is no way to avoid walking through it. It is raining lightly, to help ensure that the gooey clay mud keeps its inherent viscosity. Along with this delight, I am immediately beside the highway they are resurfacing with asphalt, so there is the noise of traffic, the smell of asphalt in the early spring, and a seriously muddy track to walk on. Just to make it worse, it seems as if all the other pilgrims have cleverly chosen the other route. There is no sign of anyone else's having been here: no boot prints, no people trudging along in the distance—nothing. I am alone in the mud.

A muddy section of the camino, made much worse by the heavy equipment being used to repair the highway to the right. Note the lonesome yellow arrow in the upper right of the picture.

Be careful what you wish for. Yesterday I bemoaned the paved and soulless track. Today I would give anything for it. I imagine an archaeologist, far in the future, finding my bones on some windblown plain and wondering why I had just lain down in the mud. As I cross a small road, I leave the worst of the mud behind. I meet a walker going the other way. He has a shock of white hair and a white beard and a big smile. He is walking from Bilbao to Strasbourg, about 2,500 kilometres. The reason he is smiling is because he is only two kilometres short of his first 1,000 kilometres. He also tells me that the track is very muddy up ahead. That's not welcome news. I tell him the same and suggest the Ventosa option. He also tells me that he is meeting about 300 pilgrims every day. If that's true, then there may be about 10,000 of us on the camino right now. That's a lot more than I had expected. We part with the standard "*buen camino.*"

The path crosses over a highway, and for about a kilometre the path is pretty good underfoot, then it starts to get muddy again. I look at my map and realize that the camino parallels this highway all the way to Nájera, about six to eight kilometres. The choice, then, is walking along the shoulder of the highway in what is now pouring rain, or slogging through ever more viscous mud. Having just been exposed to mud, I pay attention to the lesson. I backtrack to the highway, sliding down a wet grassy slope to the road. It is indeed noisy, and I have to pay close attention to the traffic, but it is by far the better option. Hey, it's *my* camino and I can do it any way I want! As I walk into an industrial area of the town — there are dozens of furniture places — I would kill for a *cafe con leche* by now, so when I see a bar-restaurant with trucks in front, I go in. I take off my soaking jacket and soaking hat. Under it I am dry, so the rain jacket was a good investment. The *cafe con leche* comes with two packets of sugar. I have not had sugar in my coffee for probably forty years, but I dump them both in today. It tastes great and I can use the burst of energy it will give me.

Then on into Nájera, and I find a small hostel with a private room. I am holed up now, having washed the mud off my boots in the sink using my trusty dual-purpose nail brush (it's OK, Carroll, I am not using it for my nails), then showering to get the congealed mud off my calves. I am warm and dry and, after a little siesta, enjoying the quiet of the little room.

Some thoughts on technology, the best and worst examples. The best? the rotary-powered toothbrush. I have not used a standard toothbrush for years, but I am using one here. I mentioned earlier that some of my senses seem heightened. One I could do without is a heightened sensitivity of my gag reflex. I cannot get through brushing my teeth without five or six seriously uncomfortable gags. With a powered toothbrush I don't have this problem, and my teeth stay in good health. So that is great technology.

The worst? The leaf blower: noisy, offensive, polluting, and for what? You get to blow the leaves and mess off your property so that they become someone else's problem. How socially responsible is that? When I get to be in charge, leaf blowers will be one of the first things to go. They are a solution in search of a problem and, in my view, a really bad application of technology. And while I am on the topic, I am also going to provide all young men — and women — who drive their cars with the windows down, so that we can admire their taste in music, with earphones and demand that they use them.

I am wandering around Nájera in search of Internet access. The Tourist Info Office is in the same place as the library, which has Internet,

Twelfth-century tombs of the kings of Navarre in the monastery of Santa Maria la Real in Nájera.

so as soon as it opens, I go up the five floors to the library. The librarian, who is a clone of librarians everywhere, says the four computers are all busy. There is no one there but us, so I ask if I can have five minutes. She agrees, with a sour face. I no sooner get on than Carroll calls on my cell phone. I answer it. Another big mistake. The librarian comes over and tells me that I cannot use the cell phone here. She is severe.

I wander some more and find the monastery of Santa Maria la Real, built over a cave entrance. The old town is sandwiched between a high, red stone cliff and the Najerilla River, which is wide, fast, and shallow. The kings of two dynasties, from 923 to 1076 and from 1135 to 1243, are buried here in the monastery. The town was taken from the Moors in 923 and made the capital of the Kingdom of Navarre. The monastery has seriously big rain chains in each corner of the interior courtyard, probably to keep the rain from damaging the court-yard's surface.

It is still raining and quite a bit cooler, around fifteen Celsius. I find a store to buy another pair of hiking socks and a pair of nylon rain pants. I also find a pharmacy to buy medicated foot powder. I don't have a fungus problem, but as Carroll points out, correctly, if I use the foot powder *before* the wet weather, I probably won't have any.

I have been quite alone all day. When I go for dinner at 2030, there is another man, likely a pilgrim, eating alone. I ask if I may join him. He is Martin, a Swiss from the Constance area, cycling the camino. We enjoy each other's company. At one point we laugh together because neither of us can remember what town we are in. *"Wir weissen nicht wo wir sind, aber wir sind. Das ist genug."* "We don't know where we are, but we exist. That is enough." It sounded more profound last evening in the German. I think maybe you had to be there. You know how painters have their periods, their blue period, their red period? I must be having my German period. This is four nights in a row that I have spent the evening with German speakers.

I must remember not to drink *cafe con leche* — or cognac — in the evening. I go to bed at 2300, but am up and wide awake at 0100.

Most of the pilgrims that I have seen are well into middle age or beyond, few young. Is it availability of time and money? Many, many solo, like me.

27 April, Nájera to Santo Domingo de la Calzada

It is day thirteen of the trip, day seven on the camino. The phone in the room wakes me at 0700; it must have been set for someone's wakeup call. Or maybe it's a hostel thing: *Get up and get going.* It is overcast and looks like light rain. I plan today to walk to Santo Domingo de la Calzada. Based on my guidebook, it is a little over twenty kilometres. I put on my rain jacket and rain pants and set out. I walk for seventy-five minutes and arrive at Azofra, the first of only two towns on this segment of the camino. This is unusual. There are usually several towns between start and stop points every day. This makes sense, since most of these towns grew up to service the medieval pilgrim trade. When I stop for a *cafe con leche,* I strip off my rain pants. Although it has not actually rained, I am completely soaked from the waist down. My pants are drenched in sweat, so the newly-purchased nylon rain pants do not work well if I am working hard. They will be okay if I am wandering around a town in the rain. It is a lovely walk today, about twenty-two kilometres, but fast. There is a good surface, little mud, cool, overcast with a breeze. I have completed about 140 kilometres so far.

I am very pleased with my legs, joints, and feet. The feet have been interesting. This detail may be an over-share, but I am finding that the feet are very, very important on this walk. I had anti-friction stuff,

Footglide, in my original pack, which Air Canada has not yet found. I have instead used Vaseline to prevent blistering, and it has worked pretty well, although I do have some colourful bits. On my right foot, the two smallest toenails are pretty well black. They don't hurt at all and do not appear to be inflamed or infected, but I expect that they will leave me at some point (the toenails, not the toes). The middle toenail on my left foot is completely white. I did not realize that the nail was a little long and was touching the end of the boot when I walked downhill. As a result, a blister formed under the nail and lifted the nail, painlessly, off the toe. It is fine now. I have trimmed the nail back and have used an antibiotic cream to prevent any inflammation, so everything is good.

There have been no livestock visible anywhere so far on this journey, not a cow, sheep, goat, or chicken (except for those in the cathedral, which I will explain in a moment, and they don't count). I have seen only sheep droppings on the road and the occasional pungent odour of manure on fields. I did hear sheep in a barn today, so I know they are around.

I note how reassuring it is for me to have the yellow arrows, the camino markers, as I walk. Sometimes there are multiple markers, which seem redundant, but I feel a real sense of reassurance each time I see one. It is external confirmation that I am going the right way. I think about how important external confirmation is for people, even if, and perhaps especially if, they seem to be very confident in their direction. This theme occurs over and over again on the camino. I shall have to remember this when I deal with people in the future.

Here in Santo Domingo de la Calzada, there is a huge cathedral, dated from 1232, with a wonderful story attached. The story predates 1350. A pilgrim family, mother, father, and son, named Hugonal, stayed overnight on their way to Santiago. The son was propositioned by a barmaid but rejected her (of course). To get even, she put a goblet from the inn in his luggage, then accused him of having stolen it. He was tried, found guilty, and hanged. That was the sole penalty for theft in those unenlightened days. As his parents sorrowfully went past his hanged body, he spoke to them, saying that he was not dead, that Santo Domingo was holding up his legs. The parents rushed to the magistrate and protested their son's innocence and told him that the boy was alive. The chief magistrate or sheriff, the *Corregidor,*[30] was just about to tuck into a meal of roast fowl and said, scornfully, "Your son is no more alive than these chickens," upon which the two chickens rose off the plate and began to crow. The son was taken down from the gallows and reunited with his parents. There is no story about what happened to the false girl, nor about the state of the magistrate's blood pressure after his meal got up off his plate. Ever since then, they have kept a rooster and a few hens in a special enclosure high in the interior of the cathedral! I was there today and saw it.

Chickens enjoying their elegant coop in the cathedral at Santo Domingo de la Calzada.

The town's motto is "***Donde la gallina canto despues de asar,***" "Where the hen crowed after roasting." Seriously, that is the town's motto.

---

30 Corregidor is also the name of the island fortress that protects Manila Bay in the Philippines. It became famous in the U.S. because during World War Two, General Douglas MacArthur was ordered by the president to leave about 11,000 American and Filipino troops there to be surrendered by General Jonathan Wainwright to the Japanese in May of 1942. Corregidor was retaken by the Americans in February 1945.

SECTION 3

CASTILLA Y LEÓN – SANTO DOMINGO TO VEGA DE VALCARCE

Castilla y León is the largest autonomous community in Spain and is also the largest region in the entire European Community. It covers 95,000 square kilometres, almost exactly the size of Indiana. It is formed of a great plain, the *"meseta,"* bounded on all sides by low mountain ranges. The population is about 2.5 million people, in nine provinces, with the capital in Valladolid. I will be walking through several of the provinces and staying in the capitals of two of them, Burgos and León. It was created in 1983 by the union of León and Castilla la Vieja (Old Castilla).

28 April, Santo Domingo de la Calzada to Belorado

When I leave town this morning, I pass over a long bridge of at least fifteen stone arches, built by Domingo in 1044 over the River Oja to assist the pilgrims who rested here on the east bank before crossing the river. *La calzada* means roadway or road, so Santo Domingo de la Calzada translates as "St. Domingo of the Road," which seems appropriate. He was canonized by the church because of his bridge-building to support pilgrims on their way to Santiago.[31] He was also

---

31 In spite of the fact that he was drummed out of two monasteries because he was such a poor student, but stubborn, you have to give him that. In addition to building bridges, he cleared some thirty-seven kilometres of road through the Oja forests, thus making the passage safer from bandits. Legend has it that when he stopped cutting from exhaustion, angels continued cutting on his behalf. You can see the advantages of persistence here. St. Juan de Ortega was a disciple of St. Domingo's.

Bridge built by Santo Domingo over the River Oja, immediately west of Santo Domingo de la Calzada.

instrumental in clearing the road through the Oja Forest, which was a haven for thieves and bandits who preyed on the pilgrims. This was a difficult and very dangerous pilgrimage during those times, completely the opposite of today. Men and women can now walk alone freely and safely the length of the camino.

This camino became famous because St. James's bones are supposed to be buried in Santiago, which, of course, bears his name. His resting place had been lost for centuries when, lo and behold, someone found his tomb just in time to help fend off the expansionist Moorish empire that occupied almost all of the peninsula from 711, except for two tiny Christian kingdoms, León and Navarre, which later became Aragon, Castilla, León, and Navarre.

The Moors were unstoppable because they had a relic of Mohammed that they took into battle as they mucked out the Christian armies. When the Christians suddenly had access to a relic of St. James, the tide turned, and over the course of about five centuries, the Moors were driven south and out of the peninsula. By 1360, the Moors held only the south coast and Granada.

Then, in 1469, Isabella, the queen of Castilla, married Ferdinand, the king of Aragon, and together by 1492 they had unified (more or less) Spain. What we now call Spanish is actually Castilian, only one of a number of popular languages of the peninsula. Unfortunately, Queen Isabella's personal confessor was Torquemada, who, as you know, was the prime mover of the Inquisition. He convinced the royal couple that, for the sake of national unity, only Christians should occupy Spain, so all others were forcibly converted (the *conversos*), driven into exile (the Jews), or murdered.[32]

"*Converso*" was the term used for anyone who converted, either from Islam or Judaism, to Christianity. People converted for any number of reasons: fear of expulsion, pogrom or legalized murder; for economic or social acceptance; intermarriage; or legitimate belief. *Conversos* were often mistrusted by both the Christians and by the religious community they had abandoned. Part of the issue was the widespread belief that *conversos* had not really converted at all, but were Christians publicly who maintained their old rituals and beliefs in the safety of their own homes. *Conversos* were also subject to pogroms and harassment by the Inquisition. This was completely unlike the Moorish empire, which had more or less allowed Jews and Christians to live more or less peacefully in their midst and practise their religions for almost seven centuries. An ironic note: many of Isabella's ancestors were Jewish *conversos*.

Ethnically pure blood, known as "*limpieza de sangre,*" was highly valued in old Spain, especially among the nobles, in much the same way as "*pur laine,*" literally "pure wool," used to describe a family of pure French blood, not tainted by intermarriage with Irish, Scots, English, or indigenous peoples, is highly valued by some, perhaps many, of the old families of Quebec. Think likewise of the Americans who claim descent from the original English settlers of the Mayflower. If all the claims are true, then the Mayflower was probably somewhat larger than the Titanic, but with a better transatlantic track record.

Yesterday, as I was walking on the wet road, I saw a snail making her way across the road. I took a picture of her (I know it was a her because of this thing she did with her eyes) on her journey, and she got me to thinking. Are my journey and her journey so very different? Is her journey different in relevance or importance to her than mine is to me? I was not able to find out, because my Escargot is even less fluent than my Spanish, but I think about all the people, past and present, who

---

32   The harassment of Jews was not new in Christian Spain. In 1391, the Jews of Burgos, Logroño, and a dozen other Christian cities were murdered in a pogrom, mostly in a cynical and deadly grab for plunder. The resident Muslims would have been murdered, too, except that there were many Christian captives in Granada, whose lives, as hostages, were at stake. The Jews and Christians were usually, but not always, tolerated and safe in Muslim-controlled areas.

make their journeys through the world and I wonder: how important is our journey? It also came to me that, while I am able to take the time to be here, I do not need to be here to think about the things I think about as I walk.

As I dressed this morning, I was reminded of a matador dressing for a fight. (I am in Spain, after all.) Each piece of clothing is carefully checked and put on, done up and fitted so there are no wrinkles that could cause chafing while I walk. I prepare my feet by making sure they are dry, putting Vaseline and my little Dr. Scholl's gems between the toes, adding a bunion ring to my right foot, just aft of the big toe—the left foot, for whatever reason, does not need one—then easing on a very thin polypropylene sock, followed by a heavier wool sock. The thin sock is to wick moisture away from the foot. Then on with the boots. As you might imagine, they fit now like a pair of old slippers. I have Lowa hiking boots, Birkenstock orthotic supports, and SAS insoles. The combination works like a dream. I can walk all day and my feet are not tired, although the rest of me often is. Then I put on my pack, pick up my hat and walking poles, and check the room visually several times to be absolutely sure there is nothing left behind. I feel like Jack Nicholson in *As Good As It Gets*.[33] I have nothing spare, so I must leave nothing behind. I fail several times in this regard, in spite of the near-obsessive behaviour.

An example: on one of my early days, I stopped in a tiny village for *cafe con leche*. When I left, I had not gone a hundred yards when I heard loud voices shouting behind me. The bargirl was running down the street with my map, which hangs in a plastic bag around my neck. This was the same place where I had had a pastry. When I asked the name of the pastry, she told me several times something which I could not get. Then she laughed and mimicked with her hand a cut across the throat and, sure enough, it does look a little like a cut throat. Dark sense of humour, these Spanish.

Today is twenty-two kilometres, almost all immediately beside a busy highway, but on a separate track. It is overcast and starts to rain. Once again, I put on my rain jacket and rain cover. The rain cover is integral to the pack, and the rain jacket lives in an external pocket on the

---

33   A 1997 movie starring Jack Nicholson as a man with obsessive-compulsive disorder.

back of the backpack, so both are easy to get at. Good thing, considering the amount of rain we are having. As the cars and trucks whiz by, I think that they may be thinking, *Poor buggers, trudging along in the rain, soaking wet, bent under the weight of their packs, cold and miserable* . . . While we—no, I can't presume to speak for others—while *I* am happy and mostly dry as I walk, thinking about the people in the cars, *Poor buggers, rushing along, slaves to time, hurrying to the next place they have to be. They are oblivious to all of the nature around them, snug and unaware in their little metal cocoons.* They must be travelling ten or twenty times as fast as I, and for what? Does it make them ten or twenty times happier or satisfied? I think not.

My camera batteries die again. This is my backup set and they lasted only two days. In the first small town, Grañon, I am able to find a shop with batteries (*pilas*). A very nice lady of a certain age runs the shop. She gives me the discount on the batteries, 1.19 euros instead of 2.25. I am also able to buy a single bottle of orange fluid—some kind of drink—from a pack of six.

I want to thank her and I am able to use two ideas in Spanish to do this. The first is *guapo* or *guapa* (handsome or beautiful, depending on the last letter—"o" for men, "a" for

Camino beside highway.

women). The other idea is using the correct form of "to be." There are two verbs in Spanish for "to be": *ser* and *estar*. The first, *ser*, first person singular *soy*, implies permanence, so I can say "*Yo soy de Canada,*" because I am always from Canada. The second, *estar*, first person singular *estoy*, implies transience, so I can say "*Yo estoy cansado,*" "I am tired now" (but it will pass). In Spanish, it is also usual to dispense with the subject pronoun if it is clear, so I would say "*Soy de Canada,*" or "*Estoy cansado.*"

A couple of days ago, after I used the wrong verb, a Spanish man warned me, with a big smile, about using *ser* or *estar* with *guapa*. If I say "You are beautiful" with *ser* as in "*Tu eres guapa*," this says that you are beautiful now . . . and always will be. If, on the other hand, I use *estar*, as in "*Tu estas guapa*," it means that you are beautiful at this moment. If you know the lady well and she is especially well turned out, all is good, but otherwise there may be the implication of, "You are beautiful at this moment, but just wait . . ." You can see how getting it wrong could be a serious social error. So I use the *ser* version, probably with incorrect grammar, but the little old lady in the shop is just delighted and ducks her head shyly. I, too, am delighted. I have the effect I seek.

All this reminds me of a small linguistic misadventure that I had back in 1963, in Belgium. I was there on an anti-tank missile course, at a Belgian army base in the rather desolate northeast portion of Belgium, near a town called Bourg Léopold, or Leopoldsburg, if you were Flemish rather than Walloon. A small number of Canadian Army officers and non-commissioned officers were there for three months. I got to be very good friends with the school's commander, a Belgian Army paratrooper named Capitaine René Possot. He invited me to join him and his wife, Louise, for a weekend in Liège, which was where she lived with her daughter, Claire. I arrived in Liège by train, was picked up at the station by René, and taken to his home.

In the evening, we decided to go out to a nightclub for a few drinks. For some reason, I was sitting in the back of their car with Louise while René was driving. It was very warm and humid, so I commented, innocently, I thought, "*René, je suis chaud*" (I am hot). He laughed and said, "I hope not. You are sitting back there with my wife!" Then the two of them explained to me with much amusement, that, in French, there are two ways of saying "I am hot." If it is the weather that is making you hot, you say; "*J'ai chaud*." Literally, "I have heat." The construction that I had used means "I am horny," which, while accurate at the time, was not what I intended to say. Happily, both René and Louise thought it amusing rather than alarming.

At the crowded and noisy nightclub, we sat next to a table where there was an attractive girl near me. We started a conversation which did not get very far because of my limited French and the incredible noise. She said something to me which I didn't catch, and she said it several more times but I could not understand what she meant. Eventually, she shrugged and got up and left. Later that evening, I asked René to translate what she had said, which was "*Déménageons.*" René looked at me in mock horror. "She was asking you to leave with her," he said. "*Déménageons* means, 'let's get out of here.'" Probably a good thing that I *didn't* understand, since I was happily married, with a wife and three small children at home. Still, I sometimes wonder . . .

Part of the time today, I walk with Georg from Bremen. He speaks good English and is a mechanical engineer. Quite a successful one, I have to imagine. He perfected his English during a three-year international project in Paris. He then decided to quit his job and travel. He and his wife spent two years in the Americas, travelling as far north as Inuvik and as far south as Tierra del Fuego. Then he shipped his car home to Germany, went to New Zealand for four months, and spent two months sailing with a French couple in the Society Islands. Now he has a forty-foot boat on the North Sea, is restoring it, and intends to sail from there around the world to New Zealand.

What a different story from Hannelore's! Georg is aware that he is wealthy enough, healthy enough, has time enough and the will to walk the camino. I also find out why there are so many Germans on the camino. A very popular German TV comedian, Hape Kerkeling, walked it in 2001, then wrote a best-seller about it. Everyone in Germany knows about the camino and many of them are here now.

In Georg's travels, he found only two places that he would like to live in, if not in Germany: New Zealand or Canada. That says very good things about Canada. I wish that the many Canadians who complain constantly about Canada could get out of it for a little while and see how the rest of the world lives. I think that there would be a lot less complaining and a lot more gratitude for the freedom, the wealth, the health, the support systems in place, the public transit, the landscapes, the boring politics (people haven't figured out yet that boring politics is a good thing—politics in Sudan, Zimbabwe, or Iraq, as examples, aren't boring at the moment) and the peaceful diversity that we share. Okay, I will grant that the winter weather isn't always ideal.

Just before I get into Belorado at mid-afternoon, there is a big to-do on the highway that I am about to cross. Motorcycle riders from the Guardia Civile[34] (I was warned earlier not to aggravate these guys, they have a short fuse and absolutely no sense of humour), some other fast motorcycles, and some cars with commercial signs, like Shimano, on the side race by. It turns out that we are on the route of the Tour de Rioja, a province-wide cycling race. And here they come! I stop just at the edge of Belorado, where the camino crosses the highway, and get a photo of the *peloton*—hundreds of cyclists—as they race by in a single tight pack.

As I enter Belorado, I see the first storks' nests on top of a ruined church. The nests are huge, perhaps five feet across.

It is difficult to find a place to stay here. Two pensions are closed, and one nice, small hotel is already full. It is only 1330, so it must have been reserved by a group of walkers who have a baggage handler and vehicle. I finally find the Hotel Jacobeo, just off the main square. It is pricey at forty-seven euros, but I have a lovely, big room. It has two twin beds, two closets, a beautifully appointed bathroom . . . and a sink that won't drain. Too bad. I wash my smalls and am off to bed for a *siesta*. Might as well nap—everything is closed until 1630. This very attractive hotel

Storks and their young in nest on a church bell tower.

is like a sounding board. I can hear every step, every murmur and laugh, every sound from the bar below—but it does not keep me awake.

This journal is interesting for me. I wonder whether it is a result of this journey or a reason for it. The journal seems to be taking on a life of its own. I have a compulsion to write these notes and send them

---

34 The Guardia Civile is a federal force, distinct from the national police, and has both military and civilian functions. They have a historical reputation of getting involved in politics.

home almost as if to have my family and friends with me as I walk. I shall have to think about this for a while. It is quite curious, since originally I had no intention of keeping a journal at all.

I have an opportunity to briefly visit the *albergue* Quatro Cantones, here in Belorado. It is dreadful, with crowded, very dark, very small quarters. Someone has written in the guest book, "*This place is fit only for pigs or chickens,*" and that would be accurate. A number of the published camino guides warn about this place as an *albergue* of last resort.

This town of Belorado, population 2,100, predates the camino by at least 700 years. It may have been a Roman settlement. It is on what was a north-south trading route, following a river. It has the major road running north-south as well as another major road running east-west, so is very untypical of camino towns, which are almost always oriented east-west, with usually only one major and one or two very minor roads. It was also another border town, this time on the Rio Tiron, the border for a while between Castilla and the old kingdom of Navarre.

Tomorrow I am off to San Juan de Ortega. There will be a major climb through thick Holm oak woods. This used to be a very dangerous part of the camino, because of the bandits who lived in the woods. The vertical profile is daunting, so I am not looking forward to the climb.

29 April, Belorado to San Juan de Ortega

As I leave Belorado, it is overcast and cold. On the right, I pass a set of old church buildings and hermits' caves in the rock. Farther along, I pass the ruins of a tiny ninth-century monastery, the Abade de San Felices, in the middle of nowhere, where the camino takes a sharp left turn to the south for a little distance. It is perhaps twenty feet by twenty feet and two storeys high. Either there were few monks or they were very crowded. It turns out that this single arch is all that is left of a major Mozarabic[35] monastery, at one time a principal religious attraction in this part of Spain. Now it is just fields of grain with this tiny ruin.

The town of Villafranca was very important in medieval times because St. James Church, built in the twelfth century, included a Doorway of Forgiveness, used by pilgrims who were so ill that they

---

35   Christians who took on Arab culture, but remained Christian.

would in all probability not reach Santiago alive. If they could reach this far and pass through the Doorway, they were granted an indulgence[36] by the church. Normally, pilgrims had to reach Santiago to receive an indulgence. The Doorway of Forgiveness was a major concession to the gravely ill, who could not reach Santiago alive and who would otherwise die believing that they were in a state of sin.

After the town of Villafranca, the camino is a steep climb for three kilometres through a dense forest of Holm oak. Remember those frightening fairy tales when you were a youngster about walking through a menacing, gloomy forest? This is that forest. The trees are old, gnarled, twisted, and covered with green fungi. I am glad it is daytime. I wonder if some of those stories were actually situated in this forest, since it was a part — and a dangerous one — of so many people's lives. Bandits lived here and thrived on what they could take from pilgrims. But there are none here now, as far as I can determine.

Holm oak forest.

The vegetation turns to heather and gorse, with lovely purple flowers. I pass a monument to Spanish Civil War victims of a massacre in this lonely area. I notice that there are fresh flowers on it. Someone remembers. The Spanish still bleed from this war that was fought from July 1936 to March 1939, which left between half a million and a million dead, thus possibly surpassing the death count of the American Civil War. The massacre here was part of the terror campaigns that

36 In Catholic theology, an indulgence is a full or partial remission of punishment for sins already committed. Many pilgrims believed that the act of making the pilgrimage to Santiago would result in a full, or plenary, indulgence. A word of caution: Indulgences are only valid for past sins, so one cannot earn credits in advance for sins not yet committed. They are not a "Get out of Hell Free" card. The misuse and sale of indulgences was a major contributor to the Protestant Reformation.

both sides conducted and that likely accounted for at least 100,000 and as many as 200,000 deaths.

There is major mud, although not as bad as several days ago. It is an interesting juxtaposition—mud and beautiful flowers, side by side. Then into coniferous forest. It is like walking on a forestry road in Northern Ontario. No vistas, just trees. I think it will go on forever, a sentiment shared by the few pilgrims I meet along this section.

I have just passed 200 kilometres so far, as I finally arrive in San Juan de Ortega. It consists of a church,[37] a ruined monastery, an *albergue*, six houses, and a tiny bar. Thirty-six inhabitants. I meet Hannelore again here. She is totally changed. She says that this is the result of our meeting the other evening. We never know what the impact of a small kindness will be on someone else. She is lively, happy, anxious to finish the camino and to go home and sort out her life.

There are no accommodation options here except for the *albergue*. It is okay, a bit mouldy, and very cold. They are just now heating one large, primitive sitting room on the ground floor, which has a stove. This is where I am with eighteen other people, sitting at trestle tables, writing, reading, chatting, or just keeping warm. There is no cell phone signal here, and when I ask in the bar about Internet access, the young fellow just laughs. We are in the deep boonies here.

Remember the new camera batteries from Grañon and the special discount rate? I have already had to replace all four batteries. They must have been years out of date, or the camera is eating batteries. Eight batteries in four days . . . and I am not taking that many photos.

Today's walk is sheer trudgery. This is a word I have made up, which means just putting one foot in front of the other. However, the hill this morning was less demanding than I expected. Either I am in better shape, I am pacing myself better, or the route is not as steep as the profile indicates . . . or all three.

This *albergue* experience: it is run by the local curé and his sister. They are justly famous for their hospitality. He is Father José Maria Alonso Marroquin, a small, dapper man, eighty years old but looks sixty, with a bushy white beard, dressed in a black suit and a black bowler hat. He speaks a little of every language that passes through here.

---

37   St. Juan de Ortega may have built at least part of this twelfth-century church himself.

The eighty-year-old curé and me in front of the albergue at St. Juan de Ortega.

There are eight bunk beds in one upstairs room, more in another adjoining room, and a few windows dingy with age and letting in only a little light. I have a lower bunk in the room with eight bunks. The downside is that one has to pass through the other *dormitorio* to get to the toilet and shower areas. This will turn out to be a challenge at night in the dark. A few chairs, no surfaces on which to put anything. What to do with hearing aids? There are three toilets and two showers for men, the same for women. No hot water; then, very quickly, no toilet paper. Happily, I have been warned and am prepared with paper. No heat in the *dormitorios*, not a lot of room. You leave your boots out in a common area.

There is no security, but there are no locals, so theft is likely not a problem. I have heard anecdotes of only two instances of theft. Neither was here. One was someone's whole backpack; the other was of a waist pouch with passport, money, etc., that someone left lying in plain view on a bed in an *albergue* for two minutes. My mother told me to never tempt an honest man. That was good advice. Theft is generally considered a problem only in the larger and more anonymous cities.

The issue of theft reminds me of a story about my own experience with theft. In 1999, I decided to sell my beloved 1983 Yamaha XV920 motorcycle. It was fire-engine red and had a beautiful Hannigan fairing and BMW saddlebags, but it was top-heavy and I was unable to pick it up if I inadvertently laid it down, which I had done a couple of times at very low speed. So I advertised it, and almost nothing happened. Over the course of a couple of months, exactly two people came to have a look at it. One of them was a mid-thirties man with a British accent, decently dressed, quiet, well-spoken. He said that his brother-in-law had exactly the same bike and he was interested in mine, but nothing came of it. His brother-in-law had broken his ankle so wasn't riding right now. By September, I was convinced that I would be storing it for another winter. Then, one evening, I was out at a nearby Chapters when my cell phone rang. It was Carroll. The quiet Brit was back and wanted to try out the bike.

There was a problem. We were leaving the next day for the weekend and the bike had been sitting in the garage for five weeks. I knew that the battery was dead, but he reassured me that it was easy to use jumper cables to start it. Did I have any? Yes I did, so while I was heading home, he went back to his home, which he said was nearby, to get his helmet. I pushed the bike out of the garage, used the jumpers and got the bike's engine running. By the time he returned, walking up with his helmet in his hand, the engine was running smoothly. He asked if he could take the bike for a short spin. I generously told him to take it for a good ride. He backed out of the driveway, took off down the road, and was gone. Gone.

A couple of hours later, I was very concerned about his welfare — the battery had had no charge — so I called the police to see if there had been a motorcycle accident in the area. There had not. The police asked if I wanted to report the bike stolen, but I did not. I was convinced that the nice, quiet Brit was just having trouble somewhere and would show up any minute.

The next morning, I had to admit that I had been fooled by a very good confidence man, so I called the police to report a theft. The policeman on the other end of the line had some questions. I had all the bike details for him. Then he asked; "Do you have the man's name?" I did not. "Do you know where he lives?" My heart sank. I did not. There was a long pause, then: "Mr. Thatcher, just how old ARE you?" I responded, forcefully; "Way old enough to know better."

We were on the way out of town for the weekend when it struck me that we had told a thief that our home would be empty all weekend. Panic stations! I called the security company and said that if there was an alarm at the house, call the police immediately, since it would likely not be a false alarm. But nothing happened. He was, apparently, a very selective thief. No household goods, only rolling stock.

A month passed. Then early one evening the phone rang. It was the police with the news that they had found my bike "or what's left of it." It had been found abandoned near a river and had been collected by Gervais Towing and taken to their compound. I had to go and identify the bike. A little heartsick, I drove over to the compound and saw the heap of rubble which was the remains of my beautiful bike. The wheels were gone, the BMW saddlebags were gone, the Hannigan fairing was trashed. To add insult to injury, I owed Gervais Towing seventy-eight dollars for carting the bike from where it had been abandoned.

There had been some warning signs, but I did not see them at the time. Why had he not driven up? Why had he not mentioned where he lived? Why had he given me only his first name? But all these questions popped up after the bike was gone. Then, more self-recrimination. Why had I not asked for ID? I began to understand why they are called confidence men. They inspire confidence in themselves by their manner. He didn't look, act, or sound like a thief. He looked, acted and sounded much like me.

Carroll and I discussed later what we could have done. I wasn't going to ride on the back of the bike while he drove it, I wasn't going to tail him in a car, and if I had asked for ID, it could have been fake; so what would have worked? Our daughter, Meredith, came up with a good solution. I could have taken a digital photo of him with the bike. Then, when he didn't return, I could have provided the police with the photo. They might well have recognized him.

Three observations came out of this. The first was that, based on the asking price of the bike and the cost of winter storage, the loss of the bike was a wash after four years. Second, I could dine out on the story for years — and have done so. Third, I would rather be me than the thief, because I can still choose to trust people, while he, because of his own propensity to remove other people's belongings, can never trust anyone. He has to assume that many people are just like him.

The story has also made me notorious in certain quarters. Shortly after the loss of the bike, I taught a short business course in Seattle with Jeff Campbell, a friend from Brigham Young University in Provo, Utah, and I told him the motorcycle story over dinner. He thought that it was the funniest story he had ever heard, and next day, told the class that I had a story to tell them. If I wouldn't tell it, he would, so I did. They, too, thought it was very funny, and afterwards one person said privately that he was relieved that he was not the only person to make such a foolish mistake. A couple of years after that, at a business convention somewhere in the U.S., a total stranger approached me, noted my name badge, and asked me, keeping a straight face, if I still had a motorcycle for sale. He had been on a course in Florida taught by Jeff Campbell, who is still telling the story. It is a tough way to be famous!

To bed at 2030. It is early but very cold, and there is absolutely nothing to do. Everyone is in bed and asleep by 2200. There is only one occasional snorer. I have to get up in the middle of the night, so without a light in the pitch black, I make my way past the bunks in this room, being careful not to wake other sleepers by making noise or shaking bunks when I touch them for balance as I pass through the door to the next bunk room, pass through it to the toilet area, shut the door, turn on the light—there goes the night vision—and relieve myself (I now understand better the term "relieve oneself"). Then I must repeat the tricky travel process in the dark, only this time without any night vision at all. Of course, if I had my missing pack, I would have my little headlamp . . .

30 April, San Juan de Ortega to Burgos

In the early morning, 0530 or 0600, some people are up, very quiet, dressing with the use of their headlamps and moving out before daylight. One person tells me that the *albergues* are very crowded, usually full by noon or 1300 at the latest, so they must leave early to get a place. That has not been my (very limited) experience so far, although I hear horror stories about the lack of beds in the section from St. Jean Pied-de-Port to Pamplona. One guy I talk to in the *albergue*, a young Italian aeronautical engineer, tells me that he walked about forty-eight kilometres from Roncesvalles to Pamplona because the *albergues* in every village between the two locations were full when he arrived. He does not remember the last five kilometres at all.

The bar next door is closed this early, but the curé's sister serves *cafe con leche* in their kitchen in a bowl, then offers cookies. I share this little communal breakfast with two Italian couples. There is genuine warmth—the human kind—at this *albergue*. It is run on donations only.

Yesterday I made a five-Euro donation. Today, after breakfast, I make another of twenty Euros. The curé and his sister need it for toilet paper and hot water, and their dedication for what they do is inspirational.

It is sunny when I leave, but it lasts for only about an hour, after which it clouds over and threatens rain. Partway to Burgos, I pass through a tiny village called Atapuerca. In 1992, an archaeological dig in limestone caves near here uncovered remains of human habitation over a million years old.[38] Yes, you read that right. These hominids (*Homo erectus*) predate *Homo sapiens*. The area is a fertile plain in a shallow bowl perhaps five miles across. When I walk here, I am walking not only in the footsteps of millions of people over the past millennium, but also where early people lived, laughed, made love and had babies, hunted, slept, were wounded, and sickened and died almost a million years ago, in their *now*. And, oh, they were also cannibals, so they also ate each other, in the old-fashioned way, in their *now*.

Just beyond the village, there is a monument beside the camino to the people who lived here. It is a sculpture of a primitive man, mounted on a plinth, life-size, shown from the waist up, heavy brow, muscular, hairy, holding a spear with a stone tip. It is excellent, but what is even better is that some wag has put a pair of wire-rimmed glasses on the man. It is wonderfully incongruous . . . and my camera's batteries are dead again.

Atapuerca is also the site of a fierce battle, in 1054, between Ferdinand I of Castilla and his brother Garcia V of Navarre. The Castilians won, and Garcia was killed in battle. As you can deduce, the Christians didn't spend all of their time fighting the Muslims. And with the ferocity and land ambition of the Castilians, it is not surprising that what we now refer to as Spanish is actually Castilian. In the long run, they won the war for land, both from the Muslims and from the other Christian kingdoms. Only Portugal survived the onslaught.

It is not yet over, though. The Basque nationalists are still active and dangerous, and when I walk in the province of Castilla y León,

---

38   As reported on the BBC news of 30 June 2007, according to the co-director
     of research at an archaeological site in Atapuerca, findings have uncovered ". . .
     anatomical evidence of the hominids that fabricated tools more than one million
     years ago."

someone has used black marker to cover the word Castilla from almost every sign that I pass. Some disgruntled Leonese is still out there, fighting the battle for independence. And with the Spanish attribute of very, very long memories, who knows? Someday we may see León and the Catalans and the Basque regain full independence from the Castilian central government.

For too brief a time today, I walk with my shadow. The sun is out for about an hour early in the day. I have missed it, the long shadow ahead of me in the morning, shortening as the sun moves overhead. In past centuries, people used the sun and their shadows to tell time of day, time of year, and direction. Something else we have lost to modernization.

I pass through a huge high pasture full of cattle. The road runs level here, no ditch, no fence, so the cattle are on both sides of the road and on the road itself. The adults are all cows — for which I am quite grateful, no territorial and aggressive bull — but the younger cattle are mixed. The young bulls are much more inquisitive than the young heifers about the people walking through their space. Probably testosterone.

I come into Burgos in fairly heavy, steady — and cold — rain through about six kilometres of light industry. This is also the camino, but it is not attractive for me. This is a city of about 185,000 people, so it covers a lot of ground. I walk and walk for over an hour looking for a hotel, asking people, getting quite alarmed and concerned as I keep walking, wet, tired, and getting cold. I finally find a hostel, get a room . . . a hot shower, it's glorious . . . hang everything up to dry — it looks like a laundry room — and go to bed for an hour. Now I am awake and warmer. Today has been a good test for my waterproof rain jacket and pack. I am very pleased to tell you they both are just fine. In the interests of real water protection, I have put each set of items inside the pack in a plastic bag. I also keep my passport and *credencial* in a separate pocket in my pants. When it rains, I move them into a waterproof pocket in the rain jacket.

By 1900, I am sitting in a little outside bar in the plaza in front of Burgos cathedral. It is considered the finest example of Gothic cathedral architecture in Spain. It is reported to be the second largest cathedral in Spain, after the cathedral in Seville. Okay, what do I know? The cathedral, its cornerstone laid in 1221, is spectacular, inside and out. It

A gate through the medieval city wall of Burgos.

was not completed until 1567, which makes it even longer than most Public Works Canada construction projects. Because I am a *peregrino*, I get in for one euro instead of four, so I have already saved three euros this trip.

Like Viana, Burgos was created on an older Celtic site in 880 by gathering the inhabitants of surrounding villages and putting them all into a fortified village to help strengthen the frontier. The Visigoth name *burgos* actually means "consolidated walled village." In the thirteenth and fourteenth centuries, Burgos was the seat of the kings of León and Castilla. Many of them are buried here in the cathedral or in St. James Chapel, in the monastery of Las Huelgas Reales ("royal amusements"), named because it was built in 1187 on a former recreational field. In the chapel is a mechanical seated St. James with an articulated right arm, used for dubbing knights. They could say, honestly, that they had been knighted by the saint!

Burgos is now best known as the City of El Cid. El Cid is buried here in the cathedral. He was actually Rodrigo Díaz de Vivar, a Castilian nobleman, who lived from 1044 to 1099. El Cid means "chief" or "lord," and is a sign of respect. He also gets a huge monument[39] on his horse Babieca, with his sword held high, cape blowing behind him, in a plaza not far from here. He was the chief general of Sancho II, who died fighting his sister Urrica for a greater share of the kingdom. Then he fought for Alfonso VI, fighting against the Moors in the *Reconquista*. Later exiled by the king, El Cid left service in Castilla and worked as a mercenary.

39　The statue is quite modern, built in the 1950s. It is known locally as "*el murcielago*," the bat, because of the flowing cape.

El Cid is considered a real Spanish hero, although as I read the history, he was actually a sword-slinger for hire, albeit a successful one. He fought on one Christian king's side against another and, on occasion, fought for the Moors. He was—and is—considered very honourable, since he remained loyal to the king who had exiled him and to his wife. In "The Song of

The setting sun illuminates the spires of the cathedral in Burgos against a dark, snow-laden sky.

El Cid on horseback in the plaza in Burgos. Of course, he is facing south.

El Cid," the citizens of Burgos, the city to which the Cid first travelled after exile by his king, cry out: "*Dios, que buen vasallo, si oviesse buen señore*" (God, how fine a vassal, if his lord were but worthy). And, as we have already seen, honour is everything to the Spaniards.

In 1272, the local nobles confronted the king, Alfonso X, here in Burgos with demands for concessions not dissimilar from those demanded by the nobles from King John of England in 1215, resulting there in the signing of the Magna Carta. The Burgos event is not nearly as well-known or remembered, at least not in the English-speaking world. Burgos has a

New World connection, because Isabel and Fernando received Columbus here after his return from his second voyage to America in 1497. Napoleon's army occupied the city from 1808 to 1813. Much more recently, Burgos was the seat of Franco's government until 1938.

However, the reason I am sitting just here is because I am waiting for the camera store across the plaza to finish charging the lithium battery of my new camera. I bought four new AA batteries this morning and they are all dead now. I did the math, and it is cheaper to buy a new camera than to replace eight batteries every day. The camera must be short-circuiting and thinks it is full on all the time. The good news is that all the pictures are safe. So I have a new Olympus (could not find a Sony to use my existing memory cards), wide angle (28mm), 5x zoom, 6 Megapixels, anti-shake, but no viewfinder.

I have decided to take a rest day tomorrow. I have walked over 225 kilometres in ten days, and a rest sure feels like the right thing to do. I will find a little better hotel and indulge myself for a day before going on.

1 May, in Burgos

It is 0940 on 1 May, and did I make a good decision yesterday about a rest day! I am lying on the bed in a comfortable three-star hotel, not a hostel, and watching the large snowflakes come down. It is three degrees Celsius out and snowing heavily.

I do not yet know the local proverb about Burgos's weather: "*Nueve meses de invierno y tres de infierno*"—"Nine months of winter and three of hell." It reminds me of the unofficial motto of Timmins, which is where Carroll was born and grew up—nine months of winter and three months of bad sledding.

It melts on the ground, but roofs are covered in snow. From my fifth-floor window, across the plaza and directly in front of the cathedral, the few pilgrims that I can see walking by below me are wrapped in ponchos, huddled and stooped under their packs. It looks totally appalling out there, like Napoleon's retreat from Moscow. Burgos sits on the eastern edge of the great *Meseta Alta*, the high plateau, so they are heading out in poor weather into an inhospitable region, wide open, flat, few trees, and few villages. Big mistake. The hell with it, I am going back to bed. Later in the week, I spoke with one of those pilgrims who chose to walk today. He told me that he walked a few kilometres from Burgos in driving snow, then hailed a cab and told the driver to take him to the nearest *albergue*. He said it really was dreadful out there.

I wake at 1400, shower in hot water in the marble bathroom, and use their fluffy towels to dry myself. I feel pretty good. This could be very seductive. I am out to eat at 1500. It has stopped snowing and is sunny and quite pleasant, although cool. I could really use a fleece, but cannot find anything in the stores.

It is my daughter Meredith's birthday, and I think about family. Carroll and the kids and my extended family are so important in my life and so much a part of me. I miss them all, but I know that if they were here, this would be a very different journey for me. It seems to me that this is a journey that I have to make on my own. There were several people back in Canada who made overtures about coming with me and I turned them all down. I have already had someone in the past couple of days ask if they could walk with me for the rest of the way, and I had to decline.

I spend three hours at an Internet place in Burgos and get back up to date. Burgos is a pretty big city, and I don't know how soon I will have Internet again, so . . .

I have an opportunity to go into the municipal *albergue* in Burgos. It makes the *albergue* with the plastic-covered mattresses in Los Arcos look really good by comparison. In Burgos, the beds are so close together that people have to turn sideways to get between them. They appear to be in one huge room with one exit, although I read later that there are three rooms. The windows are barred, and I am told that the door is locked at 2200. I doubt that there is a municipal government anywhere where this would meet occupancy or egress codes. But I am not staying there. I guess if one were a pilgrim on a journey of penance, this would be the accommodation equivalent of flogging oneself, so it might have some value in their minds. For me, it looks like massive bureaucratic indifference. Their philosophy might be, *after all, it is only for one night . . . here.* But the pilgrims who have little disposable income have to endure this kind of place day after day. It also occurs to me that it might not be bureaucratic indifference; it might just be their attempt to provide as many beds as possible at the lowest possible cost to the individual pilgrim. They may just be responding to overwhelming demand. But I would still rather not stay in this *albergue.* The only good thing that I can see is that it is in a lovely park setting.

Tomorrow is a very long walk, about thirty-eight kilometres, but I am pretty confident that I can manage it. I get the hotel in Burgos to make me a reservation at a little hotel in Castrojeriz. The guide book that I have, the replacement one from Pamplona, does not indicate any hotels or hostels in the small towns in between, so I don't want to walk all that distance and find there's no room at the inn when I arrive. The weather for tomorrow is more promising than today's, which would be easy. The forecast is for cold in the a.m., partly cloudy, chance of precipitation, but probably not. Just keep the rain gear close and wear two undershirts.

2 May, Burgos to Castrojeriz

I am on the road by 0745 with my two undershirts on, along with my rain jacket for warmth. Out of Burgos and its noise and congestion onto a high plain with fields of wheat in the good ground, barley and oats in less good soil, long vistas, no trees. The weather warms up quickly from a very cold start. It is still cool but sunny, so after thirty minutes the rain jacket is off and stowed. After two hours, the zip-off legs of the pants are off and my sleeves are rolled up . . . and yes, I've put on my sunscreen.

I make a note about camino wayfinding. Coming into Burgos, in Burgos, and on the way out of Burgos, the signage is really limited. I see a lot of pilgrims standing on street corners, trying to decide where to go. It appears as if the good burghers of Burgos never missed an opportunity to miss an opportunity. Most other places, even tiny ones, are signed to abundance. This big city doesn't much bother. And yet, the cathedral is big business here, drawing tourists from Spain and beyond by the busload. Maybe that is why they don't care about the pilgrim traffic.

Early in the day, I stop in a town for a *cafe con leche*. There is another *peregrina* there, a dark-haired girl who tells me that she is from Holland. She says that people often say to her that she does not look like she is from Holland. She explains that she is originally from Iran, moved to Holland when she was ten. I think about stereotypes. A couple of years ago, I was at a convention in the U.S. I met an Asian girl who told me that she was from Denmark. Without thinking, I blurted out that she did not look Danish. I failed the test of an English gentleman, who is never unintentionally rude. I went later to apologize for my rudeness, but never found her.

I have to remember to think at least a little before blurting out whatever is on my mind, and I have to think about how, or if, we can avoid stereotyping. It is easier for us humans to categorize people as soon as we meet them, because then we know how to interact with them. Unfortunately, it is a process fraught with peril, because people are not actually alike at all, even if they do look and sound like the person in your office whom you really do not like for very good reasons.

During today's walk, I spend several hours in the company of a Spanish man, Ferran, about forty, from near Barcelona. He wants to talk, but our only common language is German, so you can imagine the conversation—many gestures and ingenious verbal constructions to get our points across. He is walking the section from Burgos to Ponferrada, so this is his first day for this leg. On the road, we pass a genuine shepherd in a high, rocky field to our left who looks like an old man—although he is probably only in his forties—with his flock, his dogs, and his donkey. He and Ferran speak, then Ferran tells me that the shepherd says no one will be a shepherd now. He works every day from 0600 to 2300.

Ferran stops in Hontanas after about thirty kilometres. This old and mostly undiscovered—except by pilgrims—village is in a small ravine in the flat prairie, so it is not visible until we are almost there. I am hot and dry. The sight of it is very, very welcome. It is in better con-

Hontanas is tucked into a fold in the ground and is invisible until you are almost on it.

dition than three centuries ago. In the 1670s, Laffi[40] found Hontanas as hard to find as we did and very unprepossessing:

> It lies hidden in the valley of a little river, so that you scarcely see it until you have reached it. Moreover, it is small, wretched and poor. There are ten or a dozen huts, roofed with straw, that look like winter refuges from the snow, though they are occupied by shepherds. They have a strong palisade round the huts to guard against wolves, which come at night to attack them.

Given the barren wilderness through which I am walking, I am very glad that they have, I hope, resolved the wolf problem.

We have a beer together and toast each other's camino. I walk on alone for the last eight kilometres . . . which never seem to end. After this distance, almost forty kilometres, I am reaching the limits of my physical capability, so I will not do this distance again in one day. The risk of damage is too high. It is in many ways more demanding than running a marathon, which I did successfully several times in the late '70s and in 1980—successfully in that I finished in under three hours and forty minutes, not that I placed well. That was twenty-seven years ago, and the body hasn't improved over that period. Walking the distance is worse than running, because the distance between steps when running is at least twice that of walking, so the wear on the body's mechanical structure is at least two times as great. I notice this as I arrive in Castrojeriz at 1700, after nine hours of more or less constant walking, with a few short breaks for something to eat or drink.

Just before Castrojeriz, I am walking on a quiet roadway, straight for a kilometre, then a sharp turn to the left for another half kilometre, and there is Castrojeriz at the foot of the hill, dominated by the ruins of a castle. Ahead of me there are two pilgrims, a man and a woman, both quite young, and she is limping badly. She is obviously in pain. She has a large pack and I toy with the idea of offering to carry it for her, then abandon that as folly. I can barely carry my own, I am so tired. When I catch up to them, I find that he is Romanian, she is French. I think that

---

40   Domenico Laffi, *A Journey to the West: The Diary of a Seventeenth-Century Pilgrim from Bologna to Santiago de Compostella*, translated by James Hall (Leiden: Primavera Press, 1997).

if I cannot help directly, I can help later. I tell them that I will meet them in Castrojeriz and buy them a beer. Anything to improve her morale. He says to me, quite righteously, "I don't drink." With that rebuff, I ask her if she drinks. She looks at me and laughs; "I'm from Paris!" I tell them that I will meet them at what I expect to be the only bar in town.

I discover, when I ask a local woman as I enter town for directions to my hotel, that the town is very spread out, although it now only has 1,000 inhabitants. It runs in a narrow arc around the southern edge of a high hill with a ruined castle[41] on top, and is about four kilometres long. My bed for the night is about three and a half kilometres from the near edge of the town. I have to ask several times where the place is that I intend to stay, and I am very tired when I finally find it. The German medieval pilgrims called Castrojeriz *"die lange Stadt,"* the long city. It is very deceptive, because as I approach from the east, I see only its narrow edge. It is, however, amazing what a hot shower and a comfortable bed can do to improve one's mood.

On the other hand, my mood is quieter when I think about the girl from Paris to whom I have promised a beer . . . and there is no way on earth that I am going to walk back two or three kilometres to find her and buy the promised beer. I never see either of them again.

This town has been around for a very long time. In 974, Garcia I Fernandez, the Count of Castile, expanded the unofficial military draft of the time by promulgating a decree that any villein[42] of Castrojeriz who equipped a knight for battle would enter the ranks of the nobility, although not the first rank.[43] Although villeins were usually dirt-poor, obviously some managed to get some wealth behind them. It appears that Conrad Black's advance to the nobility has a long and "honourable" precedent. Even before the turn of the previous millennium, you could buy your way up the social ladder. That decree was probably just after the Muslim *razzia,* or border raid, that destroyed the castle (the castro of the name), then retreated back across the border. These *razzia* were conducted by both sides and were in search of plunder and slaves.

---

41 The castle, which precedes the Roman occupation, was used by them to guard the road to the Galician gold mines.

42 A villein was higher than a slave and had fewer options than a freeman. Being a villein did guarantee right to land, which in turn improved the chances of survival, so villeinage was preferable to the other, lower-class options: vagabond, slave, or labourer without land.

43 *Caballeria de segunda clase,* a second-class knight.

I had lots of thoughts today about the obvious parallels between walking the camino and living one's life, but they will have to wait for another day. Watch for the terms "bleak despair" and "transcendental joy."

I have Internet here. Cell phone, no, Internet yes.

3 May, Castrojeriz to Boadilla del Camino

Good morning and happy anniversary, Carroll. Forty-nine years—who knew? Since I feel only somewhere in my early to mid-forties—except when I look in a mirror in the morning—it seems totally ridiculous that I could have been married for forty-nine years. I mean, really, someone who has been married forty-nine years is really, really old. Isn't he? Or she? Carroll and I kid about how many wives or husbands we have had, all in the same two people. I have had the student nurse, professional nurse, mother, army wife, design student, interior designer, facility planner and futurist, university instructor, author, and fashion designer, all in the same person. Carroll has had a similar number of husbands—tank officer, father, missile instructor, helicopter pilot, computer analyst, university student, management consultant, businessman, university instructor, retired person, and now an author—as we have reinvented ourselves over time. This idea does not, sadly, originate with me. I borrowed it from Art Linkletter.

I was amazed to see here a young, very fat guy, ankles like tree stumps, whom I saw yesterday walking exquisitely slowly somewhere outside Burgos. He must have walked all night. I have *cafe con leche* in little

Escarpment with the camino angling up it from lower right to upper left. There are pilgrims on it, but at this distance they are too small to be easily seen.

bar built around a huge wine press. I am on the road at 0845, heading for Frómista. It is twenty-four kilometres, should be a piece of cake.

There is a huge escarpment ahead. The camino runs diagonally upwards across it, from lower right to upper left. It looks very difficult and steep and I am very concerned about how I will get up it. Then I remember my own advice. I am now on a level, good, surfaced path. I will enjoy this now and I will deal with the climb when I get to it. It turns out to be difficult and long, but one step at a time eventually gets me to the top. I am walking through fields of grain and I think about this area, which has been farmed successfully and sustainably for at least 2,500 years, possibly much longer. Then I think about agribusiness in Canada. We use herbicides and pesticides to get high-yield productivity, but at what cost? I think we are playing a fool's game. Herbicide, pesticide, suicide, homicide, patricide, matricide, infanticide, genocide . . . what part of "-cide" don't we understand? We must learn how to feed ourselves without poisoning the land, the sea, the air.

Modern windmills on a ridge line, a common sight in Spain. These are not the windmills of Don Quixote.

I see windmills—modern ones—all around me. This country, which we often think of as remote, primitive, superstitious, is serious about alternate and sustainable energy,[44] unlike Canada.

In Ottawa, the federal capital, for example, with three levels of government, as of 2004, I could not legally install a solar panel on my roof. They were waiting for government approval, while in California, with Arnold Schwarzenegger as governor, they plan to be fifty percent off-grid by 2020! We cannot trust the mainstream political parties—they

---

44　In 2004, the province of Navarre generated sixty-one percent of its power needs from renewable resources and intends to be 100 percent renewable by 2010. It leads Europe in renewable energy technology. Now that is a goal to strive for!

embrace the environment because they think it equals votes. Is there no politician anywhere, no party, that will do what is right, what needs desperately to be done, instead of reading polls and counting potential votes? The Liberals talked environment; it got worse; the Conservatives are now—only now—talking environment because they see votes in it. But both are ultimately cynical and short-sighted. I think I will vote Green next election, even though I do not expect them to get many—or any—seats, because only by showing politicians how many Canadians are serious about the environment, will they act.

We could be world leaders in alternate and renewal energy, but it is not practical. Well, neither was the first telephone. Whom can you call when you have the only phone? In 1978, when I studied computer networks under Leonard Kleinrock[45] in Chicago, there were only a few hundred points of connection—universities and labs. That wasn't practical, either, but look at the Internet now. Solar, wind, tidal, and geothermal power would be practical if we decided as a national policy to support their use. We have the money but not the will.[46] Governments do not lead, they follow; so it is up to us to lead.

En route today, I stop at the tiny ruin of the thirteenth-century Hospital[47] de San Miguel, now run by an Italian fraternity as an *albergue*. I am welcomed in for coffee. There is enormous warmth of spirit here. And, Roger, as you requested, I light a candle here for Kit, and for all the others who have died, who are sick in body or spirit, or who are mourning a loss. I do not believe in the candle thing, but it is a powerful and ancient symbol, and in any case, it does not matter whether I believe in it or not. My belief or non-belief does not change the reality. There is a sense of holiness here that I never feel in a cathedral or church. If there is a God, it is in places like this that one can sense the divine.

---

45   Kleinrock's Ph.D. thesis was on the topic of packet switching, which is the foundation of the Internet as we know it today. I should have paid more attention . . . and purchased shares.

46   In 2007, the government of the province of Ontario in Canada announced that it intends to increase Ontario's existing renewable wind energy capacity twenty-five-fold from 15 MW to over 415 MW—enough power for over 100,000 homes. This in a province of over twelve million people.

47   The term "hospital" has changed meaning since it was used in medieval Spain to describe the places that welcomed travellers, including what we today call hospitals, hotels, and hospices. The person who welcomes you is still called the *hospitalero* or *hospitalera* (feminine), and their welcome is still known as hospitality.

At about noon, I start to notice that my left shin is feeling a little strange. It feels as if I can actually feel the surface of the muscle sliding up and down over the deeper muscle. It is a little uncomfortable. This is likely not a good thing. I have no intention of stopping here in Boadilla, another tiny back-of-beyond place—population about 180—but my shin is bothering me. My planned destination, Frómista, is only about five kilometres farther, when I see a sign for a private *albergue*. It has a very unpromising entry, a barn door falling off its hinges, but that is deceptive. Inside is a little paradise, a beautiful garden, and they have a room available.

I take off my left boot and socks, and that bleak despair thing I mentioned before kicks in. My left shin is swollen, hard, shiny, red, really painful to touch, and it is painful to articulate my foot up or down. I bitterly regret my arrogance of yesterday, thinking that an old fart like me could walk thirty-eight kilometres and not have to pay for it. How on earth will I go on? I cannot walk without pain and I know that any further walking will only prolong and likely aggravate the inflammation.

It is 1430. I am sitting in the dining room of this lovely *albergue*. I have just finished a bowl of lentil soup and a second cup of wine. I am looking out over a beautiful garden. If I have to convalesce, there could not be a much nicer place. I discover that I cannot use my cell phone here in Boadilla—no service in this area offered by my provider.

I sit here with a young Finnish woman, Kirsti Antila, whom I have just met here at the table. She has long, reddish-blonde hair and very fair, almost white, skin. She seems very shy, and if you were to cast her as a nun or a missionary, she would fit the part perfectly.

I tell her about our forty-ninth anniversary and that I cannot call Carroll from here because my phone cannot get a signal. Immediately, she offers me the use of her phone, which *does* work here. I protest that it is likely expensive. She looks directly at me with a shy smile and says, "This is my present to you for your anniversary." Remember, this is a woman whom I have never seen before and may well never see again. It all seems to be part of the camino experience.

I speak to Carroll, and she tells me that, as of yesterday, 2 May 2007, I am a first-time grandfather! Christian and Beverley's baby boy, Cian, has arrived a few days early. All three are fine. The baby, five pounds fifteen ounces, is healthy and was delivered at home because the labour was unexpectedly fast, which must have been extremely good news for Bev. Although the midwife was there, our son Christian caught the baby and cut the umbilical cord. That had to be a profoundly emotional and moving experience. Of course, I have to tell everyone. Lots of toasts to our anniversary and to the new baby. It is like old home week here. Walter and Roswita, whom I last saw in Navarrette, have arrived, followed shortly after by Ferran, who has walked today from Hontana. Beer and red wine all around.

It is later now. Sitting in this beautiful garden area on a warm, nearly cloudless sunny afternoon, is like a slice out of time. Walter tells me that, as he had promised about a week ago, he has found and lit a candle in a cathedral for David Beverley of Houston. And since nowadays they have little electric candles in cathedrals, it was an effort to find a real candle and take it to a cathedral. Again, a genuine mark of respect and care from him for a man he has never met.

As I sit here, I tell anyone who will listen that, when I get to Heaven, I don't want harps and a choir. I want it to be exactly like this garden.

Still later in the afternoon, I sit and speak with Eva and Richard from Augsburg in Germany. They are together but not married. She is tiny, with a wonderful wide smile. He is recently divorced, she is ten days from her forty-ninth birthday and, I think, never married. We talk about the lovely weather, and they laugh as they tell me that Eva is always cold and Richard is always very warm. It helps that he is about twice her size. We discuss the longevity of marriage, and they ask me how I account for ours. I propose that each partner accepts one hundred percent responsibility to make it work. There is quite a discussion while five or six of us try to find the right word in German for responsibility. I think Roswita or Walter nails it down.

In the garden at Boadilla. Eva is seated to my left. Richard and Suzie are standing behind us.

As it is starting to cool down, someone says come in for dinner. The dining room is already almost full. We go in; there are three tables, two with eight places, and one with fourteen. I sit with Ferran, Eva, and Richard. It's pretty funny, sitting for dinner in a tiny, mostly abandoned town in rural northern Spain, two Germans, one Canadian, one Spaniard, all speaking German because it is the only common language.

I am explaining that it is not my birthday, it is my forty-ninth anniversary . . . and I have a new grandchild! Eva and Richard from Augsburg are seated to my left.

After dinner, the lights dim, and someone brings in two little individual cakes with a candle on each. One cake is for someone's birthday—I never do find out whose it was—and the other cake is for me. Full of good humour and red wine, I stand up to explain that it is not my birthday but my anniversary and that I am a new grandfather. I start by saying that I have to say this in English, which is definitely a minority language in the room. Then I start: "*Heute bin Ich neunundviersich Jahre . . .*" and someone beside me, I think it is Eva, says quietly, "English," so I start over and do the whole thing in English. Cheers and applause all around. I am moved to tears (there was a LOT of red wine). Then Ferran orders a round of herb brandy for four of us. That definitely caps the evening. It has been an emotionally exhilarating and exhausting day.

The only regret I have is that Carroll is not here to share this moment with me, but it's OK. We are close in spirit, if not in body, and I love her more than I can say—and that is NOT the red wine talking. So off to bed. I wonder what the morning will bring.

Overnight my left shin aches and is a little painful. Every time I roll over or move, I wake up. This does not bode well for the morrow.

4 May, in Boadilla

It is 4 May in the morning and I have to decide whether I can go on, and, if not, whether I can stay here in this *albergue*, "*En el camino*," in Boadilla. In *albergues*, the usual rule is one night only. The exception is if for some reason you are unable to continue. I walk around a little, the shin is still a little swollen and tender, but greatly reduced from yesterday. Still, there is one hard lump that has not gone down yet. I find Walter, who said yesterday that he has horse liniment with him. It really is horse liniment and he applies it to my leg and says, "I have to look after you so that you can finish the camino and go home safely to Carroll." And he is not kidding when he says this.

He and Roswita prevail on me to stay here while the shin heals. We promise to meet in León or Santiago. They are like lifelong friends, and I have known them for ten days.

At breakfast, Eva and Richard come in. We have *cafe con leche* and dry toast with some marmalade. Then, as they prepare to leave, Eva says something to Richard that I cannot hear. He asks me if I would take an extra fleece that he has been carrying. When we had talked yesterday, they were kidding about how Eva's lips are often blue because of cold and Richard, who is substantially built, walks with his jacket off and his shirt open. I try the fleece on. It is a Jack Wolfskin brand and it fits perfectly. He says now I have three choices: I can return it to him in Santiago, I can send it to his home in Augsburg after I arrive in Santiago, or I can keep it. It never occurs to me to offer him anything for the fleece and, when I think about it later, I think that he would have been insulted by an offer of cash. It is amazing how what we need most is there when we need it. As we part, Eva tells me that meeting me yesterday was good for her soul. She is a Buddhist, I am not religious, so how this works is beyond me. But whatever we talked about yesterday was a positive experience for her, and telling me this today is a very positive experience for me. I wear this fleece all day today, because the wind is biting.

I spend a quiet day, moving about very little, and what movement I make is in slow motion. All my recent friends move on, but one woman stays here, Suzie from Montreal. She is tiny, blonde, pretty, and quiet, likely about the age of my children, soft-spoken with a voice like crushed velvet. She has a sore throat and, as a professional classical singer, must be very careful. When we first met, I said I was from Ottawa and she asked me if my name was Sylvain. During the day, we speak quite a bit. She dithers about leaving or not, but finally decides to stay overnight like me. Later in the evening, she tells me that one of the reasons she asked me if I was Sylvain and stayed today was because she had heard earlier on the camino grapevine about a guy from Ottawa who was a real philosopher. She realized at some point that the guy from Ottawa was this Guy from Ottawa. We had quite a laugh about that, partly because I do not see myself as a philosopher. I just speculate about things . . . and talk to anyone who will listen.

In the garden there is a statue of two pilgrims, done in rusted and coated metal. They are on a base of large rocks. One is leaning on his staff; the other is seated and reaching for his left ankle or shin. His sandal is on a lower rock in front of him. This is most appropriate, since it is my left shin which is giving me grief right now.

At some point later in the afternoon, we get Eduardo, the happy and busy son of the owner of the *albergue*—it's a family business—to take me and Suzie into Frómista where there is a bank machine for me and a *farmacia* for her. She needs something for her throat, and I need cash. After I get my cash, I go to the *farmacia* and the pharmacist recommends a cream and a compression (Tensor) bandage for my leg. I think that I should have done this yesterday, since the only thing that I have done for my leg is get off it for a day and put some horse liniment on this morning.

I discover during the day that Boadilla used to have over 2,000

Pilgrim statue in the garden of the albergue *at Boadilla.*

inhabitants, but has been depopulating[48] for many years. It used to be an important town from the tenth century. In the thirteenth century, it was large enough to have a monastery and four churches. It has, in the only plaza, an ornate carved stone "jurisdictional" column from the fifteenth century, over eight metres high, where condemned criminals were executed by hanging.

A young woman from Hamburg joins the discussion that Suzie and I are having, over and after dinner. She is Marina, thirty-one, and could be a movie star, she is so beautiful (to my eyes, she looks like Mari-

Marina from Hamburg.

lyn Monroe, even has three natural beauty spots on her cheeks, and riveting, penetrating, grey eyes). She is about five feet four inches, full-figured, generously curved where she should be curved, and has a wonderful smile. She works as the controller for a bank in Hamburg. She is fluently trilingual — German, Spanish, and English — was on a student exchange in Guatemala, later worked for ten months for a bank in Chile. She may be the first serious Christian I have met on the trip but not, thank God, a proselytizer (that statement is a little ironic, isn't it?).

The three of us spend the evening sitting near a fireplace and talking about relationships, what works and what doesn't. They have both had failed long-term relationships and neither is in one now. I trot out the hoary, trite, but, I think, true: "It is not about finding the right mate, it is about *being* the right mate." More discussion, close and pleasant, then off to my bed in my bunk. I have been moved from my private room, which was previously booked, to the bunk below Suzie.

5 May, Boadilla to Carrión de los Condes

When I wake up, I note that the bunk above me does not contain Suzie, and I am surprised that she was able to get up and out of the bunk, get dressed, and leave without my hearing her, and sorry that we did not get to say goodbye. But there is a strange incident in the morning. I think — in fact I am sure — that Suzie has left already, because

---

48   Boadilla now has fewer than 200 inhabitants.

she has left me a postcard, so when I see a small, blonde woman walking across the room next to the *dormitorio*, I pay no attention to her, because I think she is a stranger. This is the same room where Suzie, Marina, and I had talked by the fireplace. She looks at me with a long puzzled look until I suddenly realize that this is Suzie. I tell her that I didn't recognize her, and she says, with a hurt sound in her voice: "Do I look that different, then?" She doesn't, and I think that I have hurt her feelings; it was entirely unintentional. I was so sure that she had gone that I wasn't connecting all the dots. It is funny how the brain works . . . or, in this case, fails to work.

As it turns out, she had decided to sleep on the sofa by the fire, not in her bunk, so she wasn't gone, and we do get to say goodbye after all. The postcard she left me reads:

Suzie from Montreal.

> Dear Guy, it was very heart-warming to meet you and to hear your "vignettes." Very moving stories and I somehow feel that indeed these stories will become a book of some sort and will reach the hearts of many people. This is a gift which you could not have expected but on the camino we are told to expect nothing and that everything is a gift. You will have many but these stories are no doubt part of this gift. Buen camino, fellow pilgrim, Suzie.

I will have to think carefully about what she has written to me.[49] I expect that I will see her again in the days ahead.

My leg is better—not perfect, but better. Using the cream and the tensor bandage reduced both the swelling and the pain. I will walk, I hope, to Carrión de los Condes, about twenty-four kilometres.

---

49 This book is another in a very long line of distinguished and not-so-distinguished books about the camino. The first known is the *Liber Sancti Jacobi, Book V, Liber Peregrinationis, Guide of the Medieval Pilgrim*, possibly written by Aimery Picaud, in the period from 1160 to 1173. Whoever wrote it was likely French, had a hate on for the Spanish, and described their behaviour in a very disparaging manner. It is considered the oldest tourist guide in Europe. Part of it appears to have been written by someone who was there, but other parts indicate that it was mostly a compilation of other people's work, much like a modern university paper.

Walking in early morning fog beside the Frómista Canal.

At breakfast, Marina asks me if she can walk with me for a while today. I am surprised and pleased. This is always something that is sensitive to ask of a solo walker, since he or she might really need to be alone, which is why she specified, *"for a while today."* Not me, not today. I have already had over two weeks alone. I'm sore, I expect to be slow, and she is pretty with a lovely personality. She is also an outrageous flirt who attracts men like bees to honey. I may just be protective colouration to keep predatory men away, but I hope that she wants to continue our discussion of last evening . . . and she does.

We walk in dense fog for about two hours, most of it beside the unused Frómista canal, built between 1750 and 1800, just in time for the railroads to take over heavy freight and make the canal redundant.[50] Over the lock gates, then almost dead straight beside a mostly deserted highway all the way to Carrión. The weather is very pleasant all day, just a little chilly. In Villalcazar de Sirga, we visit the magnificent thirteenth-century church of Santa Maria la Blanca, a Templar church-fortress. Given what finally happened to the Templars—they were exterminated by Spanish royalty who were not happy about the power and influence the Templars had accumulated—they should have emphasized the fortress part more. It has a huge rose window with clear glass; more Spanish royalty is buried here.

That would have been before European royalty turned with such ferocity on the Templars. At dawn on Friday, October 13, 1307, scores of French Templars were simultaneously arrested by agents of

---

50   Just like in Canada and the US at the same time.

King Philip. They were tortured, and confessed to all kinds of heresies.[51] The acts of this day may have been the origin of the unlucky Friday the 13th. The attacks widened across all Europe until all Templars had gone into hiding, were tortured, died in battle, or were executed, often by burning at the stake. It was a particularly ugly time.

The well-marked camino runs beside a highway.

In Carrión, once a city of 10,000 people, now perhaps a tenth of that, I leave Marina at the *albergue* and go looking for a hostel with a room. I strike out and am getting quite concerned, when I get the last room in the last hostel I try. A very pleasant, thin, teen-aged girl with orthodontics that remind me of Jaws in the James Bond movie, *Doctor No* (wouldn't she be annoyed with me if she knew what I thought?) finds a room for me. It is the last room available, and it is one floor away from the toilet and shower, but no matter, the room is fine.

I sleep for an hour, then wake when my cell phone rings. It is Carroll, calling from Christian's in Brooklin. I get to hear Cian, my grandson, gurgle contentedly over the phone. That's neat from thousands of miles away. Chris tells me about the birth of his son. I speak with Beverley, who is ecstatic; the birth was fine, the baby is quiet, sleeps easily, and feeds well. A textbook newborn — what could be better? Then back to Carroll. She tells me she is setting up a blog for me so the journal can continue after she leaves Canada in a few days. She is coming to join an art and architecture tour of Portugal and Spain and will meet me later in Barcelona.

I meet Marina at the *albergue* at 1800. We head for dinner, but the restaurant does not open until 1930 — and that is considered

---

51 Part of their problem was that they refused to explain what their initiation rituals were, on the grounds that they were secret. There were accusations of spitting on the cross, worship of idols, indecent kisses, and homosexuality, among other crimes, which were vigorously opposed, but torture makes men admit to practically anything. Many Templars went to their deaths proclaiming their innocence. When the order was dissolved, their property went to the Hospitallers of San Juan, and, of course, the very large debts owed to the Templars by the various royals were dismissed.

seriously early-bird here in Spain. Restaurants usually open for dinner from 2030 to 2330, with the regulars coming in very late.

There is a bar across the road. We have *cafe con leche*. Marina writes in her diary, and I use the Internet for an hour to send a message home. We meet three middle-aged Germans in the bar, and sit and talk. At about 1940, they say, as they leave, that we should go soon to the restaurant because it will fill quickly with pilgrims. This is the restaurant attached to my hostel. At lunch it was full of locals, so the food and price are probably good. They both are. Picaud[52] notes that Carrión is "an industrious and prosperous town, rich in bread and wine and meat and all fruitfulness," so that aspect of Carrión has not changed for most of a millennium.

When Marina and I go in, there are no small (two- to four-person) tables left, but there are tables for six. I see the three Germans at a table for four, so invite them to join us at a table for six. We are there only a couple of minutes when Eva from Hungary comes in and looks around. I wave her over to our table, and she joins us with a huge smile. The food is good, the red wine is good, the conversation is animated in German and English. The young Spanish waiter *really* likes Marina.

She is aware of her beauty and can use it, but is not, I think, narcissistic. She tells a story of being in an IKEA in Hamburg with a friend and finding just the right chair, but it is the last one and it is on display. She begs the (male) clerk to let her have it, but she gets the usual routine: there will be a shipment in just a few days and she could have one then. She turns to her friend and, with a toss of her blonde hair, says, "It would have worked ten years ago!" She got the chair.

I can see in the kitchen just a little. There is a woman working there, wearing gloves, and she wipes her gloved hand across under her nose. I think this would fail the health test! I am really pleased that I have finished eating. This would put me off somewhat.

Marina and I agree to meet the next morning in the same restaurant between 0730 and 0800. If I am gone, I needn't worry—she will catch me. My leg is much better after walking about twenty-four kilometres today. And so to bed and to sleep . . . but not for long. A very funny thing happened at about 2330.

---

52 Picaud, *The Pilgrim's Guide*, p. 7.

I had gone to bed at about 2230 and was fast asleep when I woke with a need to relieve myself. I likely could have hung on until morning, but one thing I have learned is not to put unnecessary pressure on any sphincter, so up out of bed, put on pants, down one flight to the john. Horrors, it is occupied. I am about to turn and go back upstairs when I hear a voice coming from the john: "*Hola.*" I am evidently not as quiet as I thought. Then the lever handle goes down and the door opens. It is Jaws, with another young girl. They are doing something exotic and mysterious with the other girl's hair. I realize that this is really a family enterprise and their home, since Jaws was also serving and clearing tables at dinner in the restaurant. I am prepared to go away but they apologize profusely — in Spanish — and head off down the hall. I go in, do my thing, and head back upstairs to sleep until morning.

6 May,
Carrión to Terradillos de los Templarios

Last evening at dinner, Eva the Hungarian was commenting about what she sees as the commercialization of the camino. In many of the *albergues* there is no kitchen, but you can purchase your meals at what I think is a reasonable price. She points out that many pilgrims are on a strict budget and need to be able to cook their own food. On the other hand, where else in the world could you go on a 700-kilometre rural walking tour and be able to get nourishment and accommodation almost every five kilometres? I did notice today at a lunch break that Eva enjoyed, as I did, a chocolate-covered ice cream, so the commercialization is not all bad.

I meet Marina for breakfast — well, just *cafe con leche* — in the restaurant, and we walk together for about an hour. A Bavarian, Herbert, catches up to us and walks on the other side of Marina. Their conversation drifts into German and I drift away from it. I find it too difficult to understand when two native German speakers are talking together. After a few minutes I deliberately slow down, and they walk on ahead. I note in passing a sense of what I think at first is jealousy, but realize very quickly is a sense of loss. I am sorry to have her leave me. The weather is again lovely, cool, and sunny. At about noon, after four hours of walking on a dead straight stretch, I catch up to them.

Marina tells me later that she had the same sense of loss as I faded away behind them.

When I say the road was straight, I took two photos ahead an hour apart. The only difference is in what is in the fields on either side of the road. This is an old paved Roman road, the Via Trajana, which connected France to Astorga.

The camino follows a Roman road, straight and flat, with no cover on the Meseta.

We eat lunch together. Then I walk on ahead. I need to keep going, because I am a little slow, still favouring my left leg. Eva catches up to me, and we walk together until 1445, when we arrive at Terradillos de los Templarios, another tiny village, owned at one time by the Templars. This is one of the very few towns on the whole camino that did not have a pilgrim hospice during the heyday of the camino, although it has one now.

Whatever the Templars did here, they did a very long time ago. From the centre of town, in the only *albergue* (and only accommodation), in 100 yards in any direction are open fields accompanied by the pungent odour of cow shit, which, for a happy reason I don't understand, we cannot smell inside the *albergue's* garden walls. Apparently we are in cattle country. The *albergue* is very pleasant, clean and warm. We (Eva, Marina, Herbert, myself, and two others) share a room with six beds, no bunks, and lots of room. It is a nice change.

Today I walk another twenty-seven kilometres, so have now completed about 330 kilometres and am approaching the halfway mark. It is hard to believe that I have come that far, although the camino has a mystique about it that is quite powerful. I am really quite grateful for the journal, since the days would otherwise blur one into the other. I know the date because it is on my watch, but not the day of the week.

From the second-floor window of the *albergue*, I see an old man stooped over, walking with canes in the street. I use walking sticks by choice. He does not appear to have that option. I have some thoughts on the transient nature of health and physical beauty, male or female.

Young people all have the beauty of physical youth and vigour about them. In a more reasonable world, older people would have and be recognized for the beauty of experience and wisdom. But our culture is obsessed with youth and tries to maintain it or recapture it through health regimes, physical fitness, and medical or surgical intervention. I won't judge people who opt for radical cosmetic surgery, since I can't actually know what problem they think that they are fixing, but I hope they achieve the satisfaction they seek.

Man walking with two canes in Terradillos de los Templarios.

Personally, I think they might be looking in the wrong place and for the wrong thing. The aging process starts at birth and seems to accelerate as one gets older. Certainly, I have here recently been exposed personally to some of the more obvious effects of aging. Parts don't work as well as I seem to remember, recovery time is longer, time to failure seems to be shrinking. After even a short rest break I start up again like a long, long freight train — that is, very, very slowly. I have noticed almost all of us pilgrims have a good low-range first gear, which we use for a few minutes after each break. Many of the older pilgrims, and there are many of us, seem to be happy in their own skins. I guess that's a goal we can all strive for.

7 May, Terradillos to Bercianos

I am in Terradillos de los Templarios, ready to leave at about 0800. I meet Heinz from Munster, northern Germany, who looks like either Santa Claus (he is a ringer, long, white, bushy beard, long white hair,

Heinz, the pilgrim from Munster, and me, starting the day's journey.

lovely happy face) or a Biblical patriarch, your choice. Also, his English is pretty good, so we can communicate readily. His long wooden staff is intricately carved with the record of his many pilgrimages. He has been doing the pilgrim thing since 1999; he walked to Jerusalem through Turkey, the only place he was ever bothered by dogs. I ask him about dogs, since this was a frequent theme in the books about the camino: "*Beware of the dogs in Spain.*" He says he tried the Francis of Assisi approach, and when that failed—it was a big pack of starving dogs—he swung his wooden staff to keep them at bay until some local villagers came to his aid and threw stones at the dogs to scare them off. They told him to say "*Tik*" each time you throw a stone. After a while the dogs respond to just the "tik" and the motion of throwing. He has never had a problem with dogs in Spain, so there is another bit of camino wisdom squelched.

We are bound for El Burgo Ranero. It is about twenty-eight kilometres, straight road and flat country. About a half hour out, we—Marina is still with me—come to a small picnic-like area on the left side of the path, where there is a whole feast of *café*, tea, and some fruit and vegetables laid out, along with a lovely wooden donation box. It is quite nice, shaded, and no one there except a few pilgrims. A few minutes later, we walk into tiny Moratinos, where, on the left side of the road, is a wall (just a wall) with a hand-painted sign in English, sub-titled in Spanish, saying: "*If you can help us, please do so.*" This is apparently some kind of construction site with not much going on. As we leave the village, we meet a local man who explains that an English couple is trying to build an *albergue* for pilgrims on that site. They also put out the food and drink that we passed earlier. I give the man a little money to give to the English couple, serenely confident that it will end up in the right hands. I am simply sure of it.

Through Sahagún,[53] a fairly large town, founded in the ninth century, we pass what looks for all the world like a grain elevator. When Marina asks a local, it turns out to be . . . a grain elevator. This is wheat-growing country. Across a big old bridge, then more flat country. The weather continues good, sunny, a little breeze but little shade. This is lovely now; it will be brutal in August.

Sahagún is the site of a battle, around 778, between Charlemagne and the Moor Aigoland with a charming legend attached. According to the legend, Charlemagne was returning from Santiago and camped with his army in a meadow on the bank of the Rio Cea, the night before the battle. As was the custom, the soldiers drove the points of their lances into the ground before sleeping. In the morning, those who will die as martyrs find their lances have sprouted leaves and bark overnight. The doomed men cut them off for the battle, but the roots remain in the ground and eventually grow into a forest where the meadow used to be. Picaud confirms this story as well as he is able: "Sahagún . . . with a meadow in which, so it is said, the gleaming lances of the victorious warriors, set in the ground to glorify God, once put forth leaves."[54]

This whole story sounds like a fable, but I can confirm at least one aspect of it from my own experience at our home in Kanata. Several years ago, we purchased some twisted willow branches, dead ones, from a local craft store and used them in Christmas decorations on the front door of the house. After Christmas, I took the willow branches and stored them in the garage. Much later that year, I was looking for something interesting to add to a berm in the lower garden. I took the willow sticks, spray-painted them bright blue, and stuck them together as a clump in the berm. They looked interesting, and I left them in through the winter.

---

53 A thousand years ago, Sahagún was a winter home for Spanish royalty. A native son, Bernardino de Sahagún, was a Franciscan missionary in the 1500s to the Aztecs of Mexico. He made it his business to record as much as he could of the native way of life and of their language. He is best known as the compiler of the *Florentine Codex*, known as the *Historia General de las Cosas de Nueva España* (*General History of the Things of New Spain*). So there is a New World connection as well.

54 Ibid., p. 8.

Sometime the following summer, we noticed some new growth directly beside where I had stuck the twisted willow sticks. To my astonishment, it was twisted willow growing strongly out of the exact location where the dead and painted sticks were stuck in the ground. The twisted willow is now, two years later, the largest growth on the berm. So the idea of dead pieces of wood stuck into the ground and growing is not without its own reality, although I remain a little sceptical that the lances of Charlemagne's knights grew bark and leaves overnight.

Shepherd with his flock and his dog sharing the camino between Terradillos and Bercianos.

At one point on the journey today, we meet another shepherd, dressed in a bright orange jumpsuit and a coat, with his dog and his flock of sheep walking towards us, this time on the camino path itself. I walk slowly as they flow around me, parting ahead of me and rejoining behind me, quite like water passing an obstacle. Marina prefers to walk on the nearby road rather than meet the sheep.

We both start to tire before we reach Bercianos del Real Camino, more than twenty kilometres, but about seven or eight kilometres short of our goal for today. We walk into Bercianos, a town of not more than a few hundred people at most. We spot a hostel as we approach the town and turn directly towards it without any discussion. Marina speaks with the people there, and we get two rooms for twenty-five euros each—this is a done deal.

I am in the room only a couple of minutes when there is a knock on my door. Am I going to get lucky? No, it is Eva, the tall, blonde Hungarian from Budapest. She was about half a kilometre behind us, trying desperately to catch up, because she has started to have trouble with shin splints and needs some cream, which I have and happily give her.

Eva is very sad because she has quite a tight timetable and is having some problems, so today she sent her backpack on ahead—this can be done thanks to a common local service — and was walking happily when her leg gave out. If she stays here, she will have to do even more on other days. If she walks to the next place, she risks being incapacitated; and if she takes a taxi to where her backpack is, she will not have walked the whole camino. The best compromise that we can come up with that she will accept is for her to start walking, but take the phone number of the local taxi with her. Otherwise, if she gets in trouble, she will really be stuck. Marina tells me later that when she saw Eva leaving the village, she had her cell phone out.

After a shower, I hand wash and hang out my clothes — they are really grungy — and Marina and I walk over to the *albergue*. It's less than five minutes away. It's a small town. We see Heinz and several others whom we recognize, sitting on a wooden bench outside the *albergue*, facing the dusty street. There are three Spanish men, Vicente, Miguel, and Vicente, *peregrinos* as well, whom Marina has met before, and one of them, Miguel, has an iPod playing Latin American music in the street. Marina takes a few dance steps that could easily be interpreted as liking the music and wanting to move to it. Miguel invites Marina to dance. My God, what a transformation! She may be a born-again Christian, but I have never seen hips do *that* before. She dances the meringue, the cha-cha, and the salsa. She is a much better dancer than Miguel, but I only have that by someone else's report, since I wasn't watching *him*. It is enough to make an old man weep . . . and several of us do. Remember, this is in the dusty street in front of an *albergue* in a tiny rural town in northern Spain. When I ask her later if this was from her time in Guatemala or Chile, she tells me that she has been taking Latin American dancing classes in Hamburg two nights a week for the past two years. Apparently she is a really good student.

Then the same guy, Miguel, puts on a Tom Jones song, "Delilah," and I am transported from here to Nicosia, Cyprus, 1969. "Delilah" was a favourite song of mine at the time. I had been stationed there on UN peacekeeping duty the year before and I had taken Carroll there on a holiday. I told her about this club where the band leader, an Egyptian, had been a friend of mine and I wondered if he was still there. When we walked into the club, he spotted me, stopped the music the band was playing, and started up with "Delilah." It was wonderful — and hearing it again after almost forty years took me right back to that time and place again.

At dinner, Marina and I talk about beauty. She tells me that when she was in Guatemala as a high school exchange student, she came to believe and act as if she were really beautiful. She was sixteen or seventeen, a busty natural blonde, long hair, big grey eyes—the people in Guatemala of course thought she was beautiful. She came back to Hamburg on what she says was "her high horse" and realized that in Hamburg she was about average; she got off that high horse and never got back on. If she is average in Hamburg . . . well, I don't think that she is average in Hamburg, unless things have really improved in Hamburg since I was there about twenty-five years ago.

Anyway, off to bed before 2200. We have a long way to go tomorrow—about twenty-seven or twenty-eight kilometres—if we are to reach Mansilla. If we succeed, then we are only one day away from León.

8 May, Bercianos to Mansilla

I am up at 0645, with an unsettled gut. What is this about? I usually have a gut like cast iron, so anything that makes me want to stay kind of close to a toilet is a little worrisome, especially if I want to walk a distance. When I come downstairs into the restaurant, there are the three Spaniards from yesterday. I sit with them, Vicente, Miguel, and Vicente, for breakfast. They have come back across town—it's a couple of minutes—to have breakfast here. They stayed in the *albergue* last night and said it wasn't too good. Noisy. They also said there were a lot of people getting up in the night to go to the john. Thought! What if the problem that I have with my gut isn't just me? As it turns out, I have no problem for the rest of the day, but it was a serious concern for the moment.

It is about twenty-seven kilometres today, an easy walk, on another section of Roman road. Marina and I discuss death and loss as we walk. I have just had bad news from Carroll about a particularly dear friend, Ted Cole, who is suffering from a recurrence of leukemia. He is such a dear man, who has given such inspiration to thousands of people over the years. As we walk, I talk about Ted and about the larger topic of illness and losing friends and family. She—Marina—has not yet had a situation where a friend gets ill and does not recover, and she does not know what to say. She has had a couple of friends with serious

Me, Vicente, Miguel, and Vicente at breakfast.

problems, but both turned out well. I tell her, say what is in your heart at that moment. When, just before I left for the camino in mid-April, I met with Peter Holtzhausen, another dear friend who is struggling for his life, I said, "Well, Peter, this sucks." He agreed. He and I talked about plans that we had had together whose priority had just changed. When I said goodbye, we were both close to tears.

At one point, Marina and I stop for a brief rest where there is one of the formal camino signs. It is a line drawing of a pilgrim, with a line under his butt to emphasize the walking person. Marina says, "Walking the camino is very good for the butt, don't you think so?" and turns and shows me her backside to make the point. Having been invited to inspect it, I do, and her butt is very good, by my standards.

Although she is almost young enough to be my granddaughter, my feelings about her are not entirely grandfatherly. I don't know what I would do if she were to come on to me, although I think that it is exceedingly unlikely to happen. I did mention, didn't I, that she was a flirt? I would hope that I would gallantly resist her, but . . . ?

I am in Mansilla de las Mulas, a day's walk out of León. The town's name is said to be derived from *mano en silla*, "hand on the saddle," and *de las mulas*, "of the mules." It turns out that the Roman name of this town, originally a small estate on the Via Traiana heading to León, was Mansella, so the whole "hand on the saddle" story is local legend only. It was once prominent as a livestock market (for mules). Granted its *fuero*—charter—in 1181, the town retains its medieval wall.

After arriving and getting settled in the *albergue* in the middle of town, we go for a drink in a nearby bar. By the way, when I use the term "bar," read "pub" or "local." These places are the social centres, often the only gathering place, of the villages.

Marina wants to know if there is a card game we can play as we sit sipping, in my case, a *cerveza* Clara (a shandy made with beer and lemonade), and in her case, just the lemonade. She doesn't drink alcohol. Not a policy, just doesn't like the taste. I propose Spite and Malice, a solitaire game for two that Carroll and I have played for years, and we ask the bargirl for two decks of cards. We get these completely foreign cards. There are four suits: clubs (a real club, the kind you hit people with), swords, cups (or chalices), and gold coins. There is no queen, but instead a second jack, this one mounted on horseback. We ask if there are other cards. After a search, the bar comes up with two other decks. Both packs are the familiar suits, but one deck is soft porn, with a bare-breasted girl on every card. However, we recognize the suits, so this works. We have the two decks we need. We are well into the game when I ask Marina if she has noticed the name on the back of the soft-porn deck of cards. She hasn't, but I have. It is Marina d'Or. She laughs at that, but she laughs even harder when I tell her that Carroll and I have been playing an extended game of Spite and Malice since 1996, and that I have won only two years out of eleven.

We eat in the courtyard of the *albergue*, along with about twenty other *peregrinos*. There is pilgrim laundry hanging everywhere — socks, underwear, shirts, pants, towels, all strictly utilitarian, except for one pair of frilly black lace panties. There are many, many jokes in several languages about these panties. The owner is almost certainly sitting here, but she — I do hope it's a she — does not acknowledge them. There are several plans concocted on how to uncover the owner, but they come to nothing, and we all go to bed with the panties still on the line. Note: They are gone in the morning.

Interior courtyard of the albergue *at Mansilla.*

The famous and unclaimed black lace panties.

Marina is taking the bus to León in the morning, so I will be walking alone for the approximately eighteen kilometres. Many people take the bus for this leg, since it is reputed to be mostly along a busy highway and through built-up areas all the way. Taking the bus does not interest me. I am not here just for the pretty vistas, although I love them.

This evening, Hannelore, who is about fifty years old and lives in Hamburg, one of the very nice German women whom I have met on the camino, tells me this horrifying story: She grew up in a very dysfunctional family. Based on her description, her mother was likely mentally ill. She never knew her father and was later brought up by a stepfather, who was quite kind to her and was, incidentally, Jewish. He must have been one of the few Jews left in Germany after the war. Some time after her stepfather died, she received a phone call from a man in the south of Germany. He claimed to be her real father and wanted to meet her. He explained that he had no other offspring and that he wanted her to come live with him and she would inherit his estate. He apparently convinced her, so she took the train from Hamburg to reunite with her real father.

When she got to the other end, she saw this little man strutting like a bantam rooster up and down the platform, who turned out to be the man she had talked to on the phone. Over lunch, it became clear that he was an unreconstructed and unrepentant Nazi and virulently anti-Semitic. He told her of his wartime exploits in the SS and then, to make his position crystal clear, he took from his wallet and showed her pictures of himself holding a pistol and shooting a young child. He explained, proudly, that the child was Jewish and that he was helping rid the world of "these vermin." His only regret was that Hitler had been killed and Germany defeated before he could complete his goal. She was appalled, got up from the table, and told him that she was leaving and never wanted to see him or hear from him again . . . and she has not.

Her never-ending nightmare is that she carries genes from this monster and cannot rid herself of the idea that the seeds of evil are within her. My inadequate consolation to her is that, whatever *he* was, she might have the potential for evil within her, but we all do. We all also have the potential for radiant goodness within us and it is clear, by her life, that she has chosen to emphasize the goodness and suppress the evil. The only difference between us is that she knows that her father was capable of the most appalling crimes which were, at that time and in that place, public policy and enthusiastically supported by the government. If I had remembered it at the time, I would have quoted Alexander Solzhenitsyn from *The Gulag Archipelago*:

> If only it were all so simple! If only there were evil people somewhere insidiously committing evil deeds, and it were necessary only to separate them from the rest of us and destroy them. But the line dividing good and evil cuts through the heart of every human being.

Just before I leave to go to bed, I am talking again to Marina about Ted Cole, about what a good person he is. She says: "There is something I can do," and, without any further explanation, goes off to find Heinz, the pilgrim from Munster. When she comes to the *dormitorio* later, she tells me: "That was funny, a Protestant and a Catholic praying for the Jewish friend of a non-believer." I agree, it *is* funny. I hope that it works. And so to sleep.

9 May, Mansilla to León

Notes on *albergue* etiquette: In the *albergue*, almost any *albergue*, both sexes are in very close proximity, common bedrooms (*dormitorios*), often common shower areas and toilets. The individual shower stalls and toilets are each segregated, so we are not actually exposed visually, but there

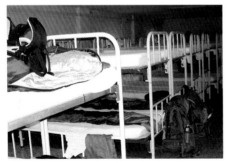

is no illusion as to what is going on. As a result, people are very polite, very quiet generally (with a few obnoxious exceptions), do not watch each other dress and undress, and avoid eye contact except when fully dressed. This last bit breaks down after a long while. You just ignore the skivvies and talk to people as if they *were* fully dressed.

Sleeping room at the Benedictine albergue in León.

Snoring can be an issue if you get people in a harmonic, but so far, so good. One woman was pointed out to me as a person to avoid at night because of her very loud snoring, but I was never in a *dormitorio* with her, so it is only hearsay. The dorms are always quiet because there are almost always people sleeping, even early in the afternoon. Lights out by 2200, no noise getting dressed or undressed, first stirrings around 0600, occasionally earlier (oh-dark-30), some gone by 0630, lights on at 0700, everyone gone at 0800.

The general rule is that a pilgrim can stay only one night in an *albergue*, except for illness or injury. The only people who can use the public (as opposed to privately-run) *albergues* are people with a *credencial* (the book in which a stamp is put each day to show where you are), and pilgrims carrying their packs, and, sometimes, cyclists. There are other "bus" pilgrims who are on a tour with a bus or van to carry their gear from place to place. They generally are not allowed in the public *albergues*. The privately-run *albergues* make their own rules, which usually restrict what kind of people can use them: *peregrinos* with *credencials*, on foot or on bicycles; and when they are open and shut, opening usually any time from 1130 to 1530 for pilgrims on foot, perhaps later for cyclists, and shutting the doors between 2100 and 2200, lights out at 2200.

I walk today to León, always on or near a major highway, often through built-up areas. It is noisy and busy and, at least at one point almost into León, frankly dangerous. The camino at this point crosses a four-lane divided highway at a curve and the pilgrim has to get across four lanes of traffic. In theory, the traffic is slower here, although one does not wish to rely on the theory. So we have this picture of individual pilgrims scurrying (as fast as you *can* scurry with a backpack and tired legs and, maybe, sore feet) across one direction of traffic, wait for another break, then scurry across the other lanes. This is really the first dangerous point I have seen so far. As you can tell, I am one of the successful scurriers.

Many pilgrims on the camino as we approach León, more than I have seen before at one time.

Then, to make the point more obvious, you walk 200 metres and take a pedestrian bridge back *over* the same highway. And I have reached 400 kilometres, with a little over 300 to go!

As I walk, I think about my friends, especially Linda, Peter, and Ted, one of whom is grieving a sudden death, the other two on what may well be the last journey of their lives. I think about death and dying, about what happens next, about Heaven and hell and resurrection. When someone dies, one of two options opens up: either some form of life goes on or it does not. Pretty clear options, it seems to me. It is my belief that, when we die, it's over. The composite parts, the molecules and atoms that we think of as "us" rejoin the rest of the earth's biosphere, either slowly through burial or quickly through cremation (I am thinking now of Western cultures). Either way, based on conservation of energy, nothing is lost. The atoms that used to be me are recycled as part of, let's say, a butterfly or a truck tire. I prefer the butterfly but I don't think I get a choice in this selection.

However, there are a lot of people who believe that life goes on. The specifically Christian belief is that the good folks get to go to Heaven and the bad folks don't. Part of my problem is the remarkably arrogant belief that, out of all the species of animals on the earth, only humans get to go to Heaven. What about the chimpanzees, with whom we share ninety-eight or ninety-nine percent DNA? What about dolphins, who are probably at least as smart as we are and, frankly, seem to have a lot more fun? What about the great apes, with those soulful, sorrowing brown eyes? What about all the other animals? What happens to them? As far as I can understand, the policy is that they all just die. No Heaven for them.

So, as I walk, I develop an alternate theory of what, if anything, happens next. (This section may offend some. If so, I am sorry that I offend you, but this is only my theory. I am not disparaging your belief. I would be happy to believe, if I could.) I postulate either there is Heaven for all or Heaven for none. We can't have it both ways. If there *is* Heaven for all, what might it look like? Well, we've already established that Heaven for humans is happiness forever, luminous light, harp music, and endless choruses of halleluiah. Perhaps a little Philadelphia Cream Cheese on the side (just joking[55]).

---

55   Kraft markets its cream cheese product with a very successful TV advertisement showing a perky and pretty angel on a cloud eating Philadelphia Cream Cheese.

I pause for a moment to wonder if some renegade, after two eons, 2,369 years, four months and seven days, whispers to the next chorister: "I am going to kill the next person who suggests the Halleluiah Chorus again. I want to get down and dirty with a little Tom Jones or the Rolling Stones—I Can't Get No Satisfaction." No, that won't do, that particular song would be proscribed in Heaven for obvious reasons. But I digress. Back to my theme.

What might Heaven for all the other species look like? Well, I imagine that they would all be pretty ecstatic about a place where humans did not exist, so that is what they get, a human-free environment. They call this Heaven, and the place where the humans are—hell. And this is just where the "good" humans are. What about the rest of us? I can imagine an environment in which the species' roles are reversed, a place where humans are kept as pets, in herds for milk, for food and clothing, and where there are protesters, probably the dolphins, objecting to the use of human skin as fun fur. This is a place where humans, with our ability to understand what is going on, live in a state of constant and unrelenting terror. "I hear that your sister Emma is going out to a steak house in Tulsa next week." This is what we humans would call hell.

Now, how about the selection process? For some, but not me, this brings to mind St. Peter and the Pearly Gates. There are lots and lots of jokes about this, but I have a queasy feeling about this whole operation. There is someone sitting at a desk, evaluating each new arrival, "You—go to the right, congratulations, pick up your choir robe at Supply. Next! Oh, you go left, sorry, stairs down just over there." Arbitrary, no appeal possible, no potential for reversal. Last time we had this type of operation on earth, we called it the selection point in Nazi extermination camps. "You, left for the showers, don't forget to take off your clothes and jewellery; you, right for the labour gang." I admit that it is a dark, dark image.

On a brighter note, since I am on the topic, what about bodily resurrection? This, it seems to me, is one of those theories that worked fine in the lab, the marketing guys love it, but production just cannot get it working well enough to affect the bottom line. My problem starts with what happens to Mrs. O'Leary, who outlives four husbands. Whom does she get on judgment day, or is polyandry finally in? What about those folks who donate their organs on their death? (And, by the way, I am *strongly* in favour of this. If you aren't using it any more, why not give this precious gift to someone else? Sign the card today.) Anyway, if I have donated my corneas, kidneys, liver, heart, and lungs to a bunch of other folks, who gets what at the resurrection? Do we have to share? You get the drift of my concern.

So I think when it's time to go, we go. And given this belief, I don't want to wait until Heaven to be good to others or to have others be good to me. Be happy here and now, share your gifts freely here and now. Treat your fellows with respect and love now. If it turns out that I am wrong, then the rest is all a bonus. (But I want more than harps and choirs. A late sunny afternoon in Boadilla in the garden of the *albergue* with friends, family, red wine, beer, and a foot massage would be fine.)

When I arrive in León about noon, I find that Marina has already arrived, been into the *albergue*, run by Benedictine nuns, found that the main part is two *dormitorios* of forty bunks, eighty people each, and has decided—correctly—that I will not like this. She has found another part of the Benedictine convent where they have small rooms. She has taken a room with two beds for us ... and it has, of course, its own light switch! It is up a two-storey wooden helical staircase and is quite lovely. We are under the eaves, with a continuous row of low windows looking out onto the street. The roof beams are exposed within the room and are ancient. We are in the convent itself, a lovely old building with paintings on the common area walls that are likely priceless.

The name León is derived from "Legion," since this was originally a Roman military garrison founded in 68 AD, later the capital of the old kingdoms of Asturias and León. León, straddling the Rio Barnesega, has a population today of about 205,000, so it is a good-sized city and, outside the ancient, well-preserved core on the east bank of the river, modern.

After I shower, we go out and visit the cathedral and the Basilica of St. Isodore. The thirteenth-century cathedral is spectacular because of the enormous number and height of the windows and the sheer size. The 125 windows cover 1,800 square metres of the interior wall. I get a sense of ancient power and beauty, engineering and architecture, but none of spirituality.

The basilica contains a library of 30,000 books from hundreds of years before the printing press. One can enter the library only as part of a guided tour, and the guide tells us that the library is still available as an active reference library for scholars. St. Isodore,[56] bishop of Seville from 599–636, is justifiably famous as a scholar, because he created the first encyclopaedia, at least in the Western world. At least ten editions were printed between 1470 and 1530. The tradition is that he preserved what Western Europeans knew of the Greek writings, including Aristotle. So how did the bones of the Archbishop of Seville end up in León?

In about 1064, Ferdinand I (the Great) was king of Castilla and was nearing the end of his life. He was a powerful king and a great fan of Santa Justa, a potter in Seville who was martyred because she would not worship Venus. He decided that he wanted Santa Justa to be moved from Seville to León, the seat of his throne. At the time, Seville was a Muslim vassal state. The king, Motadhid, was happy to arrange for this, but Santa Justa's bones could not be found. As an alternative, he arranged for the disinterment of St. Isodore's remains and shipped them north to León, where they were reinterred with great honours. Isodore is still here today, along with his extensive library. And the whole Santa Justa story has been buried under layers of time.

All sorts of kings and queens are buried here, twenty-three of them, including Eleanor Plantagenet. I had always associated the Plantagenets with England. I am going to have to brush up on my history.[57] The basilica has another of the Doors of Forgiveness, for those pilgrims who were not able to reach Santiago.

We also see a Gaudí building, the first one that I have seen here and one of only three outside of Catalonia. I will see another, more grand and more ornamented, in Astorga. Built in 1891–1892, the neo-Gothic granite Casa de Botines's four floors of apartments have four corner towers, only a slight indication of his later masterpiece in Barcelona. Just in front of the building is a bench where a life-size bronze Gaudí sits, looking at his sketchbook. I sit beside him and look over his shoulder at the book.

---

56   St. Isodore (560–636) was for over thirty years the Archbishop of Seville, a hundred years before the Muslim invasion.

57   According to Wikipedia, Eleanor Plantagenet was also known as Eleanor of England, youngest daughter of King John of Magna Carta fame.

I meet Hannelore again here, as well as Eva from Budapest and Heinz from Munster. Most of us (I can't find Eva) go out to dinner, and I have my first *paella* in Spain — at a restaurant without red wine! This is an outrage. I have to drink beer. I thought *paella* was always seafood, but there are all kinds, including chicken or vegetarian. Of course, I have the seafood option, and it is really good. We sit here in the narrow street, with a lot of fascinating pedestrian traffic and no cars, until after nine. One of the pedestrians is a smartly dressed young woman with a very little girl in red plastic boots. The woman is kicking a little ball along the street and the little girl is kicking at it but keeps missing. So the picture is of this absolutely professional-looking woman kicking a little ball up the street!

When we return to the convent, they are just about to have a pilgrims' night benediction, so we (about forty of us, mostly from the more crowded and open *albergue*) attend this very simple and pleasant service in Spanish in the nun's chapel. Since the nuns are putting us up, it seems reasonable to attend the ceremony that they are putting on for us — and it is all part of the camino experience. There are only about fifteen nuns, of whom all but one are old. And I mean old — older than time. They must have a height restriction for nuns here, because most of them are approaching five feet . . . from below.

Much later in the evening, about midnight, when Marina and I are going to sleep, I reach across to her bed, touch her hand and say "Thank you for the trust you have in me." She replies, matter-of-factly, "Guy, you are much older than you think you are." After a few silent moments, while I digest this and note, ruefully, how true it is, she laughs wickedly and says, "That was a low blow." And I agree. Then I go to sleep and sleep the sleep of the pure at heart, in spite of my "*inner Schweinhund.*" (I know, Roger Sage, that you are not going to believe this, but it's true. I swear.)

I think that I am going to take a rest day in León tomorrow. Although I think that I could go on, I am a little ahead of my schedule, and my body could use the rest. There is no need to push it, so I won't. And this is a big city with lots to look at and contemplate.

Today Carroll will arrive in Portugal to begin her tour. I am really looking forward to seeing and holding her again. This journey is making me realize how much we are to each other. Although she is not physically here, she is with me constantly. When she returned from New Zealand, she brought me a greenstone (jade) Maori pendant, which is like a Möbius strip, and which I wear all the time. It has no beginning and no end and it is like the two of us. It is my only jewellery.

10 May, in León

I have a wonderful sleep, wake up at about 0800, and get up shortly before 0900. Breakfast here in the hostel is included in the room fee, and it is at 0900. We could not take advantage of this if we were walking, because that is too late to start. Breakfast is in a large, bright room with a wall of twenty-foot windows overlooking a quite formal courtyard. It has shrubs and flowers and large, paved areas, much like an outdoor room. It is surrounded by four-storey walls on all four sides, so is likely usable even on the brutally hot summer days here. We share breakfast with a couple of nuns and a few older women who evidently live here—perhaps retired nuns. Can one retire as a nun?

We are lazy, lazy, because there is no pressure to get on the road. After breakfast, we find an Internet place, where I spend two hours

León cathedral.

adding to the blog, while Marina sits nearby writing in her diary. She complains that writing a journal is contagious. She wrote eight pages about yesterday. Then we head off to Plaza Santa Maria in front of the cathedral, sit in the sun, sip *cafe con leche,* and watch the Spanish world walk by. It's wonderful. I feel like a child who has discovered a secret cache of cookies. I sit here, content, quiet, satisfied, happy, even wearing my dorky hat. It is good to be alive and to *feel* so alive at a moment like this. A friendly middle-aged priest walks up to me as I sit, and inquires in Spanish how my camino is going. I tell him that it is going very well indeed.

Eventually I leave Marina in the plaza, head back to the hostel for a ninety-minute siesta, then back to the square, where we meet at about 1645. The weather has clouded over and it has become quite chilly and very windy. It bodes ill for tomorrow.

Marina has discovered a special tour at the side of the cathedral where, for two euros each, we can climb a ten-storey aluminum stairway, then take a bridge, also of aluminum, over to a temporary platform high inside towards the rear of the cathedral. Here a delightful guide, young, pretty, and enthusiastic, describes to us in Spanish, with much good humour and many hand gestures, the ongoing restoration of the glass. The project name is *"el sueño de la luz,"* "the dream of light." The guide has figured out that I am illiterate in Spanish, more or less, and that Marina is with me, so she takes special care to point out to Marina anything that she thinks I should note. Because of the immense area of the stained glass, about 1,800 square metres, and the subsequent lesser area of solid wall, the nave has collapsed twice in recent past centuries. Our payment helps pay for the restoration of the glass, which is intended to be preventive.

It is an enormous and painstaking project. Some of the glass is medieval glass mosaic; some is Renaissance, a mixture of mosaic and painted glass. They had discovered how to paint successfully on glass, and, of course, they could make more lifelike figures. The first colour they figured out how to use was yellow, so there is a *lot* of yellow in the early Renaissance windows. Starting at the northwest corner of the cathedral and moving clockwise as seen from above, the windows depict the events of the Old Testament. When they turn the corner at

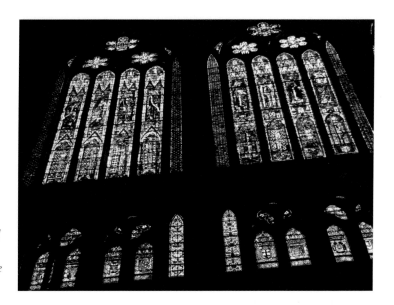

The wonderful stained-glass windows of the cathedral.

the southeast corner, where the sun falls all year, the windows show the events of the New Testament. Also the glass on the north side is thicker than the glass on the south side. I do not know whether this is deliberate engineering for some reason, or because glass is a fluid (a very slow-moving one, to be sure), and the effect of 1,000 years of direct sun has made the glass on the south side slump more than the glass on the north.

I ask if the cathedral interior will be lit up at night so that we can see the windows from outside. In James Michener's Iberia, he says, ". . . so far as sheer visual pleasure is concerned, I have seen nothing to excel León's cathedral at three in the morning, lighted from within . . ." so I would really like to experience this; but the guide says it happens only on weekends, and she is not sure if it will happen this weekend. It is Thursday today, so if I want to see it I will have to stay here for another day . . . and there is no guarantee. In the event, I decide to continue on the camino. I shall have to come back for this.

Afterwards, we repair to a restaurant where we order a beer for me, an orange-flavoured lemonade for Marina, and *churros con chocolate*, a deep-fried extruded sweet pastry fritter, dusted with icing sugar, then dipped in rich, thick hot chocolate, almost a pudding. Either one alone would be wonderful. Together they are heavenly. This is sheer decadence, and how I love it!

Marina is writing in her diary. I think she is writing her rebuttal of what I have said about her over the course of the past few days. We discuss walking solo or not and decide, at least for tomorrow, to walk together. If either of us feels the need to walk alone or to separate for any reason, we will both feel free to do so. It is a comfortable and easy arrangement.

Carroll calls at 1800, as agreed. My cell phone keeps switching itself to "Divert," so I do not hear the phone and it does not vibrate. It is annoying, and I have been unable, so far, to get the Divert function to go off or stay off. She has read my most recent blog (about my theories on Heaven and Hell) and agrees that it may well be controversial, but is comfortable with my decision to write it. I pass the phone to Marina and she and Carroll talk for the first time, but not likely the last. Marina has invited us to come to Hamburg while we are in Berlin. It is only a couple of hours from Berlin, and we hope to be able to do this.

Carroll leaves for Europe in about three hours and is ready to go. I look forward to seeing her in less than three weeks, and I look forward to having her in the same time zone, at least. I can hardly wait.

Marina and I will eat in the restaurant where we had the *churros* about an hour ago and we expect to have an early night and get on the road in the morning. Off to dinner and then back on the road. Kind of like Wayne Rostad, "On the Road Again."

11 May, León to Mazarife

Well, it is an interesting day, as in the Chinese curse. It starts off extremely well. We — that is, Marina — had arranged yesterday with Raquel, who serves breakfast at the convent, to have something available for us at 0815, instead of the usual 0900. We go down, expecting to be able to concoct something and be on our way. We underestimate Raquel. She is a rather shapeless lady of indeterminate age in baggy jeans and a shapeless, dull mustard-coloured shirt . . . and a heart of pure gold! She has a full breakfast available for us, and, just after Marina has made up a *brötchen* with ham and cheese and wrapped it in a napkin, out comes Raquel from the kitchen with a full bag of freshly baked buns with ham and cheese made up, wrapped, and ready to go for us. So we eat rather too much breakfast, with, of course, *cafe con leche*, and Marina has given me a pouch of magnesium, which her doctor had given her for muscles, so I have that in water as well.

So, light in heart, off we go, like Dorothy and the Lion in *The*

Wizard of Oz. Then, after two and a half hours of walking through downtown León (noisy and busy), and through an industrial sector of León (noisy and really ugly), we are finally out in the countryside, where we have to navigate under a maze of intersecting highways. For the first time, the camino signage fails us, or we fail to see it. There is a lot of confused yellow writing and conflicting arrows on the road surface. It looks like advertising for various *albergues.*

We are looking for an alternate route that will take us off the path beside the two-lane highway to Villadangos and into the countryside to Mazarife. Instead, after several false starts and backtracks, we end up walking for kilometres on a rough-surfaced service road directly beside a divided high-speed highway; not exactly the tranquil day we had expected. At one point, we are sitting in the weeds on the side of the road having a break, and a cyclist, clearly also a pilgrim, rides by. We realize that it does not help us to have others lost as well. We discover that we are between the two camino options, but are unable to get back easily to the option we want, and asking the locals, when we can find them, does not seem to work either, because they always want to tell us the most direct route for the camino, which is precisely the one we are trying to avoid.

This day is not turning out, so far, to be the highlight of the camino.

Eventually, at about 1330, we arrive in a village, Robledo, where we find a bar, lick our wounds, and decide to take a cab to our destination, Villar de Mazarife. Both of us are a little halt and a little lame, so striking off cross-country to get back to the camino, then proceeding for many more kilometres to arrive does not seem a good option. Did I mention we were pretty well lost?

The cab arrives, and we proceed rather rapidly (compared to our usual pace) to Mazarife. It turns out that the *hospitalero* here, Jesús, is a friend of Raquel's from León, who has sent her regards with Marina for her friend.

The place is quite nice, with only four bunks to a room and with a huge garden out back with what appears to be a mock-up of a Viking ship — it's the shields along the side — with a bull's head at the prow (we *are* in Spain) and a high cabin section at the stern. That is probably also Spanish influence.

Sitting precariously on the Spanish-Viking "ship" at the Albergue de Jesús in Mazarife. Note the ubiquitous pilgrim laundry at lower left background.

I have to tell you a very funny story that happened a few days ago. I am sitting at dinner in an *albergue* with Marina on my right and Eva on my left. Eva has come in for dinner very late, so that the rest of us at the table have pretty well finished. I had had the trout for dinner and it was good, so Eva orders the same thing. When it comes, she cuts off the head and, after asking if it's OK, puts it on my empty plate. Then she cuts off the tail and does the same thing. I note this, have a wicked lateral thought and start to snicker quietly. Marina notices this, Eva does not—this is a good thing, because Eva is quite serious about everything—and wants to know why I am snickering. I tell Marina that I will explain later.

A few minutes later, she wants to understand what it was I found so funny. I explain that it was the little piece of tail that Eva put on my plate. She looks at me, so why is *that* funny? Now I have to thread the delicate explanation of the alternate meaning of "a little piece of tail." Marina gets it quickly and then wants to know how exactly this differs from, for example, a one-night stand or making love. Could I, for instance, have a little piece of tail with Carroll? Well, no. So what is it about a piece of tail that differentiates it from making love?

Have you ever been in the position when you wished you hadn't opened your mouth? But I persevere. My opinion is that making love involves including the other person in the process, to make sure that both are happy when you finish, while a piece of tail involves satisfying yourself, using someone else's body, kind of like external masturbation. End of the story, part one.

Continuation of the story, part two: Last night, we were lying in our beds talking about language, when I think that this is a good time to teach Marina a couple of useful English phrases. Her English is excellent but, of course, does not include a lot of jargon terms. One phrase that I like is "*as thick as two short planks*," meaning "really stupid." She liked this one a lot. Another is a phrase that my brother Ance uses, "*in really deep weeds*," meaning "in really big trouble." Then I had a brainwave. To ensure that she understood these phrases, I challenged her to use all three: "*a little piece of tail*," "*thick as two short planks*," and "*really deep weeds*" in a single sentence.

You would think I'd know better, but no. She thought about this, then said to me, "Do you have a sentence that uses all three?" I didn't, but I thought about it and one jumped unbidden to my mind. This is the point where I should have said, innocently, "No, I haven't thought about it." But I did have one and I said to her: "Guy is as thick as two short planks if he thinks he can have a little piece of tail without being in REALLY deep weeds." I thought that Marina was going to wet herself, she was laughing so hard.

It is siesta time here in Mazarife. I am going to go sit in the garden, sip on my San Miguel beer, and contemplate the world.

Well, Marina is highly indignant. I told her about my most recent blog entry and she wants you all to know that at no time was she even close to wetting herself. So I stand corrected (but I still think she was).

The evening is spent sipping red wine and eating vanilla wafers in the back garden of the *albergue* with four Germans: two older guys—about my age—one of whom is Wolfgang (I haven't heard that name since *Amadeus*[58]) and two women, one of whom is Marina. She has a domestic moment and has purchased the ingredients for and made apple pancakes, which are very good and very filling. I share by going shopping with her and paying for the ingredients. I do, by the way, share my wine and vanilla wafers with all of them, although I personally eat about half of the wafers.

This *albergue*, called Albergue de Jesús, is a throwback to flower child days. The walls are bright yellow and covered with chalk drawings, snatches of poetry from the sixties, all kinds of signatures, and a chalk drawing of Heinz from Munster with his distinctive staff. He was here yesterday. By the way, Jesús is the *hospitalero* here, so the name is a clever double entendre for those who know his name.

---

58 *Amadeus*, a 1984 Milos Forman movie about Wolfgang Amadeus Mozart.

Karsten standing in the doorway of the brightly painted albergue.

There is an interesting but, I think, doomed, Romeo and Juliet courtship going on between two pilgrims here. She is tall, delicate, serene, a sweet South Korean who wears a dress down to her ankles. He is a slight, fragile-looking, lean young man with very long, very black hair falling forward over his shoulders. They wander around hand in hand, lost in each other. She looks composed; he looks either slightly dazed or slightly beatific, depending on the moment. They share a large mattress on the open second-floor balcony. I come across them there. She is sitting with her back to the wall, he is curled up with his head in her lap and she is facing straight ahead singing softly. It turns out that he is Czech, not South American Indian as some had supposed, and several people have commented—in the kindest possible way—that they would like to have some of whatever he is smoking. That may account for the beatific gaze. The Czech tells Karsten, of whom more later, that they are going to spend the next twelve days at this *albergue*. Well, it's their camino and I hope it ends well. It seems unlikely that we will ever know.

Karsten is a young German guy from Berlin, speaks excellent English with a crisp British accent, and has asked if he may walk with us tomorrow. He is lean, blond, about five foot nine, big smile, chatty, and wears John Lennon-style wire-frame glasses. There is also a very nice, quiet, German woman here, Paula. She is perhaps five-foot-seven, slim, reserved, grave, introspective. She has a lovely smile but does not often bestow it. She is travelling very light, with only a small pack.

I go to bed at 2030, since it is cold out, although the sun will not set for at least forty-five minutes yet.

12 May, Mazarife to Astorga

Our plan is to walk about fifteen kilometres today, but we walk thirty instead. The first couple of hours out of Mazarife are on a straight asphalt road, just a little traffic, farmers on tractors going out to their fields, through fairly small fields of either grain or market garden plantings. Then the path changes to a little curvy, a little hilly. The walking is very easy and the weather is good, cool and sunny, so spirits are up. Marina and I start out together, then Karsten from Berlin joins us. The three of us walk more or less together, but there is no attempt to maintain a constant group speed, so for much of the day I walk alone, with one or both of them in sight in front of me. I have no blinding revelations today (again), but the weather is kind, the track is smooth and dry and mostly even, the traffic is sparse and far away.

One jarring note: In these little medieval towns, there is still bread and general store supplies delivery, kind of a mobile convenience store. It comes in a little white truck with a piercing horn with the volume of a Mack truck's klaxon. They announce their presence by leaning on this infernal horn for about ten seconds as they pull to a stop. It is loud enough to wake the dead, so they have to be careful not to blow it near cemeteries. That would upset the natural order of things.

Early in the day, we stop at a bar for a *cafe con leche*, then walk on down the road in the village, Hospital de Órbigo. At the bar, there are posters for, I kid you not, a medieval jousting tournament to be held in

The famous bridge at Hospital de Órbigo where 300 jousts were fought in 1434.

early June in this area. As we will soon see, this is historically appropriate for here. After we leave the bar and walk for a couple of minutes, a woman comes out of her house, calls to us, and tells us that the camino is behind us. We have missed the arrows, which were just past the bar. So the stories about locals actively helping the pilgrims stay on the camino are, in fact, true. It is very kind of her, and we thank her in Spanish, German, and English, then turn back to find the camino.

Speaking of jousting tournaments, in this village, one of the thirteenth-century bridges we pass, Puente de Órbigo, is the site of the Paso Honroso (Passage of Honour), where in 1434 a love-besotted Spanish knight, Don Suero de Quiñones, decided to resolve his apparently forlorn[59] love by challenging the next 300 passing knights — I gather the peasant farmers were exempt from this idiocy — to a joust. He could do this because the only way to cross the River Órbigo here from east to west then was via the bridge, and this is a very long bridge, 400 metres and at least thirteen arches.

The challenge spread quickly across Europe and all sorts of knights took up the gauntlet. Nine Spanish knights joined Quiñones, and a great tournament was held, with 727 individual jousts. The story is that over a period of some thirty days, he fought about 300 jousts and won them all.[60] There was only one fatality reported, a knight named Claramont of Aragon, but he was killed by an unintentional self-inflicted wound. His horse shied, his own lance snapped and passed through his eye. If this story is true — and some parts of it certainly must be — then jousting was not quite as lethal as is usually seen in Hollywood movies. This story may have been the origin of the Don Quixote legend. It is also one of the earliest reported incidents of road rage.

I am in Astorga at a lovely, modern, spacious *albergue* with two bunks to a room again. The *hospitalero* here is a volunteer, a big happy, chubby German named Oskar, whom we will, unexpectedly, meet again.

Astorga, current population about 15,000, was a Roman town — originally Asturica Augusta — and some Roman remains are

---

59   She was already married.
60   Quiñones was killed in an impromptu joust twenty-four years later by one of the knights, Gutierre de Quijada, whom he had bested back in 1432, and who had threatened revenge and was obviously a sore loser with a long memory.

visible today. It stands at the junction of several major medieval trade routes and where the camino Francés—the camino I am on—and the camino from Sevilla, the Via de la Plata, merge. There were once twenty pilgrim hospitals here. There are several notable points of interest. One is the cathedral, which indicates that Astorga must have been an important town in its prime. The cathedral, begun in 1471, has a wonderful carved wooden door set in an enormous carved entryway full of biblical figures doing what biblical figures usually do.

Gaudí's controversial bishop's palace in Astorga. The palace shows some of his ideas that later blossomed in Barcelona.

Next door is the even more wonderful bishop's palace, which is notable because it was designed in the 1880s by Gaudí, the very famous and eccentric Spanish architect. The story, as I was originally told it, is that the bishop, Juan Bautista Grau y Vallespinos, a Catalan, prevailed on his good friend Gaudí, also a Catalan (Catalans stick together), to design him a palace in this rather remote region of Spain. Gaudí did so, but when it was built, the bishop did not move in, because he felt it was overly opulent for him. The end of another wonderful friendship. Gaudí was so mad at his old friend the bishop that he never came back here. He went back to Barcelona and worked on his famous cathedral until his untimely death. In 1926, he was run over by a tram on the Gran Via and died two days later in hospital. He is buried in his masterpiece, the *Sagrada Familia*, which, as of 2007, is still not finished. The due date is 2026, the one-hundredth anniversary of his death.

It turns out the Astorga story is not quite as melodramatic as the version I was first told. It seems that after six years of construction, with the palace still unfinished, the bishop died in 1893, work was halted, and the architect, Gaudí, was fired by the new bishop, who was not a Catalan. From 1905–1909 it was completed, but the bishops were ashamed to live in it. For years it stood empty, a church scandal. In the 1960s the then bishop decided that the palace would become a museum showing life along the camino in the Middle Ages . . . and that is what it is now, a fine museum.

At 2000 hrs, the main town square is absolutely full of people of every age. There is a bell tower overlooking the square with a huge bell and two life-size figures, one on either side, female left and male right, holding strikers against the bell. At the hour, the lady first, then the man, in turn swivel and strike the bell the requisite number of times. The locals no longer notice this, but we pilgrims do. It's wonderful! But there is a mystery involved here.

> The clock is struck by two mechanical figures, a Maragato and a Maragata, wearing the baggy trousers and the silver trinkets which Richard Ford (*Gatherings from Spain, 1846*) noted over a century ago, but now seen no longer. These mysterious people still exist, but no one knows their origins, though some believe they are descended from the Berbers.[61]

But it gets even better. The eleventh edition of the *Encyclopaedia Britannica*, published in 1911, tells this story:

> Near Astorga there dwells a curious tribe, the Maragatos, sometimes considered to be a remnant of the original Celtiberian inhabitants. As a rule the Maragatos earn their living as muleteers or carriers; they wear a distinctive costume, mix as little as possible with their neighbours and do not marry outside their own tribe.

So the question remains unanswered. How did the mysterious and secretive Maragatos get to be the models for the bell strikers on the bell tower in Astorga? And were they—are they, if they still exist

---

61   H.V. Morton, *A Stranger in Spain* (London: Methuen & Co., 1955), p. 328.

as a separate population—descended from the Berbers, or from the Celtiberians, or from another unknown source?

As we sit in the plaza, Karsten tells us a pilgrim horror story. He was at an *albergue* a few days ago, before we met him, and needed his clothes washed. The lady who runs the *albergue*—the *hospitalera*—offered to look after this for him at about 1400. At about 1700, he noticed laundry out on the line, but not his. He went to enquire and got the *hospitalera's* ancient mother, who told him a lot of incomprehensible detail in some dialect. He got not a word, except to understand that the lady of the house was out. A couple of hours later, she came back, and he discovered that his laundry was still in the front-loading washing machine, which had failed and could not be opened. It was now after 1900, and his laundry was neither dry nor accessible. Concern set in.

Many ineffective mechanical attempts were made to open the machine, which was quite ancient as well. (It may have belonged to the mother.) At 2130, they called the local technician, who came promptly and just as promptly told them that he could not open the door and that the machine would have to be taken to León for service. Significantly more concern set in. At that point, the *hospitalera* told them that the machine was so old that it would be okay if they had to demolish it to get out the clothes. This is basically what happened, so at about 2300, Karsten had his clothes, dripping wet and covered with tiny shards of metal. The *hospitalera* told him to go to bed, that she would fix it all up ... and she did. In the morning he had his clothes, clean, free of metal, and practically dry. She must have stayed up all night, but she had him on his way, much, much relieved—and clean—in the morning.

That's the camino.

13 May, Astorga to Rabanal

Today we walk from Astorga to Rabanal, about twenty-two kilometres. As we leave Astorga, the whole countryside starts to change. The country is rolling, a precursor to foothills ahead, which indicate some serious hill-climbing in the days ahead. In the mountainous terrain between here and Ponferrada, the Romans mined gold, silver, and other ores, which made this route critically important to the Romans—and helps explain the Roman roads. There is also weather brewing to the

Heather-covered foothills en route to Rabanal.

southwest, most of which passes harmlessly to the north ahead of us. It is extremely windy and it's a headwind. I find out later that another pilgrim, leaning into this wind, was blown off the road and suffered a serious cut to his head. The word is that he is all right and walking again. If I were sailing, I would have two reefs in the mainsail.

As we walk today, Karsten and I have a long talk about leadership. I don't know who brings the topic up, but I have lots of ideas on the subject. The first question is, of course, is leadership born or bred? Can it be taught? My answer: it depends. There is no question that there are born leaders. An example is Winston Churchill, who, from the time he was a boy, fully expected to be an important British leader. And I know from the military that leadership skills can be taught to people who have only the latent potential to be leaders. I do think that there does have to be latent potential there. It is thanks to Maryan O'Hagan, my beloved sister-in-law, that I have a real insight into leadership.

She said that what makes a leader different from everyone else is that leaders have followers. A leader must have a clear concept and sufficient communications skills and be persuasive enough to have people understand and buy into the concept, then be willing to follow him or her to bring the concept to fruition. There is no inherent morality in leadership. Gandhi, Stalin, Churchill, Hitler, Nelson Mandela, Eisenhower, Chairman Mao, and General Francisco Franco were all successful leaders. Some persuaded through fear or appealing to the beast in all of us, whereas some persuaded through shining example. When I think about Gandhi, his non-violent disobedience worked well against the British. I doubt that it would have worked against Hitler's minions.

There were very brave German men who stood against Hitler and what he stood for and most of them died in the attempt. So you have to pick your leadership method, and the circumstances in which to apply it, rather carefully.

I think about Theodore Roosevelt, who in 1913 led an expedition into the Amazon to navigate and explore a previously unexplored—at least by non-Indians—river, the River of Doubt. His leadership for this expedition was so hands-off and laissez-faire that it very nearly foundered. Three men died and Roosevelt almost lost his own life, losing twenty-five percent of his body weight through starvation and disease.

I think about Margaret Thatcher of Britain (no relation) and General Leopoldo Galtieri of Argentina, two national political leaders who cynically executed a little war in 1982 over the Falklands. Both were facing domestic unrest and nothing unites a country like a common enemy.[62]

I think about George W. Bush, who is a puppet of American commercial oil and business interests, and who has American servicemen and servicewomen dying in their thousands in Iraq in a superbly cynical attempt to secure that country's oil supply, not to mention the tens of thousands of Iraqis who are dying. Now the Americans are in another unwinnable war, like Vietnam, and George W. is not going to get them out. I expect to see him go down in history as one of America's failed presidents. I find this enormously sad, because I have so many dear American friends and relatives and because they do not understand why so much of the world dislikes them. It isn't them, it's their government and its foreign policies, but it is hard for citizens of other countries to separate Americans from their government.

On the way today, we stop in the village of El Ganso, "The Goose," at the Cowboy Bar for a little something to eat. How appropriate, when I have just been grumping about George W. Bush, the cowboy. Only in Spain on the camino could you find a bar with, over the fire-

---

62 "The political effects of the war were strong in both countries. A wave of patriotic sentiment swept through both: the Argentine loss prompted even larger protests against the military government, which hastened its downfall; in the United Kingdom, the government of Prime Minister Margaret Thatcher was bolstered. It helped Thatcher's government to victory in the 1983 general election, which prior to the war was seen as by no means certain." Internet: **http://en.wikipedia.org/wiki/Falklands_war**, 2007.

Karsten standing in the doorway of the Cowboy Bar in Ganso. It is cold today—he is wearing a fleece.

place, a painting on barnboard of a covered wagon drawn by a team of four horses, and a sign saying, "We sell scallop shells."

I am in a lovely *albergue*, el Pilar, in Rabanal, population about fifty, where, for almost the first time, I see locals using the bar of the *albergue*. (I did see this back in Lorca, as well, when the bar in the *albergue* across the road was showing the Pelota match on television.) This *albergue* was recommended by the German *hospitalero*, Jakob, in Astorga. It is sunny but very cold and windy. I am very grateful for the fleece jacket. I have walked about 472 kilometres so far, have about 230 to go. Marina and Karsten are still with me, so there must be something more that I need to learn from them. When I arrive here, I notice the book where they log in *peregrinos*, and I ask if a Canadian woman named Suzie has come through in the past day or so. Isabelle, the warm and friendly *hospitalera*, searches for her name and can't find it. Then she says, with a big grin, "*Suzie, Isabelle, Isabelle, Suzie . . . won't I do?*" I think it is in jest, but I don't pursue it.

At 1900 there is a special church service, vespers, for the pilgrims here in Rabanal. There is an ancient church here, the Church of Santa Maria, built by the Templars in the twelfth century. It is a simple barrel vault, maybe twenty-

Isabelle, the delightful hospitalera *at the Albergue el Pilar in Rabanal, and me, wearing Richard's fleece.*

five feet wide and thirty feet high, perhaps 100 feet long. There is no decoration, no gold, no glitter. There is a simple altar at the front, with two candles on the left, a crucifix in the centre, and a bunch of lilacs on the right. The service is held by two Benedictine monks from Germany, and the whole ceremony is sung in Gregorian chant. Because of the barrel vault, the two singing together sound like twenty. The ceremony is in Latin, except for the final benediction for the pilgrims, which is in Spanish.

Only the front quarter of the church is actually in use, so we are a little crowded, which is a very good thing. There are enough of us in here to generate some heat, because it is very cold outside. The rest of the church behind us is separated from us by a stout wire fence, and it is clearly an archaeological dig. They are down in places around ten feet, and you can see the layers and layers of history.

The singing takes me back almost forty years to the thirteenth-century Bellapais Abbey in Cyprus. This is the abbey that was written about by Lawrence Durrell in *Bitter Lemons*. Carroll and I visited there in 1969 and were disappointed—at least I was. It was just old stone walls, no roof, nothing in the interior. We were just leaving when four young German men arrived. They stepped in and started singing Gregorian chants. It was riveting, and this evening's ceremony is just the same. This event has been happening in this church every evening for pilgrims for hundreds and hundreds of years. Once the ceremony is over, I go and light a candle for my friends and for Kit and the rest of the family who have left the building already. I have no idea if lighting the candle does anything other than make me feel better, but it does do that. It is like a direct connection back many, many years to early days on the camino.

After the service, we go to a restaurant in a lovely old building where we order the *menu del peregrino* for 8.5 euros. It is the typical three courses: a soup or salad or pasta, followed by a second course of fish or meat with really badly done French fries. They have not mastered the French fry here in Spain, or at least not in this part. They feel it should be soggy and dripping with fat. (They may, of course, have just copied this from the British—I am joking, Roger.) Third course is the *postre*, or dessert, which will be an ice cream, yoghurt, a curd, a flan, or a piece of fresh fruit.

Having finished all this, except for the fries, I am off to bed. On to Molinaseca in the morning. The weather does not look promising. It is cold and a little rainy, with the same forecast for tomorrow.

14 May, Rabanal to Molinaseca

I am in Molinaseca and glad to be here. We walked about twenty-five kilometres today, but that does not really tell the whole story. We start in rain, wind, fog, and cold, climbing steadily uphill for about six kilometres to Foncebadón, a ruined and almost deserted village[63] . . . and I feel wonderful! I am going to have to think about the occasional disconnect between mood and the environment. There is sure no connection today. Perhaps it is because I was kind of dreading this long climb, and it turned out to be quite manageable. And in my rain jacket

The cross of iron with millions of stones placed by pilgrims.

I am warm. I am the only pilgrim walking with bare legs. I have discovered that in the rain, if I wear long pants, the pants get wet, then I get wet, and when the rain stops, the pants stay wet and I stay cold. If I wear shorts,[64] when it rains, I get wet, but when it stops, I get dry almost immediately. This works well for me, and it perpetuates the myth of the tough, hardy Canadian. Hah.

At the top of the hill is the famous cross of iron. Pilgrims in their millions have left a stone at the foot of a very tall weathered pole with a ludicrously small iron cross atop it. It is so famous that I expected it to be much larger. Again, I am misled by expectations. The custom, as it has been for ages, is for a pilgrim to bring a stone from his or her home and leave it here at the base of the cross. The pile of stones now is about twenty metres across and about eight or ten metres high. That's

---

63   Population two in the 1980s, but there is an operating bar and small hotel here now.
64   I am actually wearing a pair of pants with zip-off legs.

a lot of stones. I had brought a stone from Canada to add to this pile, but my stone is safe wherever Air Canada is storing my pack for me. So I had picked one up outside Pamplona at the beginning of this walk, carried it from there, and added it to the pile today.

The scenery is spectacular here: wild, very big hills, snow on the top of some low mountains. It is like I imagine the Scottish Highlands to be. There are patches of rain, then sunlight; we are sometimes in cloud. We are very high here. The high point is 1,510 metres (5,033 feet), just short of a mile. There are hundreds of acres of heather with purple and pink flowers, another flowering shrub in yellow — it turns out to be broom — and a third, not so common, and still anonymous in white. The hills are carpeted with this wonderful, beautiful mix.

One of the towns I pass is Manjarin, settled around 1180 and abandoned for several centuries. The town is at the top of the pass, like many on the camino route here only for the pilgrim trade (over 500,000 a year at its height), and when the pilgrim traffic dried up in the late 1600s, the town died and slowly decayed to the ruin it is today. There is one tiny, primitive[65] *albergue* here, re-established about twenty years ago by the current — and only — *hospitalero*, Tomas. No one else lives here. The Gregorian chants here are on tape.

The beginning of the end, for almost three hundred years, of the camino was the result of the incessant wars between the English and the Spanish. In 1587, Sir Francis Drake, an English pirate (according to the Spanish, but a controversial hero in England), attacked the huge natural harbour at La Coruña, just north of here on the coast, and sank between twenty and thirty ships, with the successful intent of disrupting the Spanish preparations for the armada. Drake was no friend to the Spanish royalty . . . or any other Spaniards, for that matter. The ill-fated Spanish Armada sailed from La Coruña a year later, in 1588. In retrospect, they should have all stayed home. In 1589, in the loving spirit of religious tolerance that characterized that period of history, Drake assembled a fleet with 14,000 soldiers for the express purpose of destroying Santiago, that "centre of pernicious superstition." Although it did not take place, the prospect of invasion scared off many potential

---

65   Primitive means only mattresses and an outdoor toilet and water from across the
     road. The *hospitalero* has installed a solar water heater, which is only marginally
     effective here, because there is almost always a mist.

pilgrims. In the face of this threat, Archbishop Juan Sanclemente hid the relics of the Apostle, which were lost until 1878.

The second blow, a century later in 1681, was the declaration by Louis 14th, the King of France, that the robbery and hazards of the camino were too dangerous, and no Frenchman would be allowed to make the journey. His motives were suspect—he also was no friend to the Spanish royalty—and the effect was profound. The flow of people, money, and trade goods into Spain was cut off and the camino lost its pilgrims. That sealed the fate of many of the villages and towns that had grown up to service the pilgrim route, including Manjarin. The pilgrim hospitals and hostels and the castles of the orders of knights pledged to protect the pilgrims all dwindled and died and slowly decayed to the ruins we see today. It was not until after Franco died in 1975 and his dictatorship ended that the camino was revived.

Manjarin reminds me strongly of the Anasazi ruins in the American southwest, mostly just stone walls in varying stages of decrepitude. As I leave the ruined town, at the very last wall on the left hand side, there are three men on top of the wall, setting a roof beam in place. The town is not quite dead, and the renewed pilgrim traffic may bring it back to life. I will be curious to know what this town is like in five years or so. I think about the passing of towns and cities, of states and of civilizations. The Hindus in India talk about the great wheel of life. It just keeps turning forever.

Then we start to come down; the drop is from 1,510 metres to about 600 in only a few kilometres. The camino here is rough and steep,

sometimes with large, sharp rocks, very hard on the muscles, joints, and toes. I am extremely pleased to arrive in Molinaseca. I would not want to walk even another kilometre. The *albergue* here is the converted chapel of San Roque.

Marina on a very difficult section of the camino, near the bottom of a long, steep, descent.

And now for the latest segment in the "Perils of Pauline."[66] In the pleasant municipal *albergue*, I unpack my backpack and realize, after first casually and then frantically searching the bottom of the pack, that I have left my Ziploc bag full of important papers under the bed in Rabanal! It has my schedule, Carroll's itinerary, all of my contact telephone numbers, my lost baggage tag, and all my receipts for the items I bought in Pamplona to replace the missing stuff. I am frantic, but the *hospitalero* is calming. Marina explains to him what has happened. He says, in effect, don't worry, we will look after this for you . . . and they do. When I say that I will take a cab back to Rabanal, they tell me that it will be very expensive, and is, in any case, unnecessary.

I have a couple of very anxious hours while the decision is made about what to do. It seems to be out of my hands. Lots of cell phone activity to discuss how to resolve this. You will recall Isabelle, the very nice *hospitalera* from Rabanal. She finds the papers just where I had left them, under my bunk on the floor. The options include asking a bicycle pilgrim to bring the papers, using a baggage service to carry the papers to my next stop, and several other good ideas. In the event, a Jesuit picks up the papers, drives here from Rabanal, and delivers them to my very grateful hands before I even go out for dinner. The camino really does look after its own.

We share the large upper-floor bunk room with, among others, Maxwell and his daughter, Cleo. Cleo is a delight: tall, slim, blonde, soon to be married, fluent in Spanish, planning to go off after her marriage to live in Cairo and study Arabic (I think). Maxwell is a little younger than me and has, as I see it, a lot of barely repressed anger. He spends a lot of his time sitting in the *dormitorio* dealing noisily by cell phone with what are evidently very aggravating clients. He is also having difficulty getting his laundry dry, because it keeps threatening to rain. His laundry goes twice through the only dryer at the *albergue*—it is in high demand—so Karsten takes it out and puts a different load in. Apparently Maxwell's socks were not quite dry, and he has not missed an opportunity since to take verbal shots at Karsten. It is too bad, because when he is not angry, he is quite pleasant. We have a couple of drinks together sitting in the grassed area next to the *albergue*.

---

66 A reference to a silent movie series, *The Perils of Pauline*, in which the heroine inevitably ends up tied to the railroad tracks as a train ominously approaches.

I head out for dinner with my two companions. It is about 600 metres back to the village (somehow this seems counterproductive), and we will find someplace nice to eat. It is still cold and windy, but the sun is out and the weather for tomorrow is promising. We find a tiny café/bar run by a short, tubby, happy mama, who insists on bringing all you can eat—lentil soup with *chorizo*, potatoes, spaghetti, fresh hot bread. This is the best bread I have eaten so far in Spain. It is usually some form of baguette, which I think they buy and then store for a few days to get them really hard. I am developing a theory about this. The food and feeling here is wonderful. I notice a small black line of something in one of the potatoes, but in a misguided effort to be friendly, I ignore it and eat the whole potato. This turns out to be a mistake. Back to the *albergue*, in bed by 2200, but not to sleep. I feel a little uncomfortable—something about my gut is not quite right.

15 May, Molinaseca to Cacabelos

At midnight I get up, now very uncomfortable, flounder my way through the dark space down the winding staircase to the toilet and then, with all the grace and dignity I can muster, throw up from the bottom of my boots. Back to bed, disturbed sleep for a few hours, up again at 0500 for another sortie to the toilet. The expression "sick as a dog" springs to mind. This may not be a really great day.

However, by 0830 I am okay and on the road for Cacabelos. We are almost to Ponferrada, a pretty good-sized city, formerly important for the mining of coal and iron—hence the "Iron Bridge" of the town's name—, when we meet a fellow with an enormous German shepherd coming the other way on the path. Ron is friendly, greeting us in English with a strange accent. His comprehension of English is, however, excellent, so I ask him where he is from. Birmingham. Well, that explains the strong accent. He married a Spanish girl from this area, and has lived here for fifteen years. He loves it here. When I ask him what he does here, he tells me that he teaches English to Spanish kids. It is all I can do to keep from bursting out laughing. There will be a whole generation of Spanish kids from Ponferrada who will grow up speaking English with a rich and unique Birmingham accent. Doreen Marteinson, a former British army nurse and long-time friend, who has spent her adult life working on getting rid of her Birmingham accent, will really appreciate this!

Templar castle in Ponferrada, undergoing major restoration.

In Ponferrada, we walk past the base, almost under the wall, of a huge twelfth-century Templar fortress that is being restored. It really is an imposing castle and it is right in the town itself. Marina goes off to deal with some return ticketing issues, so Karsten and I walk on alone. We will meet Marina in Cacabelos. She will join us by bus. Karsten and I talk about relationships. Yesterday, as we were finishing the descent from the high plateau, a couple passed us, at what appeared to be an unsafe pace, given the conditions of the path, the girl almost running. The girl, he tells me, was his former girlfriend from Berlin, with whom he broke up just three weeks before the camino. He is quite upset. He talks to Marina later and she gives him some really good advice. She suggests to him that all he needs to do is hang in. There is no need to actively seek out someone. It will happen in its own good time; he is much comforted by this.

As we walk, we come across a small bar, where I see Maxwell and Cleo, the father-daughter team from yesterday, sitting with a drink. We walk over to join them just as they get up to leave. Maxwell takes the opportunity to take yet another verbal shot at Karsten. Says that he has a new blister because his socks aren't dry, thanks very much, Karsten. Maxwell needs a *lot* of time on the camino. I apologize to Karsten for suggesting that we stop here and subjecting him to this abuse.

Karsten and I walk on and at one point on the path we are heading straight up a dubiously marked lane. A Frenchwoman sitting in a rest area corrects us, so we turn back and take the path to the left. After about thirty minutes and two or three kilometres, this path turns out to be the wrong way. We can see, in the distance and to our right across a divided highway, pilgrims making their way on the real camino. We walk down through a vineyard, turn right—we are now near the edge of the highway—then back up a path that eventually peters out at the base of a very steep, high incline covered in deep grass and shrubs. We climb—and I use this term advisedly, it is *really* steep and difficult—the incline and find ourselves in a field with a church in the distance, to which we walk.

From there it is a short distance to get us back to where the Frenchwoman steered us wrong. We wonder where she will be by tonight and think rather un-pilgrim-like thoughts about her. We realize that we wouldn't even recognize her. After taking a footbridge over the highway and walking about two more hours, we are almost at Cacabelos when we pass three women, one of whom recognizes us. She is the Frenchwoman who misdirected us, an older pilgrim who is extremely apologetic about what she had done. Evidently, she tried to steer another group wrong after us, but they actually knew the way and got her straightened out. She tells us that she hopes *le bon Dieu* will forgive her. I tell her that if *le bon Dieu* can, we certainly can; and so we all go on, wearily, into Cacabelos, population about 5,000.

We reach the *albergue* eventually—it seems like forever to go the last couple of kilometres. The *albergue* is a single building, a quarter-circle of two bed units, quite recently built, all joined with high partitions between, but each with its own light! I have come to realize that this is the biggest shortcoming of *albergues*: one big room with one light that goes off early in the evening and on late in the morning.

Marina arrives shortly after. She has successfully completed her business in Ponferrada, visited a couple of museums, and caught a bus from there to Cacabelos. She delights in telling us that it takes just twenty minutes and costs 1.05 euros. So she calculates that our last five hours of walking is worth 1 euro. She even has and flaunts the receipt for the fare. I may have to kill her, she is so delighted with this.

We rest, shower, wash some clothes, then head off into town for a restaurant that Ron from Birmingham has recommended. We meet the only pilgrims that we will see on the camino on horseback: two people, a man on horseback and a woman walking with her horse. Ron is right about the restaurant; it is beautiful, old, wonderfully appointed, and has, in the dining room, a full-size wood carving of a satyr, full frontal. He has a flagon of wine in one hand and a wonderful leer on his face. If I were equipped like this satyr, I would walk around with a leer as well. The food, however, is not as good as the ambience, and in the several hours that we are there, we are the only customers. The locals may know something.

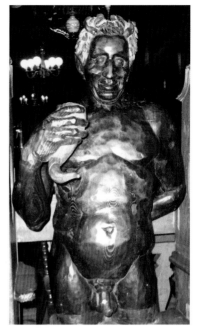

Very happy carved wooden satyr in restaurant in Cacabelos.

The plan for tomorrow is to walk about twenty-five kilometres, close to the base of the last really serious hill on the camino. Then we will send our backpacks up the hill and follow them up, looking less than usual like beasts of burden.

So off to bed at about 2145. I will have to talk later about the restorative power of sleep. Mustn't forget.

16 May, Cacabelos to Vega de Valcarce

Today the route is from Cacabelos to Vega de Valcarce, about twenty-three kilometres through a seriously narrow mountain pass. And now we are four! Paula from Bremen has joined this small, happy band. She is tall, slim, reserved, thirty-something, a nice person. We have been walking for the same distance each day, stopping each night at the same *albergues*, since Mazarife. We walk through vineyards, wonderful long vistas, then into the pass. Much of the path is beside a highway, separated only by a cement barrier. It is not elegant, but it is safe, and the path is painted yellow. Shades of *The Wizard of Oz*.[67] Apparently this used to be a dangerous section originally due to bandits and, more recently, road traffic, but not now.

---

67   The 1939 movie that made Judy Garland famous as Dorothy.

An arresting landscape on the camino between Cacabelos and Vega de Valcarce.

In a village, not long after we start out for the day, a funny incident happens. (Funny peculiar, not funny ha-ha.) We are walking together when an old woman comes out of a house on the right and stops us. She has a cell phone in her hand, shows it to us, and asks a question, which Marina answers. Apparently the woman's son has called her and left a voice message on her phone and she does not know how to get it off. Marina, being technologically competent, unlike me, knows exactly what to do, presses a few buttons, asks her a couple of questions, then hands the phone back to the woman, who holds it to her ear. Mission accomplished. She thanks us and we walk on. Picture it, if you will. A woman has a small technical problem at home, so she waits until a group of strangers approaches on the street, leaves her house and asks these strangers passing by to help. I do not think that could happen anywhere but on the camino.

In another of the tiny linear villages that dot this route, I am walking about 100 metres ahead of my three companions and I stop, turn around, and take a quick photo of them walking together as they come around a corner. As they catch up to me, Marina says jokingly, "What will you call this photo? The three disciples?" I respond, "Yes, the first three . . . and if I walk far enough, I will collect nine more." We all laugh, but I later think about what she has said. I suppose it could be seen as that type of relationship, since they have chosen to walk with me. They are all much younger than I, and it is not entirely inaccurate, but I think that it is something different. I have not asked them to come with me. I don't know whether I seem like a father figure to them, but I don't feel like one. We are just four companions who have chosen to walk together, each for our own reasons. For my part, I feel very honoured that these three young people want to walk and talk with me.

We stop for a drink and lunch at a truck stop, a place that Paula calls "this extraordinarily ugly village." Well, it *is* a truck stop. We sit outside on the patio. Karsten asks, "Have we paid?" I say, "We could run." This brings on gales of nearly hysterical laughter. It is a pilgrim insider joke. After a break like this, it is all we can do to get up, put on our packs, and walk like *really* old folks. It takes about five minutes before we can walk easily—a relative term—again. We could levitate as easily as run—hence the laughter.

Today while walking alone, I had a sense of being outside of time, in the sense of timelessness. I think about the Western world's obsession with numbers, with measurement, eyes always on the bottom line. Boy, are we missing the point. Today, I will walk for as long as it takes to go as far as it takes to get to where I need to go. The distance, the time elapsed are just meaningless numbers.

At the same time, I readily admit that I am wearing a pedometer to find out how many steps I take each day. Disconnect or what?

At 1530, we arrive at the Albergue do Brasil, run by Itabyra and ably assisted by Cristina, both Brazilians. Cristina is a bouncy, vibrant, loose-limbed, enthusiastic Brazilian volunteer, about fifty, with a big smile, great attitude, a big voice, and great legs. We can have dinner, a bed, and breakfast for twenty euros. Done deal. There is Brazilian music, food, atmosphere. It is a sunny, warm afternoon, and we are finished walking for the day. What a great feeling! I tell Cristina that I like the feel of the place. She beams.

They have the usual rules about taking off your boots and leaving them in the hall before entering the *dormitorios*, but they have an additional rule here: please do not put on any medicated ointment or perfumed cream of any kind on your feet or legs in the dormitorios, because they leave a lingering smell. This is the first time that we have been asked to refrain from this activity. Of course, that leaves all the other smells that people who have been walking for a long time can create—I am not sure which is worse.

Interestingly, Karsten tells Marina that he does not care for Cristina. I am surprised, because I really like her. She is vibrant, involved, he is intellectual, reserved. I expect that she disconcerts him because he does not understand her. With her, every emotion is right on the surface. He does not like to show any, although he is slowly opening up.

My sock liners, the inner socks I have used since I arrived, are finished. The big toe area is gone on both of them and today the right sock got wrapped around the big toe and the next toe to it and came within an ace of cutting deeply into the left edge of the right big toe. Another hour of walking and I would have had a self-inflicted wound. Also the toenail on the left middle toe came off today, painlessly. You may recall that it was the toe with the blister under the nail. If I sound a little obsessed with feet, I am, like every other *peregrino* and *peregrina*. The feet, along with the rest of the parts, are keeping us going.

I have a little sleep, a little foot massage, and I feel like new. The foot massage reminds me of one Marina gave me about a week ago. She had my foot on her lap and was massaging the calf when she leaned forward and said, "Guy, you need to relax. This muscle feels tense." I respond, with feeling: "Marina, you have just leaned forward and my foot is pushing against your breast . . . and you are asking me to relax?" She laughed and leaned back, but not before I prayed, unsuccessfully, really prayed. What I prayed for was prehensile toes.

At dinner that night, the Brazilians have a ceremony that precedes every dinner. They ask each person at the table to say his or her name, where she/he is from, and something about the camino. There are twenty of us from twelve nations. I don't know what I am going to say. As it gets closer to my turn, I get a little frantic. I really don't know what I am going to say. When it is my turn, I stand up and say; "My name is Guy, I am from Canada, and I am on the journey of my life." And I mean it absolutely. My voice breaks a little as I say the word "journey." This is a journey unlike any I have ever been on.

There is an Australian couple here, Tim and Jody. He is very tall and lean, has a short beard. She is shorter, has kind eyes and a lovely voice. They do not join the rest of the group for the communal dinner. When I ask Jody later why they stayed away, she says that they have been travelling for a long time, they have just reviewed their finances, and have realized that they are going to have to be extremely careful that they don't run out of money before they run out of trip. I think about this for a while. They are young people, they give off good vibes and I think that I can help. Quietly, I ask Jody if I can offer them a gift.

Quite warily, she says yes. I slip fifty euros to her. She tells me that they cannot repay me. I tell her that they can. Sometime later in their life, when they are more flush and come across someone who needs a little help, just provide it to them. I do not realize that Paula has seen me slip something to Jody. She asks me, when Jody has gone, if I gave her money. I respond that I did. When she asks me why, I tell her that it is because I can. I am not at all rich, but I can do this for someone who needs a little help.

Cristina tells me that she would like to visit Canada, so I give her my e-mail address and tell her that there is always a place for her when she comes. She would shake the place up at Tweedsmuir, where I live!

Off to bed in this warm and loving environment.

GALICIA – VEGA DE VALCARCE TO SANTIAGO

Galicia is the most remote of Spain's autonomous communities, situated in the north-west corner of the peninsula. Its 30,000 square kilometres, about the size of Maryland, hold a population of 2.75 million. Much of Galicia is coastal, although that is not where I will be walking. The climate here is much like that of Ireland, and for the same reason. The weather sweeps from the west off the Atlantic, having crossed over water for 5,000 kilometres, then makes landfall and bumps up against the low mountains, forcing the clouds up until they dump their load of water. Rain falls on 300 days of the year, so the countryside is emerald green. The most easterly part, where I will be entering Galicia, is mountainous and reminds me of the Scottish Highlands. The language is Galego, which is closely related to Gaelic.

17 May, Vega de Valcarce to O'Cebreiro

Today the plan is to walk to O'Cebreiro, which is only fifteen kilometres, but half of that is a steep climb. There is, however, a plot. We will send the backpacks to the destination and pick them up there, then stay overnight. It will—should—be almost as good as a day off, which my body is craving.

Before we leave this morning, we get on the Internet and find an image from *The Wizard of Oz*. We are looking for an image that shows all four—Dorothy, the Tin Woodsman, the Scarecrow, and the Lion—together. Then we recreate this image, standing together in the same left to right sequence as in the movie poster, in front of the large flag of the Albergue do Brazil. Whatever are we up to?

Over the past couple of weeks, as we have walked together, we have developed an interesting parallel story to the camino. Marina is familiar with *The Wizard of Oz*, and decides on about day three of our walking together—that would have been about 7 May—that she can be Dorothy, the part that made Judy Garland famous, and that, by virtue of my beard and my age, I must be the Lion, played by Bert Lahr in the original. Then a few days later, Karsten comes along, reserved, quiet, lean, and he becomes, naturally, the Tin Woodsman. When Paula joins us, the quartet is complete. She is, of course, the Scarecrow. She is not familiar with the story and is not delighted with this role, but we point out that she is tall, has fairly short, straw-coloured hair, and we actually do think that she has a brain. Quite a good one, in fact. Besides, we need the Scarecrow to complete the quartet. And she can make great faces!

The Wizard of Oz story has afforded us the opportunity, over days and weeks, to discuss what it means to be lost, as Dorothy is, to want to be brave, like the Cowardly Lion, to want a heart, as the Tin Woods- man does, and to want a brain, as the Scarecrow does. Of course, none of them needs to have an external solution, the real solution is in each one of them, as it is in each of us.

To add a new twist to an old story, someone brings up the *Tru- man Story*,[68] and they speculate that this whole camino thing is a staged

Paula as the Scarecrow, Karsten as the Tin Man, Marina as Dorothy, and me as the Cowardly Lion from The Wizard of Oz.

68　The 1998 movie in which Jim Carrey plays the unknowing participant in an actuality-television show.

play with Marina as the unsuspecting star, and I am cast as the host. The Frenchwoman who sent us astray last week? She is a cast member who had not read her lines correctly. As you might imagine, this leads to a lot of interesting discussion about reality, and whose reality is it, anyway?

As we leave town, the silhouette of the fourteenth-century Castillo de Sarracin[69] appears in the hills to the south. We walk in the valley of the Rio Valcarce (Prison River Valley), a reference to the narrowness and steepness of the pass itself. In former times this was a popular spot for bandits to prey on the pilgrims, so there was a strong Templar presence here. We start to climb. There are spectacular vistas to the south. We climb steadily in warm, not hot, sunny weather, about 700 metres over seven kilometres, a ten-percent grade. I think about how long, high, hill climbing is much like night autorotation in a helicopter, which is a comparison that I think many will not have made. So I will explain—I was a helicopter pilot for a few years in the Canadian army.

Many people believe that if the engine fails in a helicopter, the crew is doomed. In a helicopter, if the engine fails, there is actually an emergency procedure called autorotation that allows the pilot one opportunity—only one—for a safe landing. Otherwise, there would be a lot fewer helicopter pilots around. We are by nature optimists, but we are not completely crazy! The procedure, briefly, is to flatten the rotor blade angle to preserve rotational speed (= energy), then turn to face the aircraft into the wind (= slower ground speed), select an appropriate landing spot (= the least objectionable), and set up the best approach speed. At about fifty feet above the ground, flare the aircraft, as in quick stops in skating or skiing, to slow its forward speed and descent, then level it and land as well as you can, using the energy in the blades to slow the descent. At night, the procedure is almost the same with one important exception—you can't see the ground, so it is impossible to select an appropriate landing spot. With the black humour that most military pilots have, we say: at about 100 feet above the ground, turn on the landing light. If you don't like what you see, turn it off.

---

69   The town was founded in the ninth century by Count Sarreceno of Astorga, so "Sarracin" does not refer to "Saracen," as I had thought.

Okay, back to hill climbing. When you are walking slowly up a long hill under the weight of your pack, your eyes are fixed on the ground within a few metres of your feet. Every once in a while, you look up. If you like what you see, because you are near the top of the hill, keep looking. If you don't like what you see, look back down and keep walking. There is, I think, a real parallel to life planning here. We all trudge off into the future, looking mostly at the space and time immediately in front of us. Once in a while, we look up to the more distant future. If we like what we see, we keep looking. If we don't like what we see, we look down and keep walking. It's called "denial."

At noon, we cross the border between Castilla y León and Galicia. These mountains of Galicia are the first high land in 5,000 kilometres that the westerlies across the Atlantic hit, so, as you may imagine, the climate is very wet, some 300 rain days a year, much like the west coast of Ireland. By 1300 we are in O'Cebreiro.[70]

A palloza, a round, pre-Roman thatched structure, originally used as housing; still used for storage.

This is a very well-preserved small village, perhaps a hundred people, at the very top of an elevated east–west ridge, so that the view of the high rolling hills both north and south might be fifty miles in either direction. The word "spectacular" does not do the vista justice. Some of the structures here, *pallozas*, round houses with stone walls, no chimneys, and conical thatched roofs, are pre-Roman, still in use, and famous for their superb condition, although I expect they have

---

70 This village is noted in Picaud as the "pass of Monte Cebrero, with a hospice on the highest point of the mountain." Picaud says it is located on the "Mons Februari," which may refer to the weather. It is high here and would be bitter in any wind.

updated the thatch. When they used a fire in the *palloza*, the smoke filtered out through the thatch, keeping it free of vermin.

Three of us stay here. Paula goes on. She is a slow walker and does not want to stop here to rest, as I need to. I am very sorry to see her go, because she is nice to be with, sensible and thoughtful, as well as fun, but I expect that I will catch up to her again in the days ahead. She has a great smile, which she reserves for special occasions.

This is obviously a very popular Spanish tour spot. Buses of Spaniards are here, along with one busload of Japanese, who all get off their bus, take many, many photos, then get back on their bus for the next photo opportunity. I feel sorry for them, because they do not take the time to get the feel of this ancient place. When I mention the Japanese tourists, I remember a couple of days ago I saw three tiny Japanese pilgrims, a man and two women, walking together. Apparently they are journalists for a Tokyo daily with a readership of three million. Expect a lot of Japanese pilgrims on the camino next year.

I sleep for two hours, then wander through the village. There is a family of four from Madrid here in the small square in front of the church, with two little girls. I offer to take their picture, and ask if they will photograph me with the older of the little girls. It is a new grandparent thing. She is perhaps three, and a little reluctant to take my hand but her mother reassures her—and takes the photo—so I get the photo of me and the girl, whose name I will never know.

There are a couple of interesting stories about the little church in O'Cebreiro, built in the ninth and tenth centuries. One is the miracle of the transformation, in which a reluctant and cynical priest celebrating the mass with a single loyal parishioner, who has braved a snowstorm to be there, is faced with an actual, not a virtual, transformation of the host and the wine. That must have been a great surprise for them both. Here is the story,[71] as told by a shepherd in O'Cebreiro during a winter storm:

> "It was during a winter like this," he said, "with wind and storm and snow and frozen sheep. A monk was left here to say Holy Mass for any pilgrims who appeared at the sanctuary, but no one ever came except an old shepherd like

---

71   James Michener, *Iberia* (New York: Random House, Inc., 1968), p. 891.

me. Juan Santín was his name, and each day in the storm he would present himself before this altar to hear Mass, so the grudging monk would have to leave his fire and come to this cold place to celebrate the mystery.

"One special night, when the storm was worse than ever before, the monk aspired to stay by his fire, but Juan Santín appeared for evening Mass. It was his only pleasure in life besides caring for his sheep, so the grumbling monk had to leave his fire once more. 'Poor me, persecuted me! That I should be driven through the storm just because this idiot of a shepherd comes to hear how I pronounce a few words of Latin before this bit of bread and drop of wine.'

"And as he spoke, a clap of thunder roared through the storm, and a great flash of light filled this sanctuary, and on that altar the bread turned into the Body of Christ itself, and the wine in that very chalice which you see tonight became His blood. And the voice of Jesus Christ said to the monk, 'I too have come to hear Mass said this night, for I too am a shepherd.'"

There is a chalice here known as the Chalice of the Miracle, which relates to that transcendental moment. The other story is that the Holy Grail was hidden in this church for a few years. If only Galahad had known!

An incident happens that shows me that Marina has been paying attention to our talks. At dinner, we are seated at the kitchen bar, watching the chef, an older woman, prepare the food, including *pulpo* (octopus, a Galician specialty), in large pots on the stove. She is hot. The place is full, it's busy, and she is working hard. After the meal, Marina thanks the chef and compliments her on the food. I comment on this to Marina and she says, "How often do you get to tell the chef directly that you like the food? I am just giving her a yellow arrow." I am delighted.

After dinner, the usual pilgrim's menu, I go back to the room and to bed at 2030. It is still light out, but for me that is no problem. I can—and do—sleep anywhere at any time. Tomorrow will be a longer day, about twenty-two kilometres, and a lot of that is a serious downhill section, out of the highlands.

Northwest of here, on the coast at La Coruña—yes, the same harbour where Drake attacked the shipping in 1587 and from where the doomed Armada was launched in 1588—is the site of one of the British army's worst defeats in history. It was 1809, just shy of two centuries ago, and the site of its largest evacuation by sea until Dunkirk in 1940. The British army was here at the invitation of the Spanish to fight the French—(the Peninsular Wars, 1808–1814)—and it went very badly indeed under the leadership, if one could call it that, of Sir John Moore, who was himself killed by a cannonball on 6 January 1809 at La Coruña. It is said that one of Napoleon's greatest mistakes was killing Moore, one of Britain's worst generals, because he was replaced with Wellington, one of Britain's best generals, who eventually defeated Napoleon at Waterloo. It is said, in his defence, that Moore was the most beloved British general of his generation, and that the Highlanders who carried his mangled body from the battlefield did so with tears streaming down their cheeks.

This lovely little mountain town of O'Cebreiro is featured in the story because, during the terrible winter retreat from Astorga to the coast, in an effort to lighten the load, the paymasters had to back their wagons to the cliff edge here and dump their loads of gold coins down the mountainside, while the freezing and starving soldiers watched in horror. The officers were unable to control the soldiers as they looted and raped the local Spaniards, who were supposed to be on the same side. It was finally stopped by Moore, who had the ringleaders shot. This was the same problem that got Charlemagne's rearguard in such trouble at Roncesvalles—in 778. It seems soldiers never change.

The parish priest here, Father Elias Valiña Sampedro, who died in 1989 at age sixty, was a major player in the modern popularity of the camino. He wrote several books, helped mark the path with yellow arrows, and worked his entire life to rehabilitate the camino de Santiago. His legacy is the remarkable number of walkers every year now.

18 May, O'Cebreiro to Tricastela

Today I am off to Tricastela, a town of less than 2,000 people. It should take about six hours. I am anxious to get going in the morning, so I take off ahead of Marina and Karsten. Incredibly, I cannot find the path out of this tiny hilltop village. I find one yellow arrow and follow it out to the highway. This is not the way. Back to the village, try another route, no good. I know that I have to head west.

Finally I figure it out. They have decided to close and renovate the only *albergue* in town (at the beginning of the season for reasons known only to whoever made this decision), and the renovation has obscured all the arrows leading directly past the *albergue*. When I have this figured out, I reason that the others will have the same problem, so I sit on a rock at the beginning of the good way out of town and wait for them to appear from the village. While I am sitting there, I see at least another dozen pilgrims with the same problem. I direct them on to what I think is the correct route, then start to fuss, because what if I have just done to them what the Frenchwoman did to us a few days ago? It turns out that the route *is* correct, but I have some anxious minutes before another yellow arrow shows up. Talk about needing reassurance!

Once Marina and Karsten show up, I walk on ahead of the pair, telling them that I will stop for a drink at the first open bar. Both of them are having some foot problems, so they are going slowly. After perhaps half an hour, I find a little place, marked by a prominent plop of fresh cow shit right on the doorstep. I should have taken this as a sign. Inside, the server is a young man of perhaps thirty, who is clearly a graduate of the Madrid Sullen Service School of Hospitality. It seems that the customers, both of us, are interfering with his attempt to complete his work behind the bar. This makes me think of the attitude of people who serve others. If you have a service job, do it with grace and good humour. If you can't do that, then find some other line of work. It is not fair to inflict your bad mood on others. This guy is enough to put me off bars . . . almost, although I get over this quite quickly. Marina and Karsten do not show up, so when I have finished my *café con leche*, I go on.

After a rather steep climb of perhaps half an hour, I come out onto a crossroads and a bar, where Marina and Karsten are sitting. Surprise! Karsten tells me that he looked into the bar I was in and it looked so grubby and dark he decided I could not be there, so they went on. A better choice than I made.

Not everyone has the same motivation for the camino. There are as many caminos as there are pilgrims. People decide for themselves why they go, where to start, how far to walk each day, what route to take, and whether to do it at one go or in sections. The only common feature is that everyone eventually ends up in Santiago. I and my three companions are examples of this diversity. I am walking in one go from Pamplona to Santiago, although I had intended to start in St. Jean Pied-de-Port. I asked them where they walked from and why they were there. Marina started in late April in Logroño, the capital of Rioja. Her motivation is religious and her personal confidence shows up as well. She says,

> My only intention was to spend time with God without the demands and distraction of my daily life. Escaping the wheel of a hamster, we call it. I wanted to give space to listen and to establish a good base for the challenges He might ask of me in the future. That way I had wonderful experiences I did not ask for in advance, but also a clearly answered prayer which is always an amazing thing.
> Funny is the fact that I was not afraid of walking alone at all. It came to my mind the moment I got asked by others (mostly women) that I had not even thought about it.[72]

Karsten started in St Jean Pied-de-Port, walked with his ex-girlfriend to Pamplona, then, because of limited time, took a train 150 kilometres to Burgos and walked alone from there. He is at a transition point in his life:

> In 2006, at the end of university, I was literally exhausted and I desperately needed a holiday! But I felt that an ordinary trip to an ordinary place wouldn't do. I needed something really special. It was at that time that I first heard about the camino and I knew right away that it was absolutely the thing that I was looking for.[73]

Paula started the camino in September 2006 with a friend from Bremen. They walked for three weeks from St Jean Pied-de-Port to Sahagún. She returned this year to complete the camino.

---

72 Personal correspondence with the author; permission given to quote.
73 Personal correspondence with the author; permission given to quote.

[M]y decision was immediate and very clear, when a friend told me at the beginning of 2006 about her camino. I had never heard anything about it before. The big temptation for me was freedom, which meant no obligations but to pack my backpack every day and walk. No decisions to take, nothing to look for, just get my mind empty and clean and walk, with a destination I share with others."[74]

About an hour into the day, we arrive at one of the landmarks of the Camino, a huge, 3.5-metre-tall bronze statue of *Santiago Peregrino*, Santiago in his pilgrim guise, at the crest of the Alto de San Roque, altitude 1,270 metres. This bronze pilgrim is about three times life-size and is facing resolutely into the west, holding his wide-brimmed hat on against the wind. Again, I stop briefly with them, then go on ahead alone. Of the twenty-one kilometres today, the last six kilometres is a steep downhill section. I walk carefully and quite slowly, since it would not do to turn an ankle at this stage.

The route today is obviously heavily used by the local dairy farmers, since there is a great deal of fresh, as well as old, cow dung on the path. One has to watch rather carefully, since some of this stuff is really slippery and sloppy. The tiny villages that I pass through are quite grubby, more like clustered barnyards than villages as we understand them.

Today we are exposed to the famous dogs of Spain. One of the villages has about a dozen dogs, which the guidebooks warn about. They are large, loose, lying on the street. One of them opens an eye briefly as I walk past. These dogs have no idea how they are demolishing the myth of the vicious dogs mentioned in every single guide book about the camino.

Bronze statue of Santiago Peregrino (St. James the Pilgrim) at the top of the Alto de San Roque . . . and me, early in the morning.

74   Personal correspondence with the author; permission given to quote.

I think about the body I occupy. It is really just a big bag of bones, connected by muscles and other bits, housing a bunch of useful organs and a part on top that thinks about all this. I am reminded of some of Kurt Vonnegut's books, when he talks about the body parts with consummate irony. I have developed a theory — it is only a hypothesis at this stage — about how the body works when it is transporting "me" from place to place.

There is a sort of little puppet master sitting up somewhere behind my eyes and it is his job to keep all the appendages working. The problem is that he is a little absent-minded, much like me. First thing in the morning, as I start out, he is right on top of things, so all the parts work well. However, as the day wears on, every time I stop for a break, he gets a little behind, so that when I get up after a break after two hours of walking, he doesn't notice for about thirty seconds, so it is hard to get walking again. By early afternoon, when I take a break after five or six hours of walking, he is practically asleep, so that it takes minutes before everything is back running properly. This explains why you can see pilgrims get up from a break and hobble for about five minutes before settling down into some semblance of a normal walk. I shall have to develop a test for this theory.

I also think about sex, love, and lust. I need to point out here that this whole train of thought is not my fault. It is my mitochondria. We humans think that we are people at the top of the food chain, but we are actually just huge hosts for colonies of mitochondria, whose only interest is in perpetuating the host. Hence sex and the whole reproductive thing. As I travel on this journey, I have had occasion to notice some attractive women and, in the interest of full disclosure, like Jimmy Carter, I have to admit that I have lusted in my heart. Only in my heart, mind. And then, of course, I think about other women after whom I have lusted in my life. You would think I would know enough to stop here, but no. So then it occurs to me that I could create a list of the women who could go on the Lust List, starting with, as I recall, Cyd Charisse (which dates me a little). Then I think about the fact that there are many women, neighbours, friends, acquaintances whom I know or have known who would be horrified to find they were on my list. And then it also occurs to me that there may be other women who would be equally or more upset or furious to discover that they were *not* on my list, even if they don't much care for me, especially if it is a long list. So good sense prevails, and, although there is a virtual list, I have decided, in the interests of decency, not to say personal survival, not to write or publish this list. I *can* tell you, however, that Carroll is *still* on the list after all these years. I am looking forward to seeing her in Barcelona in less than two weeks.

Now I am in Galicia. It is very green. Since it rains 300 out of 365 days, this is not a surprise. The provincial government here has put up milestones every half a kilometre showing the distance remaining to Santiago. At the moment it is 131 kilometres. I don't think I like the milestones, because they make me feel very goal-oriented, and the goal here is not the point. It is the journey itself that is valuable. They also remind me that this journey is coming to an end, and I don't want it to end.

Here in Tricastela[75] we have caught up with Paula. She wants to have dinner with us and to walk with us tomorrow, so we will be four again. She was already in town in an *albergue*. She looked through a window and saw us walking by, fast, as if we did not intend to stop in this town. She realized that she really wanted to be with us. So she went out in a few minutes, found Karsten, and told him that she wanted to walk with us the next day. I am very pleased by this decision.

I also meet Andreas, the German guy whom we last saw on 25 April with severe tendonitis, heading off on a bus for Burgos for rest and repairs. He stayed there three or four days and has walked all the way here. He took the same bus back from Burgos to Logroño. That's dedication. It is over 100 kilometres. It is a delight to see him.

Near here are the quarries that provided the limestone used to build the cathedral in Santiago. Pilgrims passing through would carry as much as they could to the lime kilns in Casteñada, just this side of Ribadiso and only a day or so from Santiago. We don't have to do that any more.[76]

There is a pilgrims' service here at 1900, which I and many others attend. It is an interesting service, but it does not move me. There is

---

75 The three castles for which it is named disappeared about a thousand years ago, destroyed around 968 in the wars against Norman raiders.

76 But they were still doing this service in 1140, based on Picaud: "Tricastela, at the foot of this mountain in Galacia, where pilgrims pick up a stone and carry it to Castenada, to make lime for the building of the Apostle's church."

not a lot to do in these little towns, so going to the pilgrims' services is a way to keep close to other pilgrims, to see the ancient customs, and, often, to keep warm. For me, it is more like attending an equivalent type of religious ceremony somewhere in Borneo. Interesting from an anthropological point of view, but not moving.

Off to bed at 2200. Paula will meet us here at our *albergue* in the morning.

19 May, Triacastela to Sarria

Today we are off to Sarria, with a population of about 12,000. This town is important for many pilgrims because it is the closest place to Santiago where one can start walking and still get the coveted "*compostela,*"[77] just over 100 kilometres from Santiago. I am told that some of the people who start here are really not serious about the journey but about the ticket punch at the end. They are known as "Gucci pilgrims." I love the term. I expect that there may be many more pilgrims on the road from here to Santiago, but I don't yet know this. We shall see.

After having just bragged about how well I always sleep, I have a very poor night's sleep. I wake up repeatedly, not unwell but just warm. When I finally wake up as it gets light, it is 0720. Paula is joining us today, but Marina cannot bear weight on her left foot and is going to take the bus into Sarria. There is a good, fast medical clinic there that caters specifically to pilgrims. So there are again three of us, but not the same three. After Marina finishes at the clinic, she will find an *albergue* and send a text message to me and to Karsten. So now I know how to get a text message but have not the slightest idea how to create or send one.

There are three options today from Triacastela to Sarria. The northern route via Montan is the shortest—about seventeen kilometres—but also the steepest, both up and down. The middle route is less steep but is the longest, about twenty-six kilometres. The southern route is a compromise on distance, about twenty-one kilometres, but is partly along a quiet highway. We choose the highway route. We walk down through a mountain valley, with birdsong and rushing water as the predominant sounds. There is a white-breasted black bird here that

---

77   This is a document confirming the pilgrim's completion of the journey.

walks underwater on the bottom of the streambed, although it does not sing underwater. It is holding its breath. Weird! Although some of the route is directly on the shoulder of a highway, mostly it is not busy and traffic is not an issue. We come down out of the mountains into gentle rolling hills.

We share the street in town with a herd of cattle followed by the farmer's dog.

Some of the very tiny villages that we walk through are more like barnyards than villages. In some places the camino takes us between a house and its barn. Dairy farming is active here, and the camino is also used as a primary route for the cattle, with the result that, for the past two days, we have had to watch rather carefully where we step, since the cows have no sense of personal dignity and shit wherever the mood takes them. I am not the only one who notices. In John Brierley's excellent *Pilgrim's Guide to the Camino de Santiago,* revised 2006, he says: "This is rural Galicia at her best: wet and green with the sweet smell and squelch of liquid cow dung underfoot." Not exactly my sentiments. I disagree, for example, with "*the sweet smell.*"

I have been working today on a new theory. It is Thatcher's Cow Shit Fatigue Correlation Factor Theory. Here is the hypothesis. When pilgrims are fresh and alert in the morning they step smartly around every bit of cow shit on the path, whether it is freshly put down or is just a little pat of heavy dust. As the day passes and the pilgrims get tired, they are less fastidious about where they step, although they still avoid the seriously wet patches. They just walk over the dried bits. Now, this last I have not personally observed, but I suspect it to be true and this part of the camino would be the perfect place for a project. When pilgrims are just exhausted, they will take the shortest possible route with the fewest number of steps to get to the place where they can get off their feet and get their boots off. So a pilgrim close to exhaustion will walk through anything to finish. I have seen it in mud, and I suspect it to be true of cow dung as well. There should be a bursary somewhere to fund a test of this particular theory.

At this point, Karsten asks me when in the day and under what circumstances I get these "philosophical" ideas. I have to tell him honestly that I don't know. I don't have to be alone and it does not have to be quiet around me. That does not help him much. I think that being a lateral thinker is very helpful and I do not think that laterality is his strongest suit. He has a really good intellect, however, and will do well in any profession that requires careful reasoning. Since he is training to be a teacher, he ought to do well.

We stop in the early afternoon for a drink at a little bar about three kilometres out of Sarria. They also offer us a little something to eat, and I accept. The lady brings a small bowl of garbanzo beans and bits, mostly gristle, of veal. Still, it is protein, and I eat it all. Karsten leaves his bits of "veal." When we get up to pay and leave, the tab does not include the food. It is a gift from the owners of the bar. It is a nice touch and it warms my heart.

We walk into Sarria. Marina has found an *albergue* with a room for four, very nice. It has not only pillows but pillowcases . . . and sheets! The medical clinic here in Sarria diagnosed tendonitis and bound her foot up with tape, so that will help her walking. We sleep for a bit, then

En route to Sarria, we walk over this stone arch bridge, decorated with the scallop shell, one of the symbols of the pilgrim.

I go into town to find an Internet connection. The one at the *albergue* is hopeless. The keys stick, it is a Spanish keyboard, of course, and what I write looks like Greek. Sometimes it is easy to find an Internet café, but in this rather large town, I can't see anything that helps.

Again, a friendly local comes to my aid. There are three men standing on a corner. One of them says to me, in Spanish, that it is not far now to Santiago. I suppose the combination of the tan and the sandals with heavy socks gives me away as a pilgrim. I ask about Internet access and they can't think of anything. As I walk away, one of them, Pepe, comes up to me and says to accompany him, he knows where an Internet outlet is. We walk about two blocks and he takes me into an Internet place, which I would not have found on my own, and tells the owner that I am a *peregrino* from Canada and that he is to look after me. This is yet another example of the kindness that is shown to strangers here on the camino by the locals, whom you could forgive for being a little jaded about *peregrinos* — it *has* been about a thousand years that pilgrims have been wandering through here.

I compose and send the entry for 18 May, then I compose the whole entry for today, but the computer decides to loop on a command that will not allow me to post. After about five minutes of struggling, I hit the cancel command and out we go. Rats! So back to the *albergue* for supper, then back here to finish today's entry. It is now 2045 and I am going to post this, then head back to the *albergue* to plan tomorrow's leg and get a good night's sleep.

We are staying, as I told you, in a very nice *albergue,* room for four, two bunks. By virtue of seniority I get a lower bunk. I guess the others think I will likely break into bits if I were to fall out of a top bunk. I certainly don't discourage them and I don't entirely disagree with them. There is no cover on the window, and we have an excellent view of the front of the church. What we do not know is that the town fathers light up the front of the church with spotlights, and one of them is aimed directly into our room. I could have read in bed, had I been so inclined. Eventually, it is turned off at 0200. It felt like being a bomber pilot in the direct beam of a searchlight!

It has been overcast the past two days, grey, cool, but no rain, which is a real blessing. It has been comfortable to walk.

20 May, Sarria to Portomarin

Well, I am in Portomarin, another town of about 2,000 people, less than 100 kilometres from Santiago. This means, by my calculation, that I have walked over 600 kilometres in the past thirty days. It does not seem like much if you average it by day, but my body seems to think that it has been a long haul. As I walk today, I marvel at the fact that this old body works as well as it does. Some days everything seems to just tick along, but I also sometimes have the niggling sensation that all the muscles and tendons and connective bits are just a little frayed at the edges. I am being careful with the body, since it has to carry me the rest of the way. No jumping off walls, for example. As if . . .

A few of the things I see today: A man using a scythe in a field to cut hay, and in another place a family home situated above the barn so that the heat of the cattle helps heat the house. It is like a vision back two or three generations in time! This is something that has not been seen in Canada, at least not by me, for about fifty years, although I know that my older brother, Ance, in New Hampshire, has a scythe he uses to cut weeds. Claims that it is faster and easier than a weed whacker. It is certainly more environmentally friendly. No, he doesn't live above the animals.

I also start to see granaries, "*hórreos*" (pronounced ORR=ay=os), unique to this part of Spain: very, very old stone or wooden cribs, supported on two flat stones set vertically with wide, flat stones above the vertical ones and below the cribs. The flat stones overlap the verti-

cal ones on all four sides so that mice and other rodents cannot climb into the corncribs.

All four of us walk today. Paula, as usual, takes off as soon as she is ready in the morning. The rest of us are ready to go by

An hórreo, *a granary, in Galacia.*

0800, which is a record for both Marina and Karsten. Marina is determined to walk with her foot tightly bandaged and she makes it all the way today. We meet up with Paula at about 1100 and walk in very loose formation the rest of the day, arriving here about 1500, all quite tired and ready for a rest.

As we arrive at the town, we have to cross a large reservoir, Belesar, with a modern bridge over it. The original stone bridge over the River Miño was Roman. Along with the original town, the Roman bridge has been submerged by the reservoir, which was created by damming the river in 1962. The church, other monuments, and the stone steps were moved from their original locations as part of the new town. The river itself was a strategic boundary between the old Spanish fiefdoms, creating, of course, a history of turbulence and violence, because it has always been easy to cross. The Knights of Santiago and the Knights Templar guarded the southern district, while the Knights of Saint John guarded the northern parts. At times they disagreed. Violently. El Cid might have been a sword slinger here for one of the warring nobles.

At the end of the bridge is a long set of wide, steep, stone steps that lead up into the town. There is an option of taking a long road off to the right and up and back to get to the same place. We look at the steps with some dread, but they are manageable.

The countryside is now very much like Ireland, very green and misty, small fields enclosed with stone fences, rolling hills, short vistas most of the time, the paths often sided with stone fences from waist

The green fields of Galacia, which remind me powerfully of Ireland.

to shoulder high, every stone covered in moss. Sometimes small stones are piled up to make a fence, and sometimes there are large pieces of slate on edge to form the fence. To extend the sense of Ireland, the restaurants are named something like O'Mirallos, and the place we stayed yesterday was called O'Durmiñento. (And, no, I can't pronounce it, either.) I wonder if the use of "O" here is similar to its use in Ireland.[78] We hear some music today, and I swear it is Irish flute. And they have bagpipes. Apparently the language here, Galegos, is very similar to Gaelic.

As we walk today, Marina asks me how one can love someone while being very unhappy with his/her behaviour. She has had this problem. She finds this an unfamiliar concept, because how can you separate people from their behaviour? My idea is that this is actually possible, since most people, even those with bad behaviour, want to be loved or respected. They will respond positively to positive reinforcement, if they are helped to understand that they are not being judged for their behaviour alone, but for the underlying person. I admit this is not easy and I often find it difficult to separate my feelings about people from my feelings about their behaviour. But I try. I think that she is trying hard to understand this, since she has had a couple of long relationships that have eventually foundered because of the other person's behaviour, or her own. I do point out that it is not possible to change someone else's behaviour. You can only show them that their behaviour is counterproductive, that you don't like it, and that it is up to them to change it. Tell them you love them anyway.

Do you recall Wayne, the plumber from south of London, from 23 or 24 April? I remember a really funny story that he told me and that I have told the other members of -this small band. Wayne's practice is to have a siesta in the afternoon from 1300 to about 1500 in the heat of the day. One day, he is in a small town with a small park in the middle. In the middle of the park there is a hedged area, which he enters in hopes of a place to lie down for a couple of hours.

In this hedged area are a couple of benches, and he sits down on one, on which a local is also sitting. The local strikes up a conversation

---

78   I discover later that the *O'* in Galegos replaces the *el* or *la* in Castilian Spanish. In other words, it means "the."

about how much he likes Wayne's pants, which are an ordinary pair of sports pull-ons. Then he—the local—proceeds to pat Wayne's leg and slowly works his way up his leg until, as Wayne says, "He touched me Willy!" Then Wayne looks at me and says, "I was frightened [turning to me with a huge grin that splits his face] . . . and excited!"

He explained to me how he realized that he had inadvertently found himself a little gay park. He excused himself profusely and left. I realized, as I heard the story, that this could be a clever proposition, which I was very, very careful not to encourage by any comment or other indicator. I don't want some stranger, least of all Wayne, touching me Willy. Karsten and the ladies find this story, especially the part about "*me Willy,*" extremely funny, and most days the opportunity comes up to remark on someone touching "*me Willy.*"

We end up in a small private hostel in Portomarin, associated with, but physically separated from, the restaurant where we asked for directions to the *albergue* we are seeking. It turns out that it is at the other end of town, not a long distance, but we are tired, ". . . and, by the way, if you are looking for rooms, we have very nice ones at a good price." We have walked about twenty-three kilometres today and do not want to walk farther looking for the *albergue*, so this is an attractive deal and we take it. The restaurant is clearly a family business. The woman behind the bar has her daughter, perhaps five or six, with her, and later the woman's father shows up in the restaurant as well.

It is about 1830, so time for dinner and to make a plan for tomorrow's journey. It is raining, but the restaurant is close by. Well, dinner is a surprise of my own making. I decide to choose a fish dish off the menu, so I ask if they have *pescado* (generic fish). They do, so I order it, whatever it is. After all, what could go wrong? When it comes it is a set of half a dozen small tubes about the shape, size and general appearance of garden hose, each four to six inches long, clearly pan fried and it is—wait for it—eel! Another first in my life. I do not think—in fact I know I would not have—ordered eel on my own, but it is actually quite tasty. White meat, tastes like fish. Duh. I eat everything but the bones.

It is cold when we return to the pension to go to sleep.

21 May, Portomarin to Palas de Rei

As we leave Portomarin, we walk down a winding road with a stone wall on the right side. Set into the wall is a set of stone steps that look as if they have been here for hundreds of years—and perhaps they have. They would certainly not pass a safety code anywhere in Canada. The flat stone steps jut out from the wall, and there is absolutely no handrail, or even handhold, except at the very top. The path leads over a road bridge over a different part of the Belesar Reservoir. There are

Stone steps as we leave Portomarin.

actually two options here. One is to take a footbridge over the reservoir, but that entails doubling back down to a level nearer the water; or walking a little farther and crossing on a regular bridge that is at the same level and is, in fact, closer at the other end to the direction we intend to take. The footbridge is a little more romantic, I suppose, but after this many kilometres, "practical" wins easily, and I take the regular bridge.

Today's piece of the trip is a long, long one for several reasons. First, the weather is cold, blustery, and overcast, threatening rain. After half an hour, a cold mist starts to fall, changing gradually but relentlessly into driving rain. It comes from the northeast, so it hits me in the right front quarter of my body. Happily, the rain jacket continues to work splendidly, so my body core is always warm, as are my feet, but my legs are soaked through from the crotch down. I walk alone today. Marina is ahead somewhere; Paula and Karsten are way behind.

I stop at a small bar for a hot drink and a rest. There are two Spanish *peregrinas* here, both in that indeterminate—for me—age group from late thirties to early fifties, sitting together. One of them is having a very difficult moment. She is sobbing uncontrollably, and the other is attempting to comfort her. It is unclear whether the issue is physical or emotional. I would love to go over and comfort her, but I am in no position to inquire or to help. When I go to use the facilities, I could have used Wayne's help. Me Willy was hiding from the cold, wet weather. Smart Willy.

The word for today is endurance. The world is tiny, a circle of vision starting directly in front of me and encompassing the trail for a few metres ahead. The weather and general conditions take me back some fifty years to Meaford, Ontario, in November 1957. I was undergoing basic army combat arms officer training, and the final, week-long, exercise was held in Meaford. The instructors were all Second World War veterans, all with lots of actual combat experience. It was cold, blustery, rainy, and nasty, much like today. After a couple of days, mostly without sleep, we were all just staggeringly tired.

At one point, we were "shot at" (with blanks). We had to "go to ground"—that's just the army expression. Actually we had to fall down in the mud, figure out where the fire was from, and figure out how to deal with it. I was so tired that I just lay there. One of the sergeants came up to me and said; "Get up." I could not and said so. He said, "Get up" again. I said again that I could not. I was exhausted, which was true. He then said, without raising his voice: "Get up. You are an officer and your men are depending on you." and he reinforced this with a nudge with his foot, not a real kick, in the ribs.

I got up . . . and went on for three more days. That was the day when I realized that you *can* just keep going long, long after you think that you are finished. On that exercise, I did not finish, but not because I quit. They took me out with two sprained ankles, a sprained wrist, and suspected pneumonia, but I was damned if I'd give them the satisfaction of having me quit.

One of the *peregrinas* whom I passed today, in the cold rain, going up a rather muddy hill, was an old woman with her backpack and poncho, wearing what appeared to be bedroom slippers on her feet. She was shuffling excruciatingly slowly up the hill, taking two small steps, then resting before the next two small steps. It was an object lesson in endurance, and in humility, because there was nothing anyone else could do for her. She was walking her camino, and we just had to let her do it. No victim, no rescuers. Often, we try to help people who either don't want or don't need help and all we end up doing is creating a victim mentality in the other person, creating a dependency, which then allows us to see ourselves as the rescuer.

One of the older attractions of this portion of the camino is long gone . . . I think. In any case, it is cold and wet, so outdoor frivolity is the least likely of events today. In the *Codex Calixtinus*, the author complains:

> The whores, accustomed to come between the Minean Bridge and Palas del Rey in the wooded area to meet the pilgrims, are not only to be excommunicated but also are to be held in shame by all and have their noses cut off. Usually a single one appears to a solitary traveller.[79]

He does not say anything about the Johns, so even back in the twelfth century they got a break while the women got none. Doesn't seem fair.

So today is just putting one foot in front of the other until I get to where I need to be, which is Palas de Rei, about 2,000 inhabitants and about twenty-six kilometres from where I started this morning. I am exceedingly happy to be here, even if it is still raining and cold. I am indoors and I have a bed. My right foot hurts, but I think it is because I need to do a little trimming of the accumulation of toughened callus adhering to my right little toe.

The palace that gave the town its name was built, according to legend, by the Visigoth king Wittiza, between 701 and 709, when he died, still in his twenties. Wittiza was the last of a militant Christian sect, the Arians, who believed that Jesus was neither human nor divine, but supernatural. Wittiza seems to have been a just and reasonable king, considering the times, but was castigated after his death as a "Jew-lover." He was reportedly loved by the people and hated by the priests, with whom he clashed over power and doctrine. I like him already.

I also have exciting news! I have photographic proof of my theory, the one, you will recall, about the correlation between cow shit and fatigue. I was walking through a tiny town called Eirexe (if you replace the "x" with "ch," you will have an idea of how to pronounce it), when I came across not one but two fresh plops of cow shit with a fresh footprint in each. I took photos of both, since one would only be anecdotal, but two is proof! Somewhere out there ahead of me are two people who have unwittingly stepped in fresh cow dung and proven my theory.

---

79 Picaud, *The Pilgrim's Guide.*

And oh, by the way, today I just loved the milestones. They are actually kilometre stones, but that doesn't sound right to my ear. Some days it is not the journey, it's the destination, and today was one of those days. I am going to go off now, find the others, have supper, and go to bed. We are on an upper floor, with a window in the sloped roof—no view, but it does let in lots of light. It does not have any cover of any kind over it and it stays light until after 2300. The wind howls as I go to sleep. I cannot imagine what tomorrow will be like.

Milestone for seventy kilometres to Santiago.

Less than seventy kilometres to go. I can scarcely believe it.

22 May, Palas de Rei to Ribadiso

I did not mention yesterday another example of the wonderful spirit of the people who live along the camino and who endure the avalanche of pilgrims that starts in the early spring and lasts until November. Marina and I were walking along the path, watching an eagle soaring lazily above a field where a farmer was haying with a tractor. As we were watching and talking, the farmer stopped his tractor, got out of the cab, and yelled to us from a distance with gestures that we were following the wrong path. In our fascination with the eagle, we had missed a marker and the sharp right turn in the path. Absolutely nothing in it for him, except for our heartfelt thanks.

I have noticed the entire time that I have been here that there are no biting or stinging insects anywhere in this part of Spain. I do not have a single bite to show for this trip. My daughter-in-law, Laura (or TJ), would love this bug-less part of it.

The last couple of days, I have noticed many, many more people on the camino, but are they pilgrims, newbies, or wannabes? I won't judge them, since it is a matter of intent, but there is a certain cachet among the "real" pilgrims who have walked for hundreds of kilometres to get this far. I am a little suspicious of the woman who is doing this wearing her pearls and carrying no backpack, but who knows? There are lots of tour operators who offer a taste of the camino, carrying their clients by air-conditioned bus with a little walking each day, a nice hotel each evening. Their clients are not pilgrims in any sense of the word. They are tourists — and that isn't bad, it's just that they aren't pilgrims, and I am getting a little possessive of the term, it seems. I am not even sure if I can call *myself* a pilgrim yet. And a note for Bob Wilson, who asked before I left Canada: I have not seen any pilgrims doing this on their knees.[80]

Last night the wind howled, which boded ill for today, but in the morning it is overcast, not too cold, and not raining. Within an hour, the clouds are blown away. It is sunny, cool, and very windy from the northeast, but the wind is from our right or the right rear, so it is not an issue.

About breakfast time we are passing through the little city of Melide. As we walk along the street, I see a sign for a restaurant that calls itself Churrorio. This means, of course, a place where they specialize in *churros*. I am delighted and I convince the other three to join me for *churros con chocolate*. We enter the restaurant and ask for *churros*. Well, it appears that they have just run out of *churros*. This is at 0920. There are people in the place eating *churros*. We ask how long it will be before there are any more. They are not sure, it could be a while. Remember, this is in a place whose name is based on *churros*! We decide, reluctantly — and it turns out mistakenly — to have fresh croissants with chocolate. They are all right, but definitely not the same. So just because something is labelled in a certain way, don't take it for granted that it is true. Imagine, a *churrorio* without *churros*! It occurs to me later that perhaps this is a place that doesn't care for pilgrim business. We are messy, sometimes a little dirty, and we don't tip well.

I think about the remarkable restorative power of sleep versus the slowly increasing general fatigue. When I go to bed every evening, my body is tired; my legs and feet remind me of the effort that they are making on my behalf. When I wake in the morning, all the aches and general sense of physical fatigue are gone. It is truly astonishing how a few hours of sleep can renew the entire physical system, which in turn creates an overall feeling of well-being.

---

80   This comment refers to St. Joseph's Oratory, in Montreal. Pilgrims often make their
       way up the 233 steps on their knees as a penance.

Paula, Marina, and Karsten crossing a flat stone bridge.

This seems like a long, long day. Today, fatigue is winning as I walk something over twenty-six kilometres for the second day in a row. All three of the others are just ahead of me. The path is through a heavily wooded and very green area. At one point, it crosses over a small brook on large stones set on smaller stones to form a flat bridge over the water. As I walk along, I feel something banging on the backs of my heels and I look back to see that it actually *is* my ass dragging. I cannot remember ever being this tired in the past forty years or so.

Just before we arrive at Ribadiso, we walk through a small town, Casteñada, where we pass by a house with a yellow arrow, but it is not just another painted arrow. It is made from large, painted scallop shells, and this is on a private home on the camino.

I finally arrive at the beautiful *albergue* at Ribadiso at 1530. Unlike many, it is not in the town at all. It is the former Hospital de San Antón de Ponte de Ribadiso, a fifteenth-century pilgrim hospital, lovely restored buildings. It sits next to an equally lovely single-span stone bridge,

A yellow arrow made from scallop shells on a private house.

circa 572, and rebuilt twice since then, over the shallow river, hence the "de Ponte" of the name. Very old stone buildings, modern interiors, excellent facilities for showering and washing, although no toilet paper anywhere. This—the lack of toilet paper—seems to be common in *albergues* like this one that exist only on donations. I have run into it several times on this camino. We pilgrims are pretty smart about this by now. We each have our private supply of paper, usually in a Ziploc resealable plastic pouch—it is not much use when it's wet.

The *albergue* is on a large and open piece of property, edged on the east by a small river, the River Iso, more like a brook, with wide steps leading down to it, and on the west and north by fields. South is the road I came in on. Facing east, the little bridge is just to the right of the steps, and it is the bridge for the road by which we arrived here. It has separate modern buildings at the back with toilets and laundry facilities and showers with lots of hot water. The shower is a push-button system, in that you have to push a button up on the shower head to get the hot water to flow, no temperature or volume controls, and you have to push the button every few seconds to keep the water running. It is efficient for conservation, a touch annoying for function, but I manage. After a hot shower, I wash clothes, then cool my feet in the small river that runs beside the *albergue*. There are lots of people sitting and resting on the steps. The water is bitterly cold and feels wonderful on my tired feet, although I cannot keep them submersed for long.

Tired and footsore pilgrims soaking their feet on the stone steps at Ribadiso, with albergue *buildings in the background.*

There is no cellular access, no Internet here, and no place to buy food or drink, so I have to walk very slowly back up a hill about 200 metres to a little rural bar, where I have a really cold, really big glass of beer. Paradise! I was so tired when I walked past here that I didn't even see this bar as we passed it—and it is pretty conspicuous.

We four share two bunk beds, so Marina is beside me as we rest after we arrive. She has some cooling cream which she offers to apply to my tired legs and feet. The cooling effect, she tells me, is only felt when there is a breeze on the skin where the cream is, so she applies the cream, then leans forward, purses her lips and blows gently on my legs. My mind goes skittering off laterally, and I say to her, "Do you know what this is called?" She stops, laughs wickedly, and says, "Yes, it's a blow job," to which I respond, also laughing, "You know *way* too much English."

According to the milestones, we have less than forty kilometres to go, but someone says that the milestone markers are out by about nine kilometres. That just isn't right!

Today, for some reason I thought about the period near the end of my career in the military. It was 1977, and I had been selected to attend the Army Staff College in Kingston, Ontario. I was forty, about ten years older than most of the other students, and definitely not on the fast track. There was a training exercise near the end of the course, all using communications and theoretical troops (TEWT [pronounced Toot] = Tactical Exercise Without Troops). It was red army versus blue army. Blue was Canadian and were the good, defending guys, red was based on Eastern bloc (read Soviet) tactics and were the bad, attacking guys.

All the fast-track students were placed in command and staff positions in the blue force. I, on the other hand, was not a fast-tracker, so I was given a red heavy armoured division, with many, many tanks and extra attack helicopters—about 20,000 men in all. Tactically and personally, I was to act as if I were an Eastern bloc general, a divisional commander. In effect, it was my job to be ruthless. Well, with experience in tanks, anti-tank missiles and helicopters—an unusual combination in the Canadian military at the time—, I figured I knew how to use this unit. The mission was to break through the defending line of the blue army. One of the weakest points of any defensive line is the boundary between units, and I happened early on to discover the boundary between two blue divisions. I hammered at this point for two days, taking extremely heavy casualties, but I had the promise of the directing staff of the College, who were acting as corps headquarters, the next senior level above mine, that if I could break through, they would send a reserve division through to exploit the hole.

Well, after two days of relentless hammering at this perceived weak point, the opposing force collapsed—at a cost of about seventy percent of my force, including most of the tanks and all of the attack helicopters, but I had achieved the breakthrough. Then I asked the directing staff for the relieving division to push through where I had created the hole. Then I asked again . . . and again. To my astonishment, after a couple of hours, my request was refused. The reserve division was "needed elsewhere," so all the effort was in vain. Eventually the hole was plugged and the advantage lost. When I went home for the weekend I was extremely despondent. I realized that had those men been actual people, not hypothetical ones, I would have done the same thing. I would have sacrificed 14,000 men to achieve this little battlefield success, to no end. It was also appalling to me to realize that in battle I would do whatever was necessary to win, no matter how ruthless it was. I was no less bloodthirsty than any fighting general, given the right circumstances.

Years later, when I was no longer in the military, a friend of mine who was a member of the staff in the war game unit, and had been present at the time, told me what had happened during that exercise. Evidently, no one had ever succeeded in punching a hole in the blue line defences before in this exercise, and they did not want to give the other students (the blue officers, the fast trackers), the wrong impression. So it was decided at the highest level of the College to deny me the troops to push through the breach in the blue line. They denied me the opportunity to reinforce the success and, more seriously, denied the rest of the students the opportunity to deal with a "real" crisis, as opposed to a canned one.

I am not sure why I thought about this little anecdote today, but it was the climax of my disillusionment with the military. Since then, I have realized that the military, like every other organization, has to work with the people it has, some of whom are good, some of whom are great, and some of whom are simply dreadful. I had the misfortune to be at the Staff College during one of its—in my view—dreadful leadership moments. Of course, they may well have held a similar opinion about me.

I did not mention yesterday that I met a bunch of young Aussies from Brisbane, three girls, three guys, all friends, I think in their twenties: Alexis Rooney, black hair, wonderful smile and eyes, Ellen Geraghty, happy, tall, loose-limbed, big grin, Allison Margoffin, blonde and beautiful, Julian Jefferis, a BIG guy, big smile, Daniel Cahill, tall, black curly hair, big grin, and Bas, compact, intense, funny. They are walking the last section of the camino, after extensive travelling since leaving Australia. Like all the Aussies I have met, they are outgoing, exude confidence, and are wonderfully friendly. Two of the guys have spent time in Whistler. Like Canadians, they also like their beer.

The delightful Aussies from Brisbane. From left to right, Ellen, Bas, Alexis, Allison, Julian, and Daniel.

I mention them today because at the crowded bar where we go back to have dinner, there are all the Aussies, sitting and drinking beer and generally having a very good time. There is also inside the bar a table full of happy and noisy Italians . . . and there, sitting with them, is Jakob, the German *hospitalero* from Astorga! Whatever is he doing here? It turns out that last year he walked part of the camino with these same Italians and this year they have come back to complete the journey to Finisterre, and he decided to join them, so here he is. The bar is quite small and there isn't room for all of us at the tables for dinner, so we have to wait until the Italians are done. There are also three young Spanish women there, customers, who are having some kind of quiet but intense altercation with the lady who runs the bar, and she runs it with an iron fist. She has the male server, perhaps her husband, thoroughly cowed.

The Italians and Jakob are having such a good time, they keep ordering another round, and another round, lots of rousing Italian songs — I'm guessing here — and much merriment, while we get more and more hungry.

Then the altercation with the Spanish women bursts into open warfare. The bar lady tells the Spanish women that even when there is room for them, there is not enough food, so she will not serve them. They are understandably unhappy, but it appears as if they have brought this on themselves. Marina, who understands Spanish, tells me that they have been whining and complaining about the service ever since they arrived at the bar. Note to self: don't whine and complain about the service before you get the service.

The Spanish women, glowering, leave, the Italians finally understand our body language, and they get up and go outside to the patio to continue their party. We — there are five of us — sit down to eat, and the bar lady brings out enough food to feed about ten people. I guess the owner had just had it with the three whiners. Later I talk with the bar lady, who looks exhausted and who turns out to be the owner. She has been working for seventeen hours straight and she just wants to go to bed. I know the feeling.

After dinner, just after the sun sets, we walk back down the hill to the *albergue* in the deepening dark and head to bed, also in the dark.

23 May, Ribadiso to Monte do Gozo

Early last night there were thunderstorms, which I did not hear, but which were reported to me in the morning. It is clear and promising in the morning. Overnight I have to get up to go to the toilet at

Trees arch over the camino, forming a natural cathedral.

about 0500. As I walk outside in the dark on the cobbles to the next building, I can make out, in the moonlight, some really large shapes in the courtyard. There are four huge sheep lying there taking advantage of the heat retained in the stones overnight. They are not aggressive, much like Spanish dogs. One of them gets up as I approach and that is how I know they are sheep.

A few days later, I hear a very funny story from a tall Danish girl, Sophie, who is staying at this *albergue* overnight. Early in the night, she gets up to use the toilet, starts to walk to the back buildings, then decides that she can just squat by a large, low bush on the edge of the cobbles, which she does. While effectively incapacitated, she is seriously startled by the appearance of the bush's moving, then standing up beside her. It is one of the sheep. She does not tell me what happens next. I don't think I want to know.

I have a small but important disaster this morning. As I pick up my glasses to look at a map, my Maori necklace of greenstone from Carroll comes up with them, then falls to the hard tile floor and shatters. I choose not to regard this as an omen, but it is very upsetting. I have worn this every day since she gave it to me when she returned from New Zealand last year.[81]

We are on the road by 0815, stop for *cafe con leche* at 0900. It clouds over, rains lightly for a bit, just enough to force me to get out and don my rain jacket, then it clears, so off comes the jacket again. This happens twice today. The path is very good, mostly stone dust or dried bark where we walk through the eucalyptus forests. I feel really good. At times today all four of us walk together, sometimes in pairs and sometimes alone.

In this past week, I have started telling Marina and Paula separately every morning that I love them. They have chosen to walk with me for some reason, and perhaps this is part of it. I have a sense that all three of them are fragile emotionally and any reinforcement that I can provide can only help. It helps that I mean it. I really do love all of them. It occurs to me that I am telling the women but not Karsten, so this morning at breakfast with all three, I tell Karsten that I have been remiss in telling only the ladies that I love them, so I tell him that I love him too, ". . . but in the nicest possible way." Gets a big laugh, but I mean it. As I walk today with Paula, sometimes hand in hand, I conduct a little, gentle probing into her emotional state. She is very quiet and reserved, does not want to let much out, so I tell her that I sense sadness, perhaps disappointment. She says, after a moment, "Yes." Then after another long pause: "Disappointment." Somehow that resonates with her. Just those two words. I wonder what has happened to create this deep sadness in her. I remind her that she is very lovable and worthy of love and that I

---

81   This turns out to be the same day that Carroll has her purse with passport, cash, camera, driver's licence, and credit cards stolen off her lap at the restaurant in her hotel in Barcelona. So maybe it WAS an omen.

feel that she has so much to offer someone. Love is not an emotional state, not something you think about, it is a state of being.

Woman walking on the camino between villages.

We stop at 1140 and have a long, leisurely lunch, which turns out, in retrospect, to be a serious error. After lunch we continue on, and somewhere between two small villages, I pass an old woman who, for me, epitomizes this northern and rural part of Spain. It is at least two kilometres to the nearest village, and she is walking slowly along the path with a cane, her head down, in her rather shapeless dress, black stockings and sensible black shoes, and sun hat. I pass her by and say *hola,* to which she responds without lifting her head. I walk past her and realize that she would make a wonderful photo, if I can get it without disturbing her or violating her quiet dignity. I walk on a little bit, then turn around; she is behind me, her head still down, her face completely obscured, quietly intent on every step. I wonder what she is thinking.

We plan to go to Arca, about twenty-two kilometres, which will leave about twenty kilometres for tomorrow, but it does not work out at all the way we planned. My map of the camino, which we are following, is dead wrong. It shows the camino going directly into Arca, but it does not. Just before we can see Arca, the camino takes a little jog right, then skirts Arca through a dense forest, so we never are aware that we are passing by the town ... and its *albergue.* Kind of a ring road for pilgrims, but it costs us dearly.

By the time we realize that we have bypassed and missed Arca, we are one hour and almost four kilometres farther along and crossing a highway at a tiny town named Amenal. There is no bar, no store, not even a telephone, and there is no accommodation ahead on the camino for kilometres. We end up walking back along the busy and noisy highway for three kilometres, the best part of thirty minutes, to get back to Arca by about 1730, only to discover that the Aussies are already there—they were far behind us all day—and there are no beds available in the *albergue* or, in fact, anywhere in town. Despair. I am, frankly, furious at the people who carefully and ineptly made and sold a map that people walking should be able to rely on. Fury is not a good pilgrim emotion.

So we have walked almost thirty kilometres between 0815 and 1730 and do not have a place to stay. This is not fun at the moment. Marina calls an *albergue* farther down the line at Monte do Gozo, determines that there are lots of beds, then calls a cab to get us there. She says that when she talked to the *hospitalero* at Monte do Gozo and asked if he had beds, he just laughed and said, "I have *lots* of beds." Paula stays here at the *albergue*, where one last bed has been found. She does not want to take a taxi for any part of her journey. I decide, during the cab ride, that I will get a cab back in the morning to Amenal and finish the camino the way I intended, on foot. Marina will not; she is going to go on from Monte do Gozo. Karsten is undecided at the moment and will make that decision in the morning.

The cabbie drops us off at the base of a huge monument, which commemorates the late pope's visit[82] to Santiago. It is not possible to see where the *albergue* is from here, so we make a false start down the

Monument at Monte do Gozo.

---

82   Pope John Paul XXIII, in 1982.

road, which is what the cabbie said, then backtrack and follow the signs that say "*albergue*." It is just over the brow of the hill and not visible from where the cabbie dropped us off.

The *albergue* in Monte do Gozo where I stay is huge: dozens of buildings down a shallow slope, with rooms each having four bunks. There are 488 rooms, so work out the math for the size of this place. It was built about twenty-five years ago for the crowds, when the then pope, John Paul, made the pilgrimage to Santiago. (But I'll bet that he didn't walk from Pamplona!)

When we arrive, the two people with me, Marina and Karsten, both young Germans, say that it looks "like a concentration camp"—and it does. But I would not have said it to them, because I don't know whether there is any residual guilt about the Nazi atrocities still lingering in the German psyche and I don't wish to hurt either of them. This *albergue* is highly industrial, highly efficient, and can process very large numbers of people—like a concentration camp. But the beds are fine, and the rooms are quiet. This is one of the first *albergues* where there are neither pillows nor blankets, but it is heated. And, not insignificantly, hot showers and lots of toilet paper. It is an enormous change from the *albergue* in Ribadiso where I stayed last night. All efficiency, no heart.

We find out the next day that three pilgrims we know, who had beds at the *albergue* in Arca, decided, after a happy evening of eating and drinking, that they would go on at about midnight and spend the night sleeping outdoors about five kilometres past Arca. Two of them are Sturla and Mari, the Norwegian film photographers. The third is Sophie, the Danish girl; this must be the Scandinavian connection. So there were actually beds for us there, if we had only known.

One thing I have managed to do today is to use the Internet to book my flight from Santiago to Barcelona for the morning of 27 May. It is closing in on 2200 and it is time for me to go to bed. Not an entirely happy day, but it is working out OK.

24 May, Monte do Gozo to Santiago

As I intended last evening, this morning I take a taxi back from Monte do Gozo—where I can see the cathedral—back, back to Amenal, where we got to yesterday. I get picked up at the huge monument on the Monte do Gozo, which is the high point east of Santiago where, in olden days and in good visibility, pilgrims could first see the cathedral. The cabbie is the same one who brought us to Monte do Gozo last evening and he drops me in Amenal at the exact point where the camino crosses the highway. No need to tell him the location. He knows. He doesn't tell me he approves, or even if he cares, but I get the feeling that he does. (Of course, he might as likely think I am just another dumb pilgrim.) Making the decision to actually go back and walk these seventeen kilometres is one of the harder ones I have ever made. It would be so easy to just start where I am and go on, but it does not feel right to me. This is not, I hasten to add, any kind of judgment on Marina or Karsten, who elect to go on from Monte do Gozo. That is their camino, this is mine.

I start shortly after 0800, and by 1100 I am back at the huge monument where I started this morning. I think and hope that I may meet Paula on the camino, but I do not. When I stop for breakfast, I linger over a *café con leche*, hoping that she will show up, but she does not. It turns out that she is about forty-five minutes behind me. I walk alone today all the way into Santiago. So after all, I start and finish the camino alone. For today's walk of about twenty-two kilometres, I walk through eucalyptus forest for awhile. The Aussies tell me later that, for them, it was just like being at home.

Eucalyptus forest just before Santiago.

Somewhere here I pass Lavacolla without being aware of it. That is too bad, because it has a famous relationship to the camino. Lavacolla used to be by a river where pilgrims would wash themselves thoroughly before entering Santiago to greet the apostle. How thoroughly? Let Picaud tell us:

A place called Lavacolla in which French pilgrims travelling to St James are accustomed, for love of the Apostle, to take off their clothes and cleanse not only their private parts but the whole of their body. [83]

Then the landscape changes to upper-class urban, nicely manicured places, small market gardens, and finally into Santiago proper. About 100,000 people live here. You would think there would be big wayfinding signs in Santiago, of all places, for pilgrims, but no, like most of the other larger towns and cities, it is poorly marked, and I have to ask repeatedly for directions to the camino and to the cathedral. Although I can see the spires of the cathedral from a distance, once I get close they are obscured by other buildings, and it is even difficult to determine direction.

A few days ago, in O'Cebreiro, and again today, I met a young Norwegian, Sturla Pilskog, who is travelling the camino with his friend, Mari Bjørnstad, carrying a heavy camera and tripod, making a documentary about the camino at the same time as travelling it; hard work, and it makes for long, long days. It was while in O'Cebreiro that I first met Sturla. He was alone at the time and did not have a bed. Marina, who had met him earlier, made him an offer that was, in the circumstances, remarkable. I was in a tiny room with a single bed, as was Karsten, and Marina had a room with a double bed. She said that she would be happy to sleep in a double bed with me, although not with him or Karsten, and that would free up my room for him. Just how grandfatherly does she think I am? Apparently this woman has no idea what excesses my imagination is going through. Fortunately — or unfortunately, depending on your point of view — Sturla decided to go on, so I slept alone in my single bed.

During one of the periods today when I am walking alone, Sturla, Mari, and I meet and talk on the camino as it passes through a gully under the approach lights for runway 35/17 (which means it is a north-south runway) at Santiago's Lavacolla airport — we are getting very close.

While walking alone, I have an opportunity to develop a couple of new theories. One has been developing for weeks; the other is a

---

83 The present-day name of Lavacolla probably originally had the same significance as the Latin name used in the *Guide*; Lavamentula (*mentula* = genitals).

recent one. The more recent theory is that there is a small factory somewhere near Sarria (110 kilometres from Santiago, and of course you will remember the 100-kilometre rule), where they manufacture large rolls of shiny, satin-like, bright blue material, likely about five percent stretchy. This factory ships its entire production to a nearby manufacturing facility where the factory owner's brother-in-law makes many, many pairs of jackets, long sports pants, and shorts, all in this bright blue stretchy material, which they then sell through a blue sports store outlet to the pilgrims who start in and near Sarria.

This is the only way that I can account for the truly astonishing numbers of "newbie" pilgrims who are wearing this particular fashion statement. The pilgrims who have come from afar (i.e. farther than Sarria) look almost the same, except that our predominant colour is dirt. If it wasn't brown or brown-grey when you started, it is now. Also, we walk *way* slower than the more recent additions to the camino, especially uphill. It is actually hard to tell that we are moving, but just watch for a couple of minutes — you will see some movement. Part of this may be that there are many more young people now, who are faster and more sprightly than us older folks. In the first couple of weeks, there were few young people. Now there are many. I give you the Aussies as an example.

My other theory has been developing for five weeks, and it goes like this: There is a day-old bread consortium, called the Stale Bread Consortium, in Spain that collects all the bread that does not sell in the *panaderias* (bakeries) by the best-before date. It is then shipped, slowly, to a central point, where an expert woman (I don't know why, but she has to be a woman) checks each piece with her highly trained finger to ensure that it is actually stale. After the quality check, it is then shipped to tiny bars, cafés, and restaurants in northern Spain, where it is served as *bocadillos* and *pan* to unsuspecting pilgrims. As I developed this theory and tried it out on other pilgrims, some protested that we sometimes — occasionally — get fresh bread. To which my answer is, this is because when the bars and restaurants run out of the official pilgrim bread, they have to use fresh bread instead. I hasten to add, the bread is always good, just usually stale. The fuel efficiency is the same, and when it *is* fresh, it is wonderful.

As I walk into Santiago, I see a very old man with beret and cane crossing the road in front of me. An Audi driver stops to let him cross the road. STOPS! An Audi! When the old man is safely across to my side of the road, the Audi continues, and I wave to the driver in thanks. He waves back. When I reach the old man — he really *is* old — he stops me, puts a hand on my arm, and asks me, in quiet Spanish, how has the camino been for me and wishes me well. I am deeply moved by this small, loving gesture.

A few minutes later, I meet a large group of people who are going somewhere to make some kind of demonstration. They are all wearing the same green shirt, and some are carrying banners and placards that I cannot read. Most of them are very caught up in what they are going to be doing, but one of them notices me as we pass and says, "*Buen camino.*" Again, it is just a couple of words, but I am moved by the interest that total strangers — not many, but a few — take in pilgrims even in large cities.

I have arrived! Me holding hands with Suzie from Strasbourg on the plaza in front of the cathedral in Santiago.

I arrive at the cathedral at about 1230, passing through an enormous stone arch under a side building, where a single violinist is taking advantage of the acoustics, and into the huge square, Praza do Obradoiro, in front of the cathedral. It is almost empty, a few people standing or walking. I am alone, and there is no one there I know, except for one fellow pilgrim, Suzie from Strasbourg, who is sitting in the middle of the square with her boots off and her right foot swathed in bandage. She and her boyfriend have been walking for the past week and she has had a terrible time with blisters on one foot. I sit down on the stone pavement beside her and look at the cathedral. I am in Santiago, having walked about 700 kilometres since 21 April. It seems almost anticlimactic to be here.

From a text message from Marina, I know that our accommodation is less than two blocks away—I don't know how she manages this—and I go there and get rid of my pack and walking sticks and go back to the cathedral square, where I meet a couple of the Aussies, two of the guys. What I do not know at the time is that Suzie—the Canadian classical soprano from Montreal, with whom I shared a day at Boadilla on 4 May—is singing in the cathedral at the noon mass. Marina tells me that

The cathedral in Santiago.

her voice is "divine"—Marina's word. I wish that I had known. I would have gone in when I arrived, pack, boots, and all.

We—Marina, Karsten, Paula, and I—have two small but comfortable rooms in the Hotel Pico Sacro, just off the main plaza and a one-minute walk to the north of the cathedral, where I take off my boots and pack, perhaps for the last time in a long time.

So I am here. It feels quite strange to be here after five weeks of almost constant walking. Whatever will I do tomorrow? Actually, I am pleased to be here, because I have the distinct impression that my body is plotting a major rebellion for the very near future if I don't give it a break. So I will.

Some quick and first impressions after arrival—and I reserve the right to amend these dramatically later, if I feel the need. But here goes:

Epiphanies and spiritual breakthroughs: zero, although I never expected any. I was open to them, but did not anticipate them. Perhaps you have to expect one to have one.

Backpacks lost: one, courtesy of Air Canada or Lufthansa. But it doesn't matter at all.

Moments of real, intense joy and of really loving and feeling loved: many, related to the landscape, the birds' singing, the functioning of my body, food and drink, being able to feel and to sleep and to wake up without pain, being with other people from so many countries — and from gifts given and gifts received, especially after my experiences in Boadilla.

Moments of real anguish: only two, once related to leaving critical papers behind and once related to foolishly stressing the body into active rebellion. But then I ended up recuperating in Boadilla, which was one of the highlights of the camino and where I met Suzie and Marina . . . and the Finnish girl, Kirsti, who gave me her cell phone to use . . . and Walter, who not only gave me his liniment for my leg, but applied it for me . . . and Eva and Richard, the couple from Augsburg, who gave me the black Jack Wolfskin fleece I am wearing as I write. So was it bad or good? Such enormous good came out of it.

Kilometres walked: 701. That is about the distance from Ottawa to New York City, from Calgary to Vancouver, from Boston to Washington, from Monterey to San Diego, or from Tokyo to Hiroshima.

Days walked: 31, from 21 April through 24 May, with three days off.

Kilometres walked in the wrong direction: about twenty, happily not all of them at the same time.

Most frequently heard languages on the camino: German, Spanish, Italian, and French, in that order.

Most common second language: English. It is the "de facto" lingua franca of the camino.

I think about good results coming out of events that seemed really devastating at the time. My marriage to Carroll is one of those — the good result, not the devastating event. When I was just nineteen, I had completed my basic Royal Canadian Air Force flying training at Claresholm, Alberta, on Harvards, piston-driven, single-engine aircraft — fondly known as the Yellow Peril. I had been commissioned as a pilot officer (second lieutenant equivalent) and posted to advanced flying training on T-33s (the T-33 was an early jet trainer) at Portage la Prairie, Manitoba. I was, pardon the pun, flying high.

After ground school, we started flying just before Christmas. My instructor, an old guy of twenty-eight or twenty-nine, was thought by us students to drink far too much and too often, so I did not trust him much. In addition, on the third flight, we had a landing gear failure, one green light and two reds. Not good. We flew low past the tower and they reported that, of the three wheels, we had one up, one down, and one halfway down. Can't land like that, so the option was to perform high-speed stalls at altitude to shake the gear down. If the gear continued to balk, the other option was to eject. Ejection seats were not automatic in those days, either. I had been for the mandatory ride on the ejection tower, which was supposed to instil confidence but didn't, since it did not work at all well the extremely cold January day I rode the rocket.

We got the gear down, but after that, I did not trust the aircraft much, either. I now didn't trust the instructor, the aircraft, or the ejection system. It was a recipe for disaster.

On the next flight, I was very queasy, and on the next it was much worse, and on the next flight I was unable to complete the training mission. The powers decided to test me for motion sickness. The real problem was that I was afraid and I was afraid to tell anyone. I was so young and so inexperienced and so frightened that I did not tell any of the training staff my concerns about the instructor or the aircraft. So off I went to Toronto to the then Institute of Aviation Medicine, where I was tested and found to be marginally motion sick. I won't even try to describe what they did to test this. Let's just say I was on a rotating turntable and I don't want to repeat the performance. Write finis to my flying career, at nineteen years old.

But on that trip, while visiting at a friend's house — I had grown up in the Toronto area — I met Carroll and was instantly smitten. So my air force flying career was over and I was devastated, but my life's companion had shown up. In the end, I got both. I left the air force, a year later joined the army as a tank officer, and five years later was invited to apply for helicopter pilot training. They never asked me why I had left the air force, although it was in my documents when I joined the army, and I never told them about the T-33 fiasco. I never lied, but I didn't offer, either. I figured that I was older, wiser, and could handle the problem. As it turned out, I was right and never had a problem flying again, as long as I was at the controls. I may be the only person who ever washed out of military flying training for airsickness, then ended up getting the same pilot's wings that I would have if I had stayed. Lucky.

In the evening, we four go off to a restaurant, where we order, not the *menu del dia* or the *menu del peregrino*, but other food, of which we get far too much, and cannot eat it all but do manage, in celebration, to down a couple of Kahlua and milk (even Marina, who does not now drink, but confesses that when she was sixteen in Guatemala, this was her absolute favourite drink). I have promised her that I will send her the recipe for chocolate mint martinis.[84] She will *love* them.

So off back to our beds in light rain, but no one cares.

25 May, in Santiago

This morning I don't have to get up and walk. What a rush! I am awake at 0800, lie in bed until 0900, have breakfast with Marina and Paula in one little bar, then walk 100 metres and have *churros con chocolate* in another. What lovely decadence! Karsten has gone off to Finisterre by bus. If I go, it will be tomorrow with Marina by bus. Paula is going to walk to Finisterre, starting tomorrow.

I go alone to the special pilgrims' mass offered every day in the huge cathedral here at noon. As part of the daily ceremony, established hundreds of years ago, they read out, in distance order, where people started from, whether by foot, bicycle, or on horseback, what country, and how many people. I am the only Canadian who started from Pamplona on foot and finished in the past twenty-four hours, so today I am reported from the pulpit as, "*de Pamplona, de Canada, a pie, uno*"—from Pamplona, a Canadian, on foot, one. I have come a long way to hear that.

At the mass I see Eva Papp from Hungary—what a delight to see her and to hug her—and a lovely black-haired Italian girl with a wonderful open face and smile, Linda Zampacorta, and her blond, long-haired German boyfriend, Jürgen Gessner, with whom we have loosely travelled the past few days. And there is the Norwegian cinematographer, Sturla Pilskog, again, filming the ceremony and the people.

---

84   Two parts vodka, one part clear crème de cacao, one part clear crème de menthe. Serve chilled or over ice. Enjoy!

I watch as the Catholics take communion and I speculate about the nature of God, whom they believe they are receiving at the moment of communion. I think that something that we choose to call God or god or Allah or Jahweh or Jehovah or the Supreme Being or whatever you like — Gaia, perhaps — is within us but not quite for the reason they believe. I think that every one of us has internally the potential for goodness, that some of us choose to call God. There is a small internal pilot light already burning, just waiting for fuel. When we get the fuel, in the sense of the ability to demonstrate and act on our goodness to others, the light burns brighter. On the camino, where needs are reduced to real necessities, the ability to be good to others and to have others be good to us is extraordinarily multiplied, so that it is much easier to see and feel the good in others. I note that it is not much of a stretch, only one letter, from "good" to "god."

Obviously in our everyday lives it is not as easy to always remember to look for and see this essence in others. It will be one of my challenges to make sure that I do not lose this ability as the direct memory of the camino fades with time. I did not intend to keep a journal of this trip, but I am exceedingly glad that I have, since rereading it will help keep that flame burning brightly. Now I have to think about what I can do to help others get the fire burning and it occurs to me, not for the first time, that this journey might be the basis for a book about the camino, seen from my — admittedly warped — perspective. We shall see.

After the mass, I wander to a nearby outdoor bar, where there are two Spanish *peregrinas*, Ameli Vásquez and Oñati Quipuecua (Basque), in their early fifties. You will recall that I encountered them a few days ago on a rainy day in a bar while having *cafe con leche* to warm up. At that time, one of them was sobbing uncontrollably and the other was attempting to comfort her. I never did find out what the problem was, whether physical or emotional, but here they are, happy as two larks. They insist on buying me wine, more than one. What can I do — I am helpless. Can't refuse a lady and a fellow pilgrim. Sitting with them is a Dutchman, Adrie Maas, whom I did not meet on the camino but who arrived here the same day as I. He is a former telecommunications engineer who has lived all over the world and is fascinating to talk to.

We have a couple of drinks, the ladies leave, and he and I are sitting watching the world go by, when here comes Marina, walking purposefully and carrying two large plastic bags. I call her name, because she will walk right by without noticing us. It turns out the hotel has declined to look after our laundry, so Marina is walking it to a laundromat about twenty minutes away. Since some of this laundry is mine, I ask if she would like company. It's the least I can do. I am actually hoping she will say no, because then I can sit here with a clear conscience and continue doing what I am doing, which is nothing. However, she would like company, so off we go, out of the old city into a newer part of town. After depositing the laundry at the laundromat—it is not a do-it-yourself kind of place—we find it will take a couple of hours, so we walk back to the lovely Parque Alameda where there is a fiesta going on, complete with a really big Ferris wheel and requisite amusement park rides and games of chance.

There is some kind of bungee device with a trampoline so that people can leap high into the air. In one of these contraptions, there is a young—perhaps eleven or twelve—Spanish schoolgirl in full school uniform, blue top, blue skirt, bouncing up and down, black hair flying. Only in Spain. There is also a *churros* concession, where they are deep-frying them in a huge cauldron, and which we are required to support (the concession, not the cauldron). But these *churros* do not come with *chocolate*—just lots of old-artery-clogging fat.

After picking up our laundry, we walk back towards the old part of town. We come across the Aussies, who invite us to join them for dinner. I stay and wait with them, and Marina goes on to the hotel to collect and return with Paula and Karsten. Note from Karsten: Finisterre was wet, very foggy, and extremely noisy with the foghorn. He didn't see a thing.

After about fifteen minutes, I go on to find out where they are. As I walk, I run into Suzie (from Montreal, you will recall), who, it turns out, is heading to my hotel to leave me a message, since she has not found me today. Serendipity—it's wonderful! I have not seen her since Boadilla, about three weeks ago. We all repair to a restaurant where we enjoy a wonderful dinner. It turns out that Suzie lived two years in Bremen, which is Paula's home, *and* she speaks really good German, so they have a great time as well. Suzie is going to send me a copy of her

Santiago cathedral by night.

upcoming CD of Acadian folk songs, which she has worked on while on the camino, and she wants from me a copy of the book. She gives me a limit of eighteen months to get it published. The pressure! And Carroll and I will have a place to stay . . . and people to party with . . . when we get to Brisbane, which I have promised we would—and soon.

It is quite wonderful and it is all coming rapidly to an end. The pilgrims arriving now we do not know, and, although we share a common experience, I do not have the desire to throw my arms around them—with one exception. Today there is a *peregrina*, probably in her sixties, looking utterly exhausted, hobbling across the plaza in front of the cathedral. She has obviously just arrived and is in that state of shock that appears to be quite common among arriving pilgrims. I do not know her, but I walk up to her, open my arms, and embrace her. It turns out she is Bulgarian, walking alone, does not speak any language that I do, but her face is transformed when we exchange hugs and I congratulate her on arriving. That transformation from her look of anxiety, pain, and fatigue into genuine joy is worth the entire trip!

Later in the evening, Marina tells me that she has decided to go to Finisterre by bus tomorrow and to stay there overnight. I knew about her plan to go but not about her plan to stay overnight. Even if I go, I will have to return the same day, since I have to catch a flight the following day. I decide that I will probably not go tomorrow, although I will wait until morning to finally decide. I do not tell her this at the time, which in retrospect turns out to be a mistake.

Someone has told us that if you walk to the Alameda Park, then turn right and walk a couple of hundred metres, you can get a view of the whole cathedral lit up at night. Three of us — Paula, Karsten, and I — go. It is just as advertised, quite beautiful, and I take several photos, but I won't know until later whether or not they are blurred. Long exposure, no flash.

We do not get back to the hotel until after 2330, and it is time for bed.

26 May, in Santiago

This morning I get up just before 0700. The others are already up, and Marina is dressed with her backpack packed and ready to go. I tell her that I have decided to have a quiet day in Santiago, so this really is the end of the trip for the four of us. She is a little disconcerted at my decision and its timing, but she has a present for me. It is a small blue tile, with — what else? — a yellow arrow on it. It is the perfect reminder of all the discussions we have had about yellow arrows and reassurance. We say goodbye and promise to meet in Berlin sometime between 17 and 27 June, when Carroll and I will be there. She walks off and is gone without a backward glance, which is as it should be. My learning experience with her has been extraordinary, and I am very, very happy to have had this, I think, rare opportunity. As Marina said to me earlier, fooling around: "We are giving you a glimpse into a younger generation." Of course, she is also the one who, when I refer to my youth, says, "Yes, when the Mona Lisa was still considered modern art."

Paula, Karsten, and I go off to find a small restaurant to have breakfast, which we manage to do. When we finish, I go to pay the bill, which is exactly twice what we paid yesterday in the same bar for the same breakfast. The server explains that the butter and the jam are really expensive. Apparently twice as expensive as yesterday. Toast for two euros each. That is just over three dollars Canadian. It is a rip-off, not much different from my experience on my first day on the camino in Puente la Reina. So the world has not really changed — yet.

We walk back to the plaza in front of the cathedral, where Karsten and I say goodbye to Paula, who walks off, with her long, slow loping stride, hands, as always, in her pockets, for Finisterre. I do not know if I will ever see her again, but I ask her to remember every morning that I love her. Then Karsten and I go back to the hotel where we say goodbye and plan to meet in Berlin. I go back to bed for an early siesta. When I awake, he is gone.

In the square I meet the Dutch guy, Adrie, from yesterday and we go to have *café con leche*. We talk about motives for going on the camino, and he tells me two stories. One is about a Belgian guy, whose two daughters, in their early twenties, are just into final exams at university. The stress level at home is so high that he decides to go on the camino. The other anecdote Adrie tells — and is overcome with emotion as he tells it — is about a middle-aged couple whom he meets about fifty kilometres short of Santiago, who are each struggling with what is obviously an exceptionally heavy pack. When he asks them why, this story unfolds. Their only son had decided to walk the camino and had planned and prepared. He had walked a great deal, he had collected his gear, and was all ready to go when he was struck down with cancer, and was dead within three months. The parents decided to walk the camino in his memory . . . and to carry all of his gear between them, as well as their own. They will walk to Santiago, then to Finisterre and will give their son's gear to the ocean. I, too, am overcome with emotion as I tell the story.

Today is a quiet day in Santiago for me. There is no one here I walked with. The "camino" feeling of brotherhood is seeping away. I meet a fifty-one-year-old grandmother, Marlene from Munich, and we spend a quiet late afternoon and evening together, much of it walking or sitting in Alameda Park. Like me, she started the camino on 21 April and, like me, finished on 24 May, but she walked the Camino del Norte, along the Spanish coast, and walked 900 kilometres in the same time that I walked just over 700. She says the north camino is rugged, beautiful, little infrastructure or wayfinding (few arrows), the path is often very narrow, and there are bloodsuckers but no pilgrims, so you have to wear long pants . . . and she loved it (not the long pants, the whole experience).

Why is it that so many people in this era of technology — of instant gratification, of space stations, of thumbs with repetitive stress injuries from text messaging, of watching in-flight movies — why is it that so many people walk away from all this on the camino to reach a higher state, that of enlightenment?

What is missing in our lives is the *time to ponder*. Modern life is so frenetic that we forget that using engines to move us around has only occurred in the past few seconds, geologically speaking, of human history, and using other animals such as horses, only a few seconds before that. Walking the camino imposes a discipline on us that forces us to take time. We are moving at the pace that, for almost all of human history, has been the only pace of movement.

Today I think about the camino, the physical path, and my camino, which is my reaction to the path and to the many events and relationships that I have had while on the camino. Every person's camino is different and can only be experienced, not described. The dimensions that I had expected, the physical, the psychological, the spiritual, I experienced in some degree every day. What I did not expect was the emotional dimension, but that has turned out to be the part of me most affected by the camino. Most of my life I have kept my emotions tightly under control. With a British mother and upbringing, then a military career in combat arms, then a business career, perhaps the tight control is not surprising.

When was the emotional breakthrough? I think at Boadilla, on the day of our wedding anniversary and the day after Cian's birth. The gifts of the Finnish woman and the German couple were more than physical gifts; they were emotional ones as well. It seems that everything has had a greater emotional impact on me after that day. Whether the depth of emotional engagement will stay, I don't know. I guess we will just have to see. I will be leaving here early in the morning to meet Carroll in Barcelona. The people with whom I shared this journey have left already. It is time for me to go, too.

27 May, Santiago to Barcelona

I sit here in another airport, this time in Santiago, waiting for the 0830 flight to Barcelona. They allow me to carry my backpack on board, so I ought not to lose this one. The security guys discussed my walking poles intently when they saw them in the scanner (They are collapsed and inside my backpack) but decided to let me take the backpack as carry-on. I guess pilgrims are not considered much of a threat in Santiago. I think it would be different in any other airport.

It is drizzly and foggy, but who cares? I will see Carroll in a few hours. I have not seen her since mid-April. She has been so supportive of this journey of mine, and I love her deeply.

The small waiting room is silent; nine people, one other of whom is a pilgrim with his pre-teen son. No elevator music, no announcements. Across from me sits a stunning young Spanish woman, black hair in a ponytail, long legs in jeans, white shoes, listening to her iPod, clapping her hands, tapping her feet, singing very quietly, engrossed in her music . . . or maybe she is just bored.

I think about the Spain that I have experienced over the past six weeks. The camino is not the Spain of flamenco dancers and sunny beaches. It is peasant farmers, tiny rural villages slowly depopulating, huge cathedrals and churches, endless vistas, rugged terrain, small rushing rivers, people with hearts of pure gold. How many millions have walked the same roads, paths, and byways that I have just walked? It is unknowable, but I now for the first time feel really connected to them. I, too, am now and for all time one of the millions who have walked to Santiago and I can call myself a pilgrim.

There is no seat assignment. It may be a cattle call, but the flight is only ninety minutes on Clickair. CLICKAIR? Who are they? I booked with Iberia. We fly up out of the drizzle and clouds into clear air. As we overfly this sere and ancient land of crooked roads, tiny villages, and green fields, I think about the people here who generally have not lived in peace with each other but have managed to live in some kind of harmony with the land—something we might strive for. As we start to descend, the land is heavily terraced, there is a low range of mountains, and I can see the Mediterranean in the distance to the south. There is a divided highway, so we must be getting close to Barcelona. This is the same highway we will take tomorrow to Madrid. As we near the coast, there are more villages and more people. It is easy to spot the old villages — they have circular centres.

I feel different from when I started this in mid-April, more at peace with myself. I know and accept who I am. Is there anything else? I still don't know. Does it matter? I still don't know that, either. The physical camino is over, but I think that the real camino is inside me and it has just begun.

LIFE LESSONS RELEARNED

So what have I learned? There are no new lessons learned, just the same old lessons relearned. I thought that I might learn some new lessons on this journey, since it was so unlike anything that I had done before, but no. It occurs to me, reflecting back on the camino, that the lessons I observed were all the lessons that I had learned in my rather long life-time and had sometimes forgotten. It also occurs to me that I did not actually need to be on the camino to make this observation, although it came more easily here because I had lots of time to think. The lessons that follow are not in any particular order, since I think that their priority depends on the situation in which one finds oneself.

Planning and preparation are useful, but flexibility is essential. This lesson was brought forcefully home before I ever got underway, because of the loss of my backpack. Just before I left Ottawa, one of my close friends at home had asked me what I would do if my pack went astray, and I replied, flippantly, that I would just have to wait for it, since I had no plan B. After several days of waiting for the lost baggage to arrive, I realized that I either had to create and implement plan B, or go home. Fortunately, I was in Pamplona, which was large enough to have a department store with the necessary items to kit me out for the camino . . . and I had enough room on my trusty credit card to actually purchase what I needed to go. I really don't know what I would have done had I not had enough money to re-equip. That would have been a real test, and one I am glad I did not have to undergo.

It is about the journey, not the destination. It seems to me that I have always known this, but it became abundantly clear on the camino. The way itself is the reason to be on it. When I started hitting milestones showing the distance yet to go to Santiago, I did not like them, because they were forceful reminders that the journey was finite and was, in fact, coming to its end. The analogy to life is clear. I remain unconvinced that there is a destination after the end of life, so, for me, the journey is the only part that makes sense. This may be an arrogant point of view, but so far, my life experience has failed to convince me that there is anything after this life.

You can travel lighter than you think. Again, this was brought home to me, when I re-equipped with a backpack little more than half the size of the one I had lost, and all the items with which I packed it did not fill it. I was often able to rely on fellow travellers for the things I did not have, but much of what I had so carefully purchased and packed in the lost backpack, I did not need on the journey. Again, the analogy to life is clear. In the Western world, we become so used to acquiring things . . . and measuring our "success" by the count of things acquired, that we seldom realize what a burden they become. Travelling more lightly, in every sense, is something that I am going to attempt for the rest of my life.

You don't have to walk fast to walk far. The Chinese saying, "A journey of a thousand miles begins with the first step," is exactly right. When I trained for the camino, I was able to walk about six kilometres each hour. When I started the camino, I planned on being able to keep up that pace. Of course, I could not. The pace each day depends on many variables, among them weather, ascent or descent, road surface, personal health, state of the feet, joints, and muscles. Often, I delay starting something because I think that it is going to take a long time to finish it. Of course, logically, if anything is going to take a long time to finish, that is the best reason for starting as soon as possible.

There is no such thing as too much reassurance. The painted yellow arrows and the formal markings on the camino were always welcome, even when there were many of them at a single point. Their presence reassured me that I was at the right place and heading in the right direction. Their absence alarmed me when it extended over a distance. In cities, I kept asking for directions to reassure myself that I was going the right way. I think about how important external confirmation is for me and for other people, even if—and perhaps especially if—we seem to be very confident in our direction. This theme occurs over and over again on the camino. I shall have to remember this when I deal with people in the future.

You are stronger than you think, physically and mentally. The act of walking over 700 kilometres was a challenge for me in both dimensions, but not an insurmountable one. I was pretty confident when I embarked that I would be able to complete the plan, but one never knows what can happen between plan and execution. "There is many a slip 'twixt the cup and the lip."[85] I read back over what I have written and I see that, although I was very unhappy when I pulled up lame in Boadilla, the downtime was only a day, and the affected part, my left shin, did not give me any more grief after that.

Do not judge others—and do not be too hard on yourself. I have spent my whole life judging others and have found most of them wanting, that is, insufficiently like me. What I have learned again is that different is not bad, it is just different. I have been very proud of my excellent hand-eye coordination, something that I did not learn or work hard for. It was simply there and I was lucky enough to have been able to use it in my career. I have thought of myself as very smart and quick. I have always been a quick learner, although I have not always successfully retained what I have learned. Hence the life lessons *relearned*.

In fact, I was so stupid that I thought I was smarter than Carroll, and she was so smart that she let me continue this fantasy until I didn't need it any more. If we were to know all the background of anyone else, we could probably understand his or her behaviour, even if we strongly disagree with it. Judging at first sight was a common and valuable human trait when we lived in tribes and could never trust the motives of a stranger from an adjacent tribe. It still has its place, but can cause us to make decisions about others that prevent us from learning from them.

The body is marvellously resilient. However, you have to treat it like the fine tool that it is. I trained a long time to walk the camino, and my body was ready for it, in most ways. The training that I did not do was to walk over twenty kilometres every day for an extended period of time. What I found, at the end of each day, was

---

85   Ancient Greek proverb.

that I was physically tired. Thirty minutes' sleep would provide enough recovery time to allow me to enjoy the rest of the day. The overnight sleep provided time to allow the body's mechanisms to rewind, purge the accumulated poisons, and let me wake up refreshed in the morning. The rest days were exceptionally good at allowing a deeper recovery. I did not take a rest day during the last fourteen days on the camino, from León to Santiago, and in retrospect that was a mistake. I abused the body a little and I felt it when I arrived in Santiago. I was bone-weary. I could have prevented that, had I included a rest day each week, as my original schedule had planned.

Life is all about relationships. This is the most powerful lesson that I relearned on the camino. For some people, life is about power or money, but not for me. I thrive, I expand, I positively bask in relationships. I walked from 21 April to 3 May alone, and I was quite happy. I needed the solitary time to think, but I was also very happy when Marina asked if she could walk with me, and then Karsten, and then Paula. I liked the fact that they had chosen me to walk with. Our relationships were simple, probably because we all knew that they were temporary. While I was almost two generations older than they, I hesitate to use the word disciples, because it wasn't quite like that. We were learning from each other, giving when able and taking when needed. I gave them the benefit of my longer life experience. They gave me the benefit of their youth and enthusiasm.

The life of a hermit, while attractive in many ways, is not for me. I am happy alone, seldom lonely, but I have a deep-seated need for approval. I crave the applause of the audience. I realized this when Carroll told me how many people were reading the daily stories of my journey that I was passing back to her. This realization was an enormous incentive for me to keep writing. I also realized, once again, how much I depend on and value the relationship between Carroll and me. I never doubt her commitment to our lifelong relationship and that stability has been, and remains, a major part of my life.

The map is not the ground. This lesson must be very important to me because I had the opportunity to relearn it three times on the camino. The first time was with Wayne on 23 April, just at the beginning of the camino, when we missed the alternate camino to

Villamayor. The second time was in Melide at the *Churrorio* that had no *churros*. The third time was on 23 May, almost at the end, when I misled my companions around, instead of to, Arca. Each time, I relied on a map or a sign, and each time the information was wrong. It did not accurately represent the thing it purported to represent. Both times when the map was wrong, I had to walk farther and for longer than I had intended, when I was already tired. To make this lesson more relevant to life: The data base is not the inventory and the bank statement is not the money. In these examples, what one observes is information *about* something, rather than the thing itself. I can't assume because I read it, hear it, or see it on television that any information is correct or complete. That is why good journalists always seek a second source for controversial information. I must remember that, if it affects me, I need to check it out independently.

Security of your person and of your belongings is important, but absolute security is a myth, and giving it up is liberating. During the first few days on the camino, I usually found a small hostel or hotel to stay in. I did this because I was concerned about actually having a place to stay, where I could be alone, secure with my pack behind a locked door, where I could change and shower in privacy. I would walk each day, and almost every day I would spend some time talking to other people from many different lands. Then I started to realize that, each evening, I was giving up the companionship and fraternity of the people with whom I was sharing this rather unusual journey. A significant part of the value of the journey was in what other people could teach me. And I was giving up this connection for security and privacy.

The trade-off, for me, was not worth it. I discovered, during the rest of the journey, that I could safely leave my opened pack on a bed in a common room of bunk beds, shared by people of whom I had no knowledge, except that they, like me, were walking the camino. I was not foolhardy about it, though. I did not leave cash, credit cards, or passport in plain view. As my mother told me, never tempt an honest man. My privacy was a small issue, since everyone had the same lack of personal space. The only thing that I missed from having my own room was not the lockable door or the private shower and toilet, but the lack of control over the lighting of the room. The towels were nice, too, but hardly worth giving up relationships for.

If you really have a dream—really want to do something—commit to a start date, closer than is comfortable, plan your preparatory tasks backwards from that date, and just go do it. A wish without a date is only a dream. I had known about the camino for perhaps ten years, then about three years ago started to feel the compulsion to do it. I did nothing about it for a while, just thought that I would like to do it. Time passed, and I realized that unless I set a date, it was never going to happen. And I am at the stage in my life when, if you don't act on dreams, they are going to, at some point, become physically impossible. So I set a date for 2007, then narrowed it down to spring, then targeted mid-April for the start date. Then I agonized for two years about whether I could actually do it, when push turned to shove. Even sitting in the airport in Ottawa, on my way, I wondered if this was a smart move or just plain stubbornness, unwilling to admit that I had bitten off more than I could chew. My method of commitment, I can see in retrospect, is that I tell everyone what I am going to do . . . and then am too embarrassed by the possibility of failure to *not* do it.

The weather is something that you can't change, so dress for it and go anyway. I found that the weather was such a minor factor on the camino that I cannot really remember what the weather was like on any given day. The only days that I remember the weather clearly are the first day, when I walked over the Alto de Perdón in the dehydrating noonday sun, the day I walked into Burgos in a cold, steady rain, and the next day, when it snowed. Possibly if the weather had been more extreme, I would have been more aware of it. But as a Canadian living in Ottawa, one can't really hide from the weather except by hibernating all winter. Just be aware that Mother Nature is neither benign nor malignant. She is indifferent, as the English pilgrim who perished near Roncesvalles discovered.

Now is the only real time there is, so experience it. The only real now that we have is the one we are experiencing in this moment, and so it becomes important that we are mindful of now and experience the only moment in which we exist. The Romans had it right—*Carpe diem.*

WHATEVER HAPPENED TO . . .

After I arrive in Barcelona, I am reunited with Carroll, drive with her to Madrid to pick up her replacement passport (the Canadian consul service in Madrid is excellent), continue on in southern Spain for another week, spend two weeks in Croatia (but that is another story), then fly to Berlin. With our dear friends Ginette Parent and Hubert Miller waiting for us at the airport is Karsten! And when we drive up to Bergfelde, just on the northern outskirts of Berlin, there is Marina waiting for us at our friend's house. We have a wonderful and happy reunion with our old and new friends, then Karsten returns home to Berlin and Marina goes back the next day to Hamburg. Carroll and Marina get along famously, especially when they discover that they have sewing, as well as me, in common. After exploring Berlin and the rivers and lakes north of Bergfelde with Hubert and Ginette for a few days, we return to Canada at the end of June.

After seeing him in the Austrian *albergue*, I never run across Wayne, the English philosopher-plumber, again.

The Norwegian friends, Sturla Pilskog and Mari Bjørnstad, who were filming their journey on the camino, return home, where they get very busy creating a documentary about the camino. It premieres in Oslo on 28 June 2008, and Carroll and I are invited to attend. We intend to go. Sturla offers, with enormous generosity, to allow me to announce and publicize my book at his premiere. He even offers to include information about it in the invitation that will be sent out! Now that is a generous spirit. The Web site for more information about this film is **www.caminosantiago.no**.

I continue to keep in close touch with my three travelling companions.

After returning to Bremen after the camino, Paula travels to Madrid to sing with her choir, meets there a man in a park, sitting side by side on a bench and, completely out of character, spends a couple of hours speaking with him. While still in Spain, I have sent her an e-mail:

> I felt a real sense of loss as you walked out of the plaza
> in Santiago on your way to Finisterre. I hope that you
> understand how important your company was for me as we

walked across Spain. I think that you are a lovely and loving person and I hope that you find that special person who you would like to have in your life. I think that you will be a wonderful life companion for someone who will, I think, be a very lucky person to have you in their life.

She tells me, in a later response:

> I'm really grateful I met you, it was very special for me because you are such a loving and caring person, and you kind of "cracked my shell" by telling me all your affection-ate thoughts about me. I'd like to be a little like you when I'm "old" (I know you are not really "old," I just mean "rich in years" :=)).

Her relationship with Agustin has deepened wonderfully and they are going to spend their lives together.

After the camino, Karsten returns to Berlin, where we meet in mid-June. I send an e-mail to him, which says:

> I felt a real sense of loss as we parted in Santiago. . . . I enjoyed your incisive mind and your sense of humour and compassion. I think that you are a fine and loving person and I hope that you find that special person that you would like to have in your life.

He responds about the camino: "[I] feel enriched in my heart and in my memory and that indeed feels really good."

After meeting us in Berlin, he visits Marina in Hamburg, where, for the first time, he sees the movie *The Wizard of Oz*. He is going to teach in France for the next seven months, and, more important, he meets a Canadian girl, Olivia, from Vancouver, with whom he falls in love. At Christmas he travels with her to Canada to meet her family and he is taking her to Paris at Easter. I think that this is serious as well.

Marina goes back to Hamburg and has her foot X-rayed. She has a broken bone in her foot, so when we meet in Berlin, she is sport-ing a large and cumbersome cast. She walked for the last three weeks of the camino with a broken foot. That is determination and German grit. She says about her baptism, which occurs a week after we meet in Berlin: "My baptism was great. A day like a wedding should be one day: no stress and a lot of joy. I was smiling all day long."

She is now dancing again, taking up swimming, enjoying her circle of friends, and undertaking religious studies, but does not have a permanent man in her life and she would like that a lot. She sends me a message: "I miss our talks, Guy . . . There is nobody like you here." She intends to go to Oslo in June 2008 for the premiere of Sturla's movie, so we will meet there. I am looking forward to it.

I expect to see the couple who gave me their fleece in Boadilla, Eva and Richard from Augsburg, after I arrive in Santiago, but they are not there. I keep the fleece until I go home to Canada, then return it to them, along with my deepest gratitude and with a book about native Canadians, because I know that Germans have a deep and abiding fascination with anything to do with North American Indians. We get a thank you for the fleece and the book and, later, a Christmas card with a photo of both of them at a dance, looking really happy.

I send Walter and Roswitha, from Cologne, pictures of my new grandson, and I get a lovely e-mail back. They are moving into a flat in downtown Cologne.

Suzie, whom I met in Boadilla and again in Santiago, returns to Canada and resumes her hectic international schedule, singing in Canada, Europe, and Japan. While she was on the camino, she was thinking about the creation of yet another CD, this one about Acadian music. Her ancestry is Acadian. One evening back home in Ottawa, months later, we are delighted to see a special TV program about her and her Acadian music. We will be hearing her sing in Ottawa at the end of July 2008.

I meet Eva Papp from Hungary for the last time in Santiago. She invites us to come and visit in Budapest. Her e-mail address fails, and I have not been able to locate her again.

Ferran, with whom I walked for most of a day, and with whom I ate dinner on my anniversary in Boadilla, walked on the next day and I did not see him again on the camino. I know that he is from near Barcelona, but I do not have a last name for him.

After León, I do not see Hannelore again. I hope to see her in Santiago on the 25th of May, because that is her birthday, but I do not. I do not know her last name and do not know how to contact her. I hope that her newfound enthusiasm for life continues and that she is able to put her loneliness and nightmares behind her.

After my one day's experience with Kirsti Antila, the Finnish woman who lent me her cell phone in Boadilla, I never see her again. And I have no way to find out how to contact her. Then I receive a message from Sturla Pilskog, the video photographer from Norway, and there on the e-mail, as one of the other recipients, is Kirsti Antila, so I send her a message and she happily responds. I will probably see her in Oslo.

My dear friend Peter Holtzhausen dies in late June 2007, just before we return to Canada.

Another dear friend in Canada, Ted Cole, is alive and doing well. You will remember him as the person for whom Heinz and Marina prayed on 8 May. He and his wife, Elaine, have just been blessed with their first grandchild, a girl.

At the end of December 2007, I once again lose the year's games of Spite and Malice to Carroll, making it now two years out of twelve that I have won. I am working now on best out of twenty-five. It will take me until 2020 to win the series.

My unaccompanied airline baggage, my backpack and its contents, never does arrive, not in Spain, not in Canada. They cannot give me any idea as to where it could have gotten to. In the fullness of time, I get a cheque from the airline for about sixty percent of the value of the contents of the backpack. In an eerie replay of the event, in February of 2008 we fly from Florida across North America to the Okanagan valley in British Columbia to go skiing. My ski gear is in my unaccompanied baggage, which does not arrive the whole time we are there, so I have to rent or borrow everything. Carroll's gear arrives with us. I feel especially bereft because the bag also contains my trusty hiking boots, which survived the trip to Spain, and a favourite red fleece that Carroll made for me. About a week after we return to Florida, I get a phone call from Norway. It is an SAS found baggage handler, who has my suitcase. It went to Norway, months before I am due to go. Who knows? I am tempted to ask if they happen to have seen my backpack.

And so it goes.

GLOSSARY OF SPANISH TERMS

a la Romana	breaded and deep-fried
a Pie	on foot
Agua	water
Agua del grifo	tap water
Albergue	hostel
Alto	high, height or hill
Asparragus	asparagus
Bocadillo	sandwich, bun
Bodega	winery
Buen Camino	greeting: have a good walk
Caballeria de Segunda Clase	a second-class knight
Café con Leche	coffee with warm frothed milk
Calzada	roadway
Camino	path, way
Cansado	tired
Cerveza	beer
Chorizo	sausage
Churros con Chocolate	deep-fried fritter with hot thick chocolate
Cinco	five
Ciudadela	citadel
Compostela	certificate of completion of the camino
Conversos	Christians converted from Islam or Judaism
Corregidor	chief magistrate, sheriff
Credencial	official pilgrim booklet
Dormitorio	sleeping room
Dueña	chaperone
El Camino de Santiago	the path to Santiago
El Sueño de la Luz	the dream of light
Estar	to be (temporarily)
Farmacia	pharmacy
Fuente	fountain

Fuero	charter
Ganso	goose
Guapa	pretty
Guapo	handsome
Guardia Civile	federal civil guard
Hola	hello, hi
Hórreo	Galician granary structure
Hospitalero, Hospitalera	concierge at an albergue
Lavadora	washing machine
Limpieza de Sangre	pure blood
Main Nue	bare hand
Mas	more
Menu del Dia	menu of the day
Menu del Peregrino	pilgrim menu
Meseta	plateau
Muy	very
No Comprendo	I don't understand
Palloza	pre-Roman thatched stone structure
Pan	bread
Panaderia	bakery
Peloton	squad, group of racing cyclists
Peregrina	female pilgrim
Peregrino	male pilgrim
Pescado	fish
Pincho	a small piece
Puente	bridge
Razzia	raid
Reconquista	reconquest
Reina	queen
Sagrada Familia	Sacred Family cathedral in Barcelona
Secadora	clothes dryer
Ser	to be (permanently)
Sidra	cider
Tortilla	potato pancake
Uno	one
Vino	wine
Vino Blanco	white wine
Vino del Año	new wine
Vino Tinto	red wine

BIBLIOGRAPHY

Allende, Isabel. *Zorro.* New York: HarperCollins, 2005.

Brierley, John. *A Pilgrim's Guide to the Camino de Santiago.* Findhorn, Scotland: Findhorn Press, 2006.

Gitlitz, David, and Davidson, Linda Kay. *The Pilgrimage Road to Santiago.* New York: St. Martin's Griffin, 2000.

Harrison, Kathryn. *The Road to Santiago.* Washington, D.C.: The National Geographic Society, 2003.

Hoinacki, Lee. *El Camino, Walking to Santiago de Compostela.* University Park, Pennsylvania: Pennsylvania State University Press, 1996.

Laffi, Domenico. *A Journey to the West: The Diary of a Seventeenth-Century Pilgrim from Bologna to Santiago de Compostella,* translated by James Hall. Leiden: Primavera Press, 1997.

Mackay, A. *Spain in the Middle Ages.* London: MacMillan Press, 1977.

Menocal, Maria Rosa. *The Ornament of the World.* Boston: Little, Brown, 2002.

Michener, James A. *Iberia.* New York: Random House, Inc., 1968.

Morton, H.V. *A Stranger in Spain.* London: Methuen & Co., 1955.

O'Callaghan, Joseph F. *A History of Medieval Spain.* Ithaca: Cornell University Press, 1975.

Picaud, Aimery. *The Pilgrim's Guide, a 12th-century Guide for the Pilgrim to St. James of Compostella.* London: Confraternity of St James, 1996 (originally published circa 1140).

Roddis, Frey, et al. *Walking in Spain.* London: Lonely Planet Publications, 1999.

Rupp, Joyce. *Walk in a Relaxed Manner.* Maryknoll, NY: Orbis Books, 2005.

Shrady, Nicholas. *Sacred Roads.* San Francisco, CA: HarperCollins, 1999.

ABOUT THE AUTHOR

Guy Thatcher served in the Canadian regular armed forces from 1955 to 1980 as a tank officer, helicopter pilot, anti-tank missile instructor, and computer analyst, serving in Germany, Belgium, Cyprus, Texas, and Alabama, as well as at various bases in Canada. He then pursued a second career for a further twenty-five years as a management consultant, working primarily in the field of facility planning and management. He holds a degree in Computing and Information Systems from Queen's University in Kingston, Ontario, is a Fellow of the International Facility Management Association, and is a lifetime Certified Management Consultant. He developed and taught postgraduate courses in Information Management for Facility Professionals at Michigan State University, delivered worldwide over the Internet. He has written or contributed to several business books and workshop manuals. He continues to teach in the Caribbean, successfully combining work and pleasure.

He continues to be married to Carroll Thatcher, with whom he has four grown children and one new grandson, clearly the most beautiful baby in the world. For the past seventeen years, he has been a home support volunteer for the Hospice at May Court. He skis, travels as much as he can, gardens, scuba dives (occasionally), reads voraciously—mostly history and science—, square dances, teaches, and plays a truly dreadful game of golf.

All of this, however, has nothing to do with the walk he took across Spain . . . or perhaps it has everything to do with the walk he took across Spain. He lives in Ottawa, Canada, and you can contact him at **journeyofdays@yahoo.ca.**

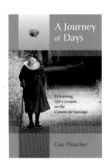